Sendmail

Theory
and
Practice

Sendmail

Theory and Practice

Frederick M. Avolio

Paul A. Vixie

Digital Press
Boston • Oxford • Melbourne • Singapore • Toronto • Munich • New Delhi • Tokyo

Recognizing the importance of preserving what has been written, Butterworth-Heinemann prints its books on acid-free paper whenever possible.

Library of Congress Cataloging-in-Publication Data

Avolio, Frederick M.
    Sendmail : theory and practice / Frederick M. Avolio, Paul A. Vixie
        p.   cm.
    Includes index.
    ISBN 1-55558-127-7
    1. Sendmail. 2. Electronic mail systems. 3. Mail receiving and forwarding services—Computer programs.   I. Vixie, Paul A. II. Title.
HE6239.E54A96   1995
004.6'92—dc20   95-29078
                                       CIP

British Library Cataloguing-in-Publication Data
A catalogue record for this book is available from the British Library.

CP/M is a trademark of Digital Research, Incorporated. DEC, DECnet, ULTRIX, VAX, and VMS are trademarks of Digital Equipment Corporation. SCO UNIX is a trademark of the Santa Cruz Operation. Interactive 386/ix is a trademark of Interactive Systems Corporation. SunOS is a trademark of Sun Microsystems Corporation. HPUX is a trademark of Hewlett-Packard. OSF/1 and Motif are trademarks of the Open Software Foundation. X and the X Window System are trademarks of the Massachusetts Institute of Technology. Z-mail is a trademark of Z-code Software Corporation. UNIX is a trademark of UNIX System Laboratories, Incorporated.

The publisher offers discounts on bulk orders of this book.
For information, please write:

Manager of Special Sales, Digital Press
Butterworth–Heinemann
313 Washington Street
Newton, MA 02158–1626

Order number: EY–S421E–DP

10 9 8 7 6 5 4 3 2

Printed in the United States of America

For our families.

Contents

4. Aliases and Local Delivery

5. Configuration Design

6. Configuration Basics

7. Using IDA "dbm" Tables

8. Configuration Details

9. Maintenance and Administration

Foreword

Here's the short version: Sendmail can be scary. This book takes away the fear. Do you want to hear more? OK, read on.

Sendmail is a strange beast, wild at heart and hard to tame—or so, at least, it's easy to imagine after having stared too many hours at lines like $*<$+@$-.$=w>$* while wondering why, *oh why,* don't any messages find their way out of the black hole that currently makes up your computer. So why is it so hard to use Sendmail?

Well, Sendmail is a peculiar program. Its basic function is to take incoming electronic mail messages and send them on their way to their final destinations. Pretty simple. Yet the nitty gritty details on how it achieves this are many and complex, mainly for two reasons: (1) The world isn't quite as simple as it looks, and (2) Sendmail's configuration language is, shall we say, somewhat on the terse and cryptic side.

At the heart of Sendmail is an AI-like rule-based engine that performs routing decisions and address rewriting. This engine makes Sendmail very flexible and is often thought of as its greatest strength. However, because it is difficult to harness, the same flexibility can also be considered Sendmail's most serious weakness. It is simply *too easy* to make small changes that are hard to control and that have dire consequences. I sometimes wonder if misconfigured sendmail.cf files haven't cost more in time and effort than can be considered reasonable compared with the cases where Sendmail's power really was needed to solve a problem.

Yet we all depend on Sendmail running smoothly.

Electronic mail is the lifeblood of the modern organization. The system administrator is the person responsible for the often thankless task of keeping it flowing. As long as things are running fine, everyone is happy—in fact, they will take this for granted—but the moment something goes wrong, the world literally comes to a grinding halt. For the sysadmin, this means an emergency late night session trying to repair the damage or at least contain it.

In 1984 I was a system administrator at a recently networked university in Sweden. At that time, all we basically had was a UUCP dialup connection from a PDP-11 running BSD 2.9 with Delivermail to a backbone node in Stockholm. The PDP-11 was in turn connected to our DECsystem-20 mainframe via a slow serial line over which we ran our own home-brewed mail-forwarding software. It was fairly slow and not very reliable, but it was *connectivity!* What was at first an exotic demonstration of technology quickly become an important infrastructure in our everyday lives.

The PDP-11 was soon replaced by Sun workstations and Delivermail by Sendmail. As the world became more complicated and our connections grew, so did our Sendmail configuration file. At some time in 1986, it was taking more time to maintain and administer than I was willing to spend, so in an effort to clean things up, I decided to rewrite it from scratch. There were also a several other features that I wanted—such as consolidated From: addresses—that were hard or impossible to do by simple changes to sendmail.cf. Fortunately, the source to Sendmail was freely available, so I started grinding along. Access to *dbm(3)* files was one of the first extensions to be added; then came embedded ruleset calls, multi-token class matches, split envelope/header rewriting and so on. By 1987 our Sendmail had reached a respectable size and was becoming generally useful enough that I decided to publish it on Usenet. Thus the IDA Sendmail Enhancement Kit was born. Today, IDA Sendmail and its derivatives are in widespread use at innumerable sites around the globe.

Paul Vixie was one of my early supporters. He had written to me in the early stages of the IDA Kit and kept encouraging me throughout. Paul is a strong-minded person with fire in his belly and a passion for his work. He was until recently the longstanding maintainer of one of the cornerstones of the ARPA Internet and Usenet (DECWRL), and is now heading a group working on the BIND implementation of the Internet Domain Name Service. He is also the author of King James Sendmail, a conservative and more performance-oriented offspring of IDA Sendmail.

Fred Avolio is in many ways Paul's east-coast counterpart. He used to run DEC's Maryland gateway and has been giving Sendmail tutorials at DECUS every year for the past ten years.

It has been said that working with Sendmail is not for the feeble minded or weak hearted. It is true that it often can be a time-consuming and frustrating experience, but in the right hands, Sendmail can be an incredibly powerful tool that keeps your mail traffic swift-flowing (and your users happy). Setting up a network for mail handling can be tricky, but having a mentor to help you get the details right helps greatly. This book not only describes Sendmail with all its bells and whistles, but also tells you how to use it *in practice* based on the authors' expertise and experience with sites spanning the few workstations of a small business and worldwide organizations with thousands of nodes. It is my great pleasure to introduce you to their work. I'm confident that you will find it useful. It may even be able to make you smile, too.

Lennart Lövstrand
Palo Alto, California
March 1994

Preface

It might surprise the reader to learn that we, the authors, are both on a mailing list called `sendmail-haters`. Do we really *hate* Sendmail? If we do, why write a book about it? And, why "Theory and Practice" ?

The sublime truth of the matter is that we both enjoy a love/hate relationship with Sendmail. Each of us has, over the years, created and been responsible for electronic mail gateways to networks that varied in size from a few hosts to multinational corporate Internets. During its infancy, electronic mail was not taken seriously by anyone except its most stalwart users; therefore, running mail gateways was considered dirty and irrelevant work, and those of us who spent our time that way learned to make the most of whatever resources we could acquisition, covertly, from our unwitting and potentially unwilling employers. Tools were used, reused, misused, abused; they were written, rewritten, merged, broken apart, cribbed from, modified; everything that could be made to work was so made; everything that could be broken was broken and fixed and broken again. Sendmail, even with all its warts, does its job, does it well, is widely used, and is part of most commercial "open" systems today. What is even more important, Sendmail is readily available in source code form, which makes it easier to abuse, rewrite, modify, crib from, merge with, break, and fix than most of its competitors.

Software that is available in source code form tends to scatter to the winds and mutate according to local custom. Sendmail and its Postmasters have developed different customs and habits in each Internet locality; we came to Sendmail from very different angles and were using it in wildly opposing ways by the time we met each other. Today we run the same software and configurations, but the road to where we are now is littered with the corpses of many local customs that could not hold out against stronger and more viable customs that had come to life elsewhere. We like to think that the way we do things today contains only the strongest elements of our separate and very different heritages—that merging our code and our ideas has resulted in a new and stronger breed of Sendmail.

We've also answered a few questions and taught a few seminars on the subject of Sendmail configuration. Whetherin Usenet's `comp.mail.sendmail` newsgroup or at DECUS Symposia all over the world, the question continually comes up: "Is there a book we can read to learn more about Sendmail?" The answer has always been "No." We got tired of giving that answer.

Which leaves the question: "Why 'Theory and Practice'?" We decided that if we were going to write a book about Sendmail, we would have to demystify it in a way that would allow any intrepid soul to understand its depths if she so chose; however, we would also have to provide enough "cookbook recipes" and simplified explanations so that a moderately disinterested Postmaster could make Sendmail do what she wanted it to do, without delving into the source code to find out "how." Sendmail can be arcane, and because of its monstrous size and complexity, most Postmasters never feel that they know what's going on. This book was written so that those who want to know what's going on can know, and those who don't want to know can still get Sendmail working and be comfortable that they aren't doing anything "wrong." We expect that the reader knows a bit about electronic mail and computer networks, at least from a user's perspective, and has an interest in learning more about Sendmail and how it works and how to manage a mail system.

We have chosen to speak of users and Postmasters using the pronouns "she" and "her." Neither author is female and neither is a "feminist"; however, we believe that since the overwhelming majority of literature throughout history has used male pronouns, some balance is called for—if for no other reason than to break up the monotony.

The mail addresses used in the examples, unless otherwise specified, are just that: examples. The reader would be wise not to waste time and network bandwidth in trying them out. In some of the examples, we use addresses in the DEC.COM Internet domain or otherwise talk about Digital's network setup. This reflects the fact that we both worked for Digital Equipment Corporation throughout most of the preparation of this book.

Some relevant RFCs[1] are mentioned throughout this book, in particular RFCs 822 934, and 1123. A section of RFC 822 can be found in Appendix I as can intructions for obtaining these RFCs and others.

This book will show you how and why Sendmail does what it does and how and why we do what we do. We believe you will be edified. Some parts are certain to make you think hard. Others parts will, we hope, make you smile.[2]

---

[1] An RFC is a "Request For Comment," the way to float ideas for new standards or mechanisms on the Internet.

[2] "If a man insisted always on being serious, and never allowed himself a bit of fun and relaxation, he would go mad or become unstable without knowing it." From *Histories of Herodotus,* Volume 11, Chapter 173, c. 420 B.C.

Acknowledgments

Authors are necessary but not sufficient to the creation of any book. Many others helped or were inconvenienced (or both) during this book's writing and as we acknowledge some, there is little doubt we will forget others. Of those we beg forgiveness and ask that they let us know and buy a lot of copies of this book, so there can be a second edition in which we can correct this mistake.

Our greatest debt is to our families for their support and their patience. There were times when we should have been available and we weren't. Thanks, especially, to Lisa and Victoria for filling in the gaps that we left during this time.

This book was conceived and mostly completed while we were employed by Digital Equipment Corporation. We thank our supervisors and colleagues for their support and encouragement, and we thank Digital for the use of the ULTRIX RISC workstations and PrintServers.

We had some terrific and ruthless reviewers, and we thank Eric Allman, Peter Churchyard, Jon "Maddog" Hall, Allen Leibowitz, Marcus Ranum, Win Treese, and Lennart Lövstrand for their comments and suggestions, which smoothed out (repaved, really) the rough spots. Tim Guarnieri's drive to the post office during rush hour deserves special mention. Cynthia Livingston swooped down on our stalled effort and pulled it back from the brink of oblivion; without her, this book would not be in your hands now (or ever?).

Thanks to Lennart Lövstrand for the title of the book, which we cribbed from his original IDA Sendmail paper with his permission. And, of course, additional thanks to Eric Allman. If he hadn't written Sendmail, this book would have been much thinner.

Fred Avolio <fma@al .org>
Paul Vixie <vix@al.org>
1994

"Neither snow, nor rain,

 nor heat, nor gloom of night

stays these couriers

from the swift completion

of their appointed rounds."

Adapted from Histories of Herodotus, Volume VIII,
Chapter 98, c. 420 B.C.

Carved into the facade of the General Post Office on 8th Avenue in New York City by order of William Marshall Kendall, one of the architects for the building, in 1914.

1

Background and History

While many people use electronic mail (hereafter "e-mail") in today's internet-worked world, comparatively few people are concerned with the details of its delivery. This is as it should be. Just as we don't have to know the details of "physical mail" (or postal mail, hereafter, "p-mail") to be able to use it, we would normally prefer to go about our business of using e-mail without knowing its inner workings. In e-mail as in p-mail, only the Postmasters have to know how it works. Sendmail is a tool of the e-mail Postmaster, and as of this writing, it has handled more e-mail than any comparable tool. Sendmail is to e-mail as delivery vans, airplanes, sorting machines, letter carriers, and all the rest of the postal system are to p-mail. If you have received only one e-mail message in your life, chances are better than even that Sendmail had a hand in its delivery.

1.1. A Brief Introduction to Sendmail

On the Internet, the majority of hosts run the Berkeley UNIX operating system or some derivative thereof (such as SunOS, ULTRIX, HPUX, or OSF/1). Sendmail is the program most of these systems use to handle e-mail. Some systems include alternate mail transport agents such as MMDF (which ships with SCO UNIX) or SMAIL (which ships with Interactive 386/ix), but even on these systems you will very likely find Sendmail lurking in a corner somewhere, deprecated by the vendor but available if you want it.

Sendmail was written by Eric Allman to handle the problems of address mapping between heterogeneous mail and network environments and to "help bridge the gap between the totally ad hoc world of networks that know nothing of each other and the clean, tightly coupled world of unique network numbers."[1] The design plan was to have all e-mail pass through Sendmail for processing. Sendmail would be able to switch mail between just about any mail user agent (hereafter "UA" — any one of many programs you might use to read and send e-mail) and message transfer agent (hereafter "MTA" — a program that moves mail between hosts using a particular network protocol or language). One of Sendmail's design goals was to easily accommodate the addition of new UAs and MTAs with only minor configuration changes (see Figure 1-1).[2]

Sendmail supports distribution lists in the form of "aliases" for people or sets of people. It supports the use of individual user .forward files to allow forwarding of incoming e-mail to programs or to other mailboxes. Sendmail also facilitates the rewriting of e-mail addresses to allow for gateways — which deliver mail between different kinds of mail networks — and to provide a mechanism for bridging various gaps between different systems. We will see examples of this later.

Further, Sendmail provides for message queuing when a retryable error is encountered (e.g., when a host or a network is temporarily unreachable), automatic routing, and returning the e-mail to the sender when an unrecoverable error is encountered (such as mail addressed to nonexistent users or hosts).

Sendmail is freely distributable software that works with many versions of the UNIX operating system, but its full glory can only be realized on systems that provide the BSD "socket" interface.

1.2. History

In the beginning, there was no such thing as IP/TCP or Ethernet or the Berkeley UNIX operating system ("BSD") or the Internet as we know it today (1993). Words had 16 bits, and we felt lucky to have that many. Networking meant serial (RS232) links in which "high speed" was 9600 baud, or it meant simplex coaxial point to point links at a whopping 2 megabits. The wide area networks of the time mostly used X.25 or SNA, and most traffic on them was between timesharing hosts and remote terminal users.

"Peer to peer" communication, as it was called then, meant that programs on one computer would speak directly to programs on some other computer; the protocols could be designed for programmers and programs rather than for humans and teletypes. Peer to peer was a distant ideal to most programmers, since the vendors were competing to provide proprietary visions of the future; the only way you could get

---

[1] Allman, Eric, "SENDMAIL — An Internetwork Mail Router."

[2] Sendmail is also an MTA as it contains an implementation of the SMTP protocol.

one vendor's computer to talk to some other vendor's computer was with serial links and programs like Kermit. Even in the unlikely event that all the "peers" you wanted to speak to were on other computers made by the same vendor as yours, you still had to learn your vendor's unique programming interface to their networking layer. Woe would frequently visit unto thee if your computer did not have a direct link to whatever other computer you wanted to "peer" with, since this would imply that some computers in the network had to be gateways and nobody, either vendors or system administrators, had enough expertise about running gateways. (This is arguably still true.)

One of the interesting lost technologies of this era was Berknet. Berknet was a web of then called "high speed" serial asynchronous links. The BSD tty driver had

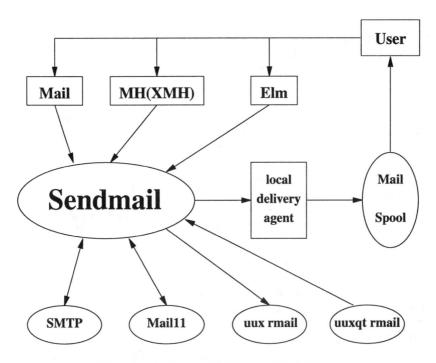

Figure 1-1. Sendmail's External Data Flow

a line discipline for Berknet that allowed a user level process to send and receive full speed serial data without flow control or special character interpretation. Berkeley Sendmail included vestigial Berknet support in its configuration files as recently as R5 (1993).

This situation was quite grim. But ultimately the technology got cheaper and faster and bigger and better, and things that had once seemed to be pie in the sky began to look implementable. The biggest single influence on subsequent events was, obviously, the UNIX operating system and the C programming language, both from Bell Labs. These two artifacts had the same effect on minicomputers (and, later, workstations and some mainframes) that CP/M had on the 8 bit microcomputers of the 1970s: vendors were no longer encouraged to develop their own proprietary programming environments but, rather, to "port" the common UNIX and C environment to their computers so that customers could theoretically buy "iron" from any vendor and get the same basic look and feel. Programs that ran on any UNIX computer could supposedly run on any other UNIX computer. This was only a theoretical ideal because vendors being vendors, there were always local "enhancements" that made your code unportable if you used them; if you did not use them, your code ran poorly or not at all. In fairness, the wide array of hardware also caused some of UNIX's portability problems: All CP/M computers have Intel or Zilog CPUs; all MSDOS computers have Intel or Intel compatible CPUs — however, not by a long shot do all UNIX computers contain DEC CPUs. UNIX has more bases to cover, in terms of portability, than any previous system.

Since UNIX's portability comes at the source code level (rather than at the binary level as in CP/M or, later, MSDOS), and because the C programming language is so flexible and because vendors were, and are, so excited about providing proprietary enhancements to the environment, UNIX's portability ideal was never realized — programs that ran fine on one UNIX computer probably would not even compile on most other UNIX computers. But the work needed to get a working UNIX program to run on other UNIX computers was still quite a bit less than, say, getting a HP9000 Pascal program to run under VAX VMS. So although UNIX's full ideal has yet to be realized, it still represents a vast improvement in software reusability over the bad old days when software only ran on a single kind of CPU.

In parallel to the spiraling ascension of UNIX and C, computers were getting faster, memories were getting larger, network pipes were getting fatter, and everything was getting cheaper. Smart programmers everywhere were getting their hands on all this new hardware, along with the UNIX source code, and new and improved versions of UNIX and its subsystems began sprouting up all over. One such sprout occurred at the University of California at Berkeley, which was more ambitious and better organized than most other places and so its version of UNIX actually got a name — BSD — and was widely distributed to other UNIX license holders.

Meanwhile, the United States Department of Defense Advanced Research Projects Agency (ARPA) had sponsored the creation of a wide area network connecting its various research contractors for the purposes of general research collaboration and the basic network specific research that later led to IP and TCP. This network was called ARPANET and is second only to UNIX and C in its influence on the modern computer industry. ARPA sponsored the programmers at Berkeley to port their BSD UNIX software from the PDP-11 to the VAX, and then to add networking capability so that BSD UNIX computers could connect directly to the ARPANET, which by this time was switching from NCP to TCP as its reliable stream protocol. (Historians will note several gross oversimplifications in this account, but it's close enough to explain where Sendmail came from.)

A few years later, ARPA declared its ARPANET experiment a success and decided to stop funding it; the National Science Foundation decided that more research in wide area internetworking would be useful and, further, that many of its grantees would benefit from being connected to a wide area IP/TCP network. Thus was born the NSFNET, which was originally proposed as a way to link the NSF Supercomputer Centers together but which has become the backbone of what we now call the Internet. We're all waiting to see what happens next.

1.2.1. Sendmail Arrives

Given that background, it now makes sense to declare that Sendmail came out of the BSD effort at the UCB Computer Science Research Group (CSRG). Sendmail was written by Eric Allman, who also wrote the syslog subsystem and contributed code and ideas to many other parts of the BSD UNIX system. Sendmail was originally an expanded and generalized version of Eric's previous mail transport, called deliver-mail. Delivermail had its 15 minutes of fame, and these days, the only reason people know about it is that Sendmail's documentation mentions it.

The syslog facility was originally part of Sendmail and used only by Sendmail. This is evidenced by the fact that in 4.2 BSD (and in operating systems whose syslog facilities have not been updated since 4.2 BSD), the syslog file (which contains the actual logged data) is still in Sendmail's queue directory (/usr/spool/mqueue). Because syslog was a general tool, it migrated into the base BSD system and is now used by almost all of the BSD UNIX system for logging of background daemon activity. Several other BSD UNIX library calls also trace their origins to Sendmail. Eric wrote his support routines as generally as possible, and many of them turned out to be so general that they belonged in the global BSD UNIX C library (libc.a).

1.2.2. Sendmail R8

During the preparation of this book, Eric Allman renewed his interest in Sendmail's development, and Sendmail resumed its long evolution. Sendmail R6 was released and then quickly renamed Sendmail R8 to go out with 4.4BSD. We chose not to alter the book to cover Sendmail R8's new features, which are legion, since all system vendors of which we are aware still ship Sendmail R5. Also, we believe that the fundamental philosophy of Sendmail is the same in R8 as in R5. The things you need to know to be a successful Postmaster using Sendmail are mostly the same for R5 as for R8; R8 adds many new features, but does not change the underlying architecture.

1.3. Summary

In summary, we see that Bell Labs spawned UNIX and C, which in conjunction with the technology curve spawned BSD UNIX, which in conjunction with the ARPA and ARPANET and IP/TCP spawned VAX BSD, which contained the first freely redistributable implementation of the IP/TCP protocol stack, including a set of working applications. Among these was Sendmail. That gets us to 1980 or 1981.

So, why are we still using Sendmail? Given Sendmail's many suboptimal design features (an obscure configuration file, monolithic "one program does it all" packaging, extreme ease of misconfiguration, catastrophic failure modes, and so on), why are we still using it? Why, a dozen years or so after Sendmail was written, are we writing a book about it instead of building — or writing a book about — something better?

Inertia, mostly. Sendmail comes free with every modern UNIX system, which makes it a fairly attractive way to solve the average computer's mail transport problem. Also, the cost of switching has yet to be lower than the cost of living with things as they are. There are alternative mail transport agents such as MMDF, PP, and SMAIL, and these each have strong and loyal user communities with more or less active ongoing enhancement and development. However, in the opinion of many people (including those who choose the mail product strategies for the major UNIX vendors), the alternatives to Sendmail all have worse problems. Some are too large and have an even larger configuration matrix than Sendmail's (MMDF and PP); some are too small and have no configuration variables at all other than what you choose at compile time (earlier versions of SMAIL).

Sendmail, once you get it working, works *really well*. Unless you run a large mail gateway, you don't have to spend much time watching or reconfiguring Sendmail. This, combined with the fact that Sendmail comes with almost every UNIX system sold, makes it a solid winner with no relevant competition. Here, perhaps, is an instance of "good enough" being the enemy of "the best," but we can't argue with the results.

2

The Groundwork

We will start our examination of e-mail and Sendmail by laying groundwork and defining some terms so that we can delve more deeply into the subject. We will also examine Internet e-mail address formats and discuss how they are used. As this is not a general purpose text on e-mail, we will touch only lightly on some of these subjects.

2.1. A Metaphorical View

To describe in everyday terms what Sendmail does, we must define some mail terms. It might help if you can remember back to your youth when you first learned to write a business letter. This is going to seem basic, but indulge us.

A business letter that you send through the postal system has some standard parts to it. On the envelope there is a place for recipient (or addressee) information and a place for sender information. On the letter itself there is also sender and recipient information, though perhaps with less detail. The date is included. Following those items are the greeting, body, closing, and signature. In a *proper* business letter, all these parts should be present. If it is a memorandum, things are in a different order, but the same information should still be there.

The envelope may contain different information than the addresses inside the letter. You must have received such mail. The envelope has your name and address on it, but in the letter (or memo) the address indicates a mailing list ("To: Technical Staff," for example, or "Dear Parent"). We can think of instances where the sender information might be different as well.

We'll carry this a bit further in describing what Sendmail's job really is, still using the example of p-mail going from one location to another. Let's pretend that at each mail transfer point (the post offices or mail rooms where mail is handled) there are three basic operations:

Focus

> Look at the address on the envelope, put the address into *canonical* form, and then *focus* on the *most important piece of information* (hereafter "MIPI"). Putting it into *canonical* form means putting it into a standard format for internal handling.

Route

> Determine things such as which mail slot or mail bag in which to dispose of the mail, what mail to bundle together, and so on, all based on the destination information provided by the Focuser.

Transport

> Take the mail package and carry it to the next handling facility on its journey. This entails not only what transports it but also the method used to do the transporting.

As stated, one of the Focuser's jobs is to focus on the MIPI on the envelope needed for delivery. It ignores (we can even think of it as *hides*) everything else. Let's assume that the Router can only see one piece of information at a time. What is the MIPI on the envelope? That depends on where the mail is in relation to where it is going — that is, how close it is to its final destination. Figure 2-1 is an example of an envelope's addressee information. Note that while we are using a U. S. mail address in this example, every p-mail address on the planet can map into this model. Of course, every country has its own unique rules for address formats — some put street address first, some put it last — and this also is an exact analogue to the e-mail world.

If we mail the letter in Figure 2-1 from Paris, France, the MIPI on the envelope is the country designation (USA). If the letter is sitting in the Gotham City Post Office, the ZIP code is not at all important for delivery because it is already at that ZIP code location. In the Gotham City Post Office, the MIPI is the street address. Once the letter gets to the mail room at the Acme Giant Magnet Company, the MIPI is not the

---

```
Ms. Jane Doe
Office of the President
Acme Giant Magnet Company
1600 Main Street
Gotham City, NY 98765
USA
```

Figure 2-1. P-Mail Address

---

street address (since it is already there) but the mail stop (in this case the "Office of the President"). Once Jane's secretary gets the letter, the MIPI is not the country designation, not the ZIP code, not the street address, and not the mail stop, but the name of the addressee (since, presumably, Jane's staff gets mail addressed to the office of the president also).

Finding the MIPI is the job of the Focuser. However, the Focuser is not very bright, and so it does its focusing one step at a time. It *tries* to find the MIPI and send it to the Router.

The Router's job is to direct and deliver mail to an MTA, which moves the letter closer to the intended recipient in the process, or to a local UA if the letter is for a local person. The Router receives the envelope with the MIPI highlighted. The *only* other thing it can do is recognize when the MIPI is redundant or useless information, for example, the letter's destination given as ZIP code 98765 when it is already *in* 98765. The Router uses the MIPI to move the letter closer to the recipient in relation to its current position.

Now, let's follow the letter to Jane in a few steps (we'll skip many of the stops it might really make).

(1)   The Paris Focuser focuses on the country name and hands it to the Router.

(2)   The Paris Router sees the country designation and notices that is it not for France, so it gives the letter to the proper MTA (via air) to send it to New York.

(3)   The New York City Focuser focuses on the country and hands it to the New York Router.

(4)   The New York Router sees the country, knows that it is already in the USA, and gives it back to the Focuser, saying something like "Try again, this is useless information to me."

(5)   The Focuser focuses on the ZIP code and hands it to the Router.

(6)   The Router sees the ZIP code, notices that it is not a New York City ZIP, and passes the letter via the proper MTA to the next city on the route to Gotham.

(7)   In this city the Focuser and Router go back and forth on the country information.

(8)   The Focuser tries the next MIPI — the ZIP code (meaning *Gotham City*, perhaps).

(9)   The Router sees this information and sends the letter via the proper MTA (the truck to Gotham) to Gotham City.

(10)   The Gotham City Focuser and Router go back and forth about the country.

(11)   The Gotham City Focuser gets the letter and points out the ZIP code to the Router.

(12)   The Gotham City Router sends it back (it is already at that post office!). He is not much smarter and is just as patient as the Focuser.

(13)   Gotham's Focuser focuses on the street address information.

(14)   The Gotham City Router puts the letter in the sack of the letter carrier for that street address (the proper MTA in this case).

Well, the letter isn't in Jane's hands yet, but you get the idea. The same function gets carried out in the mail room at Acme and then in Jane's office.

2.1.1. The Analogy Comes Home

When a message is given to Sendmail, part of the information associated with the message is envelope information, including the address of the remaining recipients. Sendmail copies the mail into its mail queue directory, selects an MTA, and attempts delivery.

It then tries to pass along each piece of mail, via an MTA, for delivery. A mail message going by the same MTA to the same foreign host, but to multiple users on that host, gets sent — only one copy — in one transfer to that host. A process at the final destination makes and distributes separate copies. If it gets a temporary (or "soft") error (a valid host is currently unreachable, for example), the mail gets left in the queue to be tried later. If it gets a permanent (or "hard") error (the host says that there is no such user, for example), an error message, possibly including the message, is sent back to the sender. If Sendmail detects that the mail message has been in the queue, unable to be delivered, for longer than a set period of time, the mail is returned to the sender as "undeliverable."

2.2. Internet Addressing

Sendmail was originally called an "internetworking mail router," and though this use of the term internetworking predates the existence of the Internet, Sendmail has grown up with the Internet and is strongly oriented toward Internet technology.

Consider, for example, that the only transport (or delivery) protocol that is actually built into the Sendmail program is SMTP, the Internet "simple mail transport protocol." That is, while Sendmail has to spawn a subprocess to deliver mail via UUCP or DECnet or even to deliver to a local mailbox, it has built into it the logic needed to open an Internet SMTP connection or to listen for incoming SMTP connections from other hosts. Sendmail is as general as possible in its interface to various other message transport agents, but SMTP is something it wants to handle on its own. In fact, many modern mail transports that know they will be living on the same computer as Sendmail will actually use localhost SMTP to speak to Sendmail rather than execute Sendmail as a subprocess, because SMTP is a more robust protocol than just blasting a message over a pipe and hoping for the best.

While not strictly true, it is therefore useful to believe that Sendmail is an Internet mailer that happens to have the ability to speak to foreign, non-Internet mail transports if you happen to need that ability. This Internet centricity shows up in Sendmail's internal use of @ notation to determine whether an address is qualified for the operation of the C mailer flag (read about mailer flags in Appendix C); you can also see it when you consider that almost all sendmail.cf files use Internet @-notation for their *canonical form*, even if they are used on a host that has no Internet connectivity.

Some Sendmail afficionados may see Sendmail as UUCP centric, or DECnet centric or even, in times gone by, Berknet centric. Be that as it may, we are Internet centric, and most of the Sendmail community is Internet centric, and we are going to focus our discussion of e-mail address formats on Internet addressing.

2.2.1. Relevant Internet RFCs

The Internet standards documents relevant to this discussion are RFC 821 and RFC 822. An RFC is a *request for comments*, and the number following the "RFC" designation is sequentially assigned in order of publication. RFC 821 describes the SMTP protocol, which includes the exchange of sender and recipient *envelope* addresses. RFC 822 describes the format of Internet mail headers, which includes the sender and recipient *header* addresses.

The overlap between RFC 821 and RFC 822 is obviously that they both describe mail address formats, and where they both speak of addresses they tend to agree — that is, almost everything allowed or specified by one is likewise allowed or specified by the other. The exceptions come in the areas where one offers a capability that would not make sense for the other. For example, RFC 822 specifies *list address* format for those cases where you want to be able to send to a list of recipients whose addresses do not appear in the headers of the message. The envelope *must* contain the real addresses, or the mail will not go anywhere. Therefore, it makes no sense for RFC 821, as an envelope specification, to provide the capability of a syntactically correct but semantically empty recipient, even though RFC 822 has and needs such a capability. However, the most common usage (*user@domain*) has the exact same specification in RFC 821 as in RFC 822. We recommend a thorough reading of both RFC 821 and RFC 822, even though most Sendmail administrators do not need to know the details at that level and both documents are quite dry.

You would probably not regret having read more RFCs; to help you avoid some of the bad ones, our favorites are: RFC 934, RFC 937, RFC 974, RFC 976, RFC 1034, RFC 1035, and RFC 1123.

2.2.2. Local Addresses

The basic address is of the form

user

which refers to some user on the local host or, if there is an alias for this user, to the processing specified by that alias. Strictly speaking, the "thing" to which you are mailing should not be called a *user*, since it may be a distribution list or even the standard input of some program. Because of the ambiguity in knowing exactly what kind of object an address refers to, this part of the address is often called the *local-part*. For the purposes of this explanation, however, we will refer to this part of the address as a *user*.

2.2.3. Nonlocal Addresses

Statistically speaking, most Internet users are not on your local host. The address format used to reach remote users is

user@domain

where *user* is as before and *domain* is some name in the Internet Domain Name Service (DNS). Even though many people, when they see *user@thing*, think of the *thing* as a *host* rather than as a *domain*, this is an erroneous view. The *thing* really is, and must be, a *domain*. All host names are also domains, but not all domains map to host names. Mail sent to paul@vix.com will reach one of us, yet there is no such host as vix.com. Mail sent to paul@gw.home.vix.com will also happen to reach the same author of this book, and gw.home.vix.com happens to be a real host. For this reason we say that Internet @-notation addresses are of the form *user@domain* rather than *user@host*.

2.2.4. Internet Source Routing

There is a deprecated but still valid form of Internet address called a *route-addr* (pronounced "route adder"). This is of the form

@dom1 , @dom2 , @dom3 : user@domain

where everything before the "`:`" is called a *route*. This route means that to reach this recipient the mail should be sent to a host that is responsible for *dom1*'s mail; we call such a host *dom1*'s *mail exchange*. This host will remove the *@dom1* term of the route and forward the message to whatever host answers for *dom2*, which does likewise and sends the message to the host responsible for *dom3*; *dom3*'s mail exchange removes the *dom3* and sees the

user@domain

which it then handles in the normal way. The table below shows this process in detail.

Address	Host
@dom1,@dom2,@dom3:user@domain	local host
@dom2,@dom3:user@domain	*dom1*
@dom3:user@domain	*dom2*
user@domain	*dom3*
user	*domain*

Route-addrs are used when you need to dictate an exact forwarding path (called a *route*) used to reach a recipient. This would be necessary if, for example, you could directly reach the mail exchanges for *dom1* but not for the other domains shown in our example, or if you wanted to circumvent normal routing to avoid some specific host or mail exchange.

In practice, route-addrs are very rarely used, since it is almost always possible for a domain administrator to set up her mail exchanges such that at least one of them will be reachable from anywhere on the Internet. Because of a standardization gaffe, route-addrs cannot be used to encode foreign network names, because all the domain terms (*dom1*, *dom2*, *dom3*, and *domain* in our example) must be real Internet domain names, registered with the DNS. In addition, RFC 1123 makes it legal to look ahead in the route-addr and deliver to the last named domain (which is *domain* in our example.) With no requirement that the leading *dom1*, *dom2*, etc. terms be respected, and a requirement that all domains appearing must be registered with the DNS, route-addrs are virtually useless. What little they can still do can be done better with MX RRs, which we will explain later.

The lack of any real need for route-addrs, combined with the many dangerous things that can happen when they are misused and combined with the intrinsic ugliness of addresses encoded in this format, caused the route-addr syntax to be deprecated in RFC 1123. To be "deprecated," in this context, means that the Internet Engineering Task Force recommends that this format be accepted but never generated. The example `sendmail.cf` files in this book follow this recommendation. Please note that a route-addr is the only valid format that contains more than one "@."

2.2.5. Summary of Internet Addressing

The address formats shown in the previous section are the only ones recognized by the Internet standards for e-mail. "But wait," we hear you cry, "What about UUCP and DECnet and all the other things that aren't part of the Internet?" The answer is contained in your question. Those other networks exist, but the Internet address formats make no special provision for them. If an address contains an "@," then, unless it is a route-addr, everything to the right of the "@" is a *domain*, and you can deliver mail to it by finding that domain's mail exchange and opening an SMTP connection to that host. If there is no "@," then the whole address is considered a *local-part*, and each host is allowed to interpret this any way it wants to. Now, it happens that there are many other address forms in use that all hosts tend to interpret in the same way; we'll get to those later.

2.3. Anatomy of a Mail Message

In this section we examine the format and parts of an e-mail message by dissecting two example messages, one very simple and the other somewhat complex. Then we'll take a look at the concept of *forwarded* mail, and finally at some less commonly used headers.

2.3.1. Dissecting a Simple Example

In Figure 2-2, we see a short e-mail message being sent. This transmission uses comp, which is part of MH, the Rand Message Handler mentioned below, but any other user agent could have been used. It prompts for the To:, Cc:, and Subject:; more headers such as From: and Date: will be added by Sendmail when it gets its hands on the message. Everything above the first dashed line is header information; everything below it is the body of the letter. The dashed line is added by comp for clarity — it isn't actually contained in the mail as received by the recipients. Each recipient will see the headers, followed by a blank (i.e., empty) line, followed by the text (called the *body*) of the message. Each header contains a field name, followed by a colon, followed by more information. We'll look at different types of header fields in detail shortly; for now, just remember that the headers are at the top and that the first blank line ends the headers and introduces the body.

We cannot tell by looking at the address lines of the message whether the addressee reviewers is a local user named reviewers, a personal alias that will be replaced by the real address or addresses of the addressees, or a system alias or distribution list. We'll pretend that in this case reviewers is a transport level alias such as a system distribution list (in the Sendmail `aliases` file). Aliases are explained more fully later in Chapter 4. Their use in this example should be "intuitively obvious":

```
reviewers:
        peter@lister.london.uk, norman@gadfly.utoronto.edu,
        al@netwolf.dco.frobozz.com, win@netwolf.dco.frobozz.com
```

Depending on our mail network configuration, Sendmail may have to send out multiple copies of this letter. In the case of a machine that can or does directly connect to all of these hosts, Sendmail sends the message out in three different mail transactions. Each transaction contains a message that looks for all practical purposes like the example, except that as mail leaves our host, Sendmail adds our host or domain name to local addresses (for example, `avolio` becomes `avolio@dco.frobozz.com`). Also, a `From:` line will be added that looks like

```
From: Frederick M Avolio <avolio@dco.frobozz.com>
```

One copy goes to `netwolf.dco.frobozz.com` for users `al` and `win`. Another copy goes to `gadfly.utoronto.edu` for user `norman`. A third copy goes to `lister.london.uk` for user `peter`.

Each of the recipients gets a copy of the message with header lines indicating that it came from `avolio@dco.frobozz.com` and that it was sent to `reviewers@dco.frobozz.com`. However, there is nothing showing the individual addressees in the `reviewers` alias. The only address information that is among the different copies of the messages is the envelope information.

```
% comp
To: reviewers
Cc:
Subject: Review of Book -- Chapter 1
--------
I am sending in a separate message a draft of chapter 1.
Please get back to me in 2 weeks with your comments.

Fred
^D
--------
What now? send
%
```

Figure 2-2. Sending a Simple Mail Message

Recall the e-mail envelope information we discussed earlier. Thus, the message to `peter@lister.london.uk` would show in the header `To:` line that the mail is for `reviewers@dco.frobozz.com`, but on the envelope, it would be addressed to `peter@lister.london.uk`. We'll see shortly how the envelope sender and recipient information is associated with the mail message.

2.3.2. Dissecting a Complex Example

Although the body of the message is usually the most important part of the e-mail in the eyes of its intended recipient, for our study the headers are more important and more interesting. We will now look at a more elaborate e-mail message and discuss the different header lines.

In Figure 2-3, all the lines up to and including the `Date:` line are the headers. First, we should notice that some of the lines begin with a blank or TAB character. A header line which starts with a blank or TAB character is treated as a continuation of the previous header line. There is no design limit to how many continuations one is allowed to have.[1]

The next thing to notice is the variety of formats for addresses we have on the `To:` and `Cc:` lines. The individual mail addresses are separated by commas. If the address is in angle brackets (`<address>`), the other strings in the address area between the commas are taken to be a comment. Typically this is used for the person's name. If there is nothing in angle brackets, anything outside of parentheses is considered to be the address. All of these will get to the same person:

```
Paul Vixie <vixie@pa.frobozz.com>
vixie@pa.frobozz.com (Paul Vixie)
Paul <vixie@pa.frobozz.com> Vixie
vixie(Paul Vixie)@pa.frobozz.com
```

Now, let's look at the different header lines. The `Return-Path:` and the `Received:` lines are there to provide an electronic trail of mail message handling. The `Return-Path:` should provide a route back to the sender. `Received:` header lines are added by every RFC 822 conformant mail transport as the message is handled. This information is useful for tracing problems in the mail network.

The `From:` (or `Resent-From:`) field is required and is the address of the person, or persons, whom the mail is, well, *from*, not necessarily the *sender* of the mail. In

---

[1] Versions of Sendmail earlier than 5.61 have a limit of 2,500 characters for the values of the headers (including continuation lines) and would silently dump core if this limit were overrun in the message.

this example, we see that while the mail is *from* Ed Gold, the *sender*, indicated by a
Sender: header line, is joe@pa.frobozz.com, who, we might assume, is Ed
Gold's secretary or administrative assistant. The Sender: header, if it exists, should
always contain a valid mail address for the person who actually sent the mail. The
From: header must always be some individual's mailbox.

A Reply-To: header indicates the address(es) to which replies should go. While
it is possible to send replies to everyone having anything to do with the mail, often

---

```
Return-Path: <joe@pa.frobozz.com>
Received: by gildor.dco.frobozz.com (5.57/fma-030592);
        id AA11614; Thu, 4 Jun 92 19:29:05 -0400
Received: by weir.pa.frobozz.com;
        id AA12989; Thu, 4 Jun 92 16:28:53 -0700
From: Ed Gold <gold@pa.frobozz.com>
X-Organization: Frobozz, Inc., Network Systems Laboratory
X-Phone: +1 415 555 1212
Sender: <joe@pa.frobozz.com>
Reply-to: <gold@pa.frobozz.com>, <joe@pa.frobozz.com>
Errors-to: <joe@pa.frobozz.com>
To: Marcus Open <mjo@dco.frobozz.com>,
        Fred Avolio <avolio@dco.frobozz.com>,
        Brit Reed <reed@pa.frobozz.com>,
        Win Chung <chung@crl.frobozz.com>,
        Allen Lowenbrau <lowenbrau@det.frobozz.com>,
        corey@vix.com (Corey James)
Cc: interest@pa.frobozz.com
Message-Id: <9206042328.AA12989@weir.pa.frobozz.com>
Subject: new software on gatekeeper
Date: Thu, 04 Jun 92 16:28:52 -0700

A new version of the "glock" program, which is the heart of the
server on gatekeeper has been installed.

Let me know if there are any problems.  I think I've tested all
the features, but there are always bugs...

Ed
```

Figure 2-3. A Complex Message

---

we want to (often we should) reply only to the originator. This header gives us some flexibility. In this case both the originator and the sender (Ed and his secretary) will get copies of the replies.

There are other times when you would make use of this header line. Let's say that we are guests on an out of town machine, using a temporary account or someone else's mail account. We could send out mail from that account, but prefer that all replies go to our *real* mail address. Adding the header

```
Reply-To: avolio@dco.frobozz.com
```

will allow this. The `Errors-to:` header tells Sendmail the address to which error messages should be sent.

The "Recipient" fields are probably obvious. We are familiar with `To:` and `Cc:` fields. The `Bcc:` field is also valid, but usually you won't see this one unless it is in the original mail and you typed it in. The `Bcc:` (for "Blind Carbon Copy") line has addresses of interested people who receive the message without others on the recipient list being aware. There are many reasons for doing this. You might want to flame someone and make sure her boss gets a copy, but you might not want to invoke the full policital implications that an explicit `Cc:` would have. This is not always ethical but it does happen and Sendmail will help you do it.

The `Message-Id:` (and `Resent-Message-Id:`) gives a unique identifier to the piece of mail. There is no standard for creating this unique *identification stamp*, but RFC 822 defines it to be in the form *unique-id@host-name*. Often, as in this example, an identifier is formed by joining the date and time in numeric format (in the current example, `9206042328`, which says 92, as in 1992, the 6th month and the 4th day, and the time of 2328, UT[2]), the queue identifier (`AA12989`) and the system name (`weir.pa.frobozz.com`). This is a unique identifier, since there could only have been one e-mail message generated with that queue identifier on that one system at that one instant in time.

This mail has a `Subject:` field, although `Subject:` fields are not required. Mail can also have a `Comment:` field, but this is rarely used.

The `Date:` field is required (also, `Resent-Date:` on resent mail) and is usually tacked on by the first MTA to get the mail. Thus, when Sendmail gets mail from an UA, it adds on the `Date:` header line. You'll notice that rather than indicating PDT for the timezone (Pacific Daylight Time) the notation `-0700` appears, indicating 7 hours less than (west of) UT measured from the Prime Meridian. This is preferred to the character string indicating a time zone, since there is no worldwide standard for time zones, but `-0700` is completely unambiguous.

---

[2] UT is Universal Time, formerly Greenwich Mean Time (GMT).

Finally, the fields that begin with x- are "user defined" fields for adding more information. Actually, you could put any field in the message header area since Sendmail ignores those it doesn't care about. But RFC 822 requires that no subsequent standard will ever specify headers beginning with "x" so an "x-" prefix is guaranteed to be "safe." Hence, X-Organization: and X-Phone: in Figure 2-3.

2.3.3. Forwarded Mail

Most UAs support forwarding of e-mail by taking the whole message and repackaging it with new headers, the old headers becoming part of the body of the new message. RFC 822 supports "resent" fields for mail user agents that support forwarding of mail without changing the headers. Instead of the message being repackaged, the original mail message — headers and all — is used as the resent message with the addition of Resent-From:, Resent-To:, Resent-cc:, and Resent-Bcc: lines. The "resent" headers then take priority, and the others are left intact but treated as historical information. What about resending a mail message that has already been resent? Multiple "resent" header lines are not supported by RFC 822. In other words, they are undefined. Think about this. Since mail header lines can appear in any order, there is no way, given numerous Resent-To: headers, for example, to tell which were added in what order. We recommend forwarding mail messages in the bodies of other messages for this reason.

Let's look at three examples. Figure 2-4 is an original mail message. We have removed some of the header lines in the interest of clarity.

```
Return-Path: kirk@starfleet.mil
Date: Thu, 13 Aug 92 23:21:48 -0400
From: kirk@starfleet.mil (James T. Kirk)
Message-Id: <9208140321.AA05738@enterprise.starfleet.mil>
To: spock@vsa.edu (Spock)
Cc: sulu@starfleet.mil (H. Sulu)
Subject: Happy Anniversary

Happy Anniversary, you wascally wabbit!
```

Figure 2-4. Original Mail Message

Next, Figure 2-5 shows the message from @Ref(Figure, "Original Mail Message") after having been "resent," and finally, Figure 2-6 shows the same message after having been forwarded as the body of another mail message. This message format is specified by RFC 934.

```
Resent-Date: Thu, 13 Aug 92 23:21:48 -0400
Resent-Message-Id: <9208140323.AA05757@excelsior.starfleet.mil>
Resent-To: mccoy@luna.edu (Bones)
Resent-From: sulu@starfleet.mil (H. Sulu)
Date: Thu, 13 Aug 92 23:21:48 -0400
From: kirk@starfleet.mil (James T. Kirk)
Message-Id: <9208140321.AA05738@enterprise.starfleet.mil>
To: spock@vsa.edu (Spock)
Cc: sulu@starfleet.mil (H. Sulu)
Subject: Happy Anniversary
Comment: Dr.  This is resent to you from me. Sulu

Happy Anniversary, you wascally wabbit!
```

Figure 2-5. "Resent" Message

```
Date: Thu, 13 Aug 92 23:24:46 -0400
From: sulu@starfleet.mil (H. Sulu)
Message-Id: <9208140324.AA05768@excelsior.starfleet.mil>
To: uhura@starfleet.mil
Subject: Forwarding funny message

This is a message for you to see.

-------- Forwarded Message

Return-Path: kirk@starfleet.mil
Date: Thu, 13 Aug 92 23:21:48 -0400
From: kirk@starfleet.mil (James T. Kirk)
Message-Id: <9208140321.AA05738@enterprise.starfleet.mil>
To: spock@vsa.edu (Spock)
Cc: sulu@starfleet.mil (H. Sulu)
Subject: Happy Anniversary

Happy Anniversary, you wascally wabbit!

-------- End of Forwarded Message
```

Figure 2-6. "Forwarded" Message

2.3.4. Less Common Headers

Many of the less common headers are not shown in these examples. `Full-Name:`, if it is present, is used to supply a value for the originator's full name. Usually, this information is on the `From:` line in a comment or passed to Sendmail on the Sendmail command line.

If `Return-Receipt-To:` is one of the headers of a message, a return receipt is sent to the addresses specified on this header line when the mail is delivered to its final destination. Please note, this *sounds* like a wonderful idea, but it might not be supported by the final deliverer, in which case it will have no effect. Also, a return receipt only indicates that the mail got to the mailbox, not that it was read. `Return-Receipt-To:` can cause problems, as well. For example, a Postmaster at Pennsylvania State University found it to be a bother, according to the following article, which he posted to Usenet:

> One of the professors here sent mail to someone in India. Apparently their spool partition was full, because the mail bounced with the error message
>
> `/var/spool/mail/foo: Cannot append`
>
> This in itself isn't that bad. But the bounce messages all included a `Return-Receipt-To:` header (from the placement of this header, it looked like it was part of the default headers in their `sendmail.cf` file). So when we got the bounce messages, our Sendmail obediently sent the return receipt. But, since their spool was full, the return receipt bounced! So, their mailer bounced our return receipt .... and so on, and so on, and so on. ARGH!
>
> We finally got tired of this, and we couldn't determine who the postmaster was, since it was on the other side of a UUCP link, so we ended up compiling a version of IDA Sendmail with the "`Return-Receipt-To:`" functionality commented out :-).

`Apparently-To:` is added to mail when the only recipient information it has is on the envelope. You would think that Sendmail would just add a `To:` header line, but a `To:` line carries with it the implication that the sender addressed this mail to that or those addresses. An absence of a `To:` line lets us know that we have no idea what the addressee list was. Finally, the `Precedence:` header line, if present, sets the value of the precedence of the mail message to the value indicated.

```
Precedence:   first-class
Precedence:   500
```

More on precedences later.

This is not meant to be an exhaustive list of headers. We didn't mention `References:`, `In-Reply-To:`, or `Keywords:`, all of which are available and defined for adding more information to the header of a letter. For further and deeper detail on all of this, please see RFC 822.

2.4. Architecture and Terminology

The literature about e-mail makes some specialized use of otherwise harmless looking terms. To write much more about e-mail, we'll need to use some of these terms, and they are obscure enough and subtle enough that we need to explain them up front.

The ISO/OSI documents about networking tend to create "reference models" for each branch of technology they address. While very few implementations will be layered in precisely the way ISO describes, the descriptions are still quite useful. So it is with e-mail.

The reference model thinks in terms of protocol stacks, layered in such a way that entities at the same level hold a virtual conversation with each other, but only by holding actual conversations with entities above and below them in the stack. If you are like most people, that description does not make any sense to you at all, so have a look at Figure 2-7.

In the figure, there's a user on the left who sends mail to the user on the right. ISO figures that ultimately there will be users sending and receiving mail, which, except for vacation programs and archive servers, is a reasonable assumption. The user sends mail by typing characters at her user agent, often with an editor of some kind. The user agent hands off the mail to the transport agent, which hands it off to the other transport agent, which hands it off to the recipient's user agent (often just a program that appends the message to a file where the user can read it later), and finally the recipient reads the message by typing commands at her user agent.

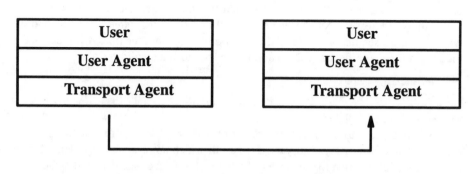

Figure 2-7. Ideal Mail Protocol Stack

This is all nice and simple and straightforward — and wrong. Or, at least, not exactly true in Sendmail's case.

Sendmail's place in this picture is "transport agent."

Sendmail does not do the entire job of transport agent, however. It needs other programs (which it calls "mailers") to, at the least, append incoming mail to local recipients' mailboxes and sometimes get mail from the sender's system to the recipient's system. So, if we were to redraw the ISO diagram to reflect Sendmail's reality, it would look more like Figure 2-8.

Figure 2-8 shows a "Sendmail layer" in which the two Sendmail instances talk to each other, except that in Sendmail's case they sometimes talk directly and sometimes have to talk through mailers. The recipient's user agent is really two programs: one is the "mailer" used by Sendmail to get the mail into the user's mailbox; the other is the program that the user actually uses to read (and, most likely, delete) the mail. Coming up with a diagram that shows what's really going on and is not more confusing than this paragraph of explanation is an area of active research.

2.5. Other Transport Agents

Sendmail is not the only bilge pump on the sea. Non-UNIX systems can't run Sendmail at all, for example. And on UNIX systems, there are alternatives such as MMDF,

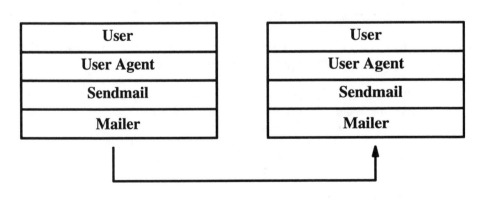

Figure 2-8. Actual Mail Protocol Stack

PP, and SMAIL. Each of these transport agents has its own set of mailers, which is why the ISO/OSI diagram in Figure 2-7 seems generally worthless rather than just specifically so in Sendmail's case. Some of these transport agents include user agents and sometimes the interface between user and transport agent is so stylized that you can't use the same user agent if you switch transport agents. (An example is the mailbox format: Sendmail doesn't have one, but depends on the local delivery agent to handle that detail; MMDF has one, and it is incompatibly different from the one used by everybody else.) We aren't going to say anything else about MMDF or PP or SMAIL, since this is, after all, a book about Sendmail. But if you want to check them out, try Archie (see Appendix K) and see if you can dig up the sources.

2.6. Mail User Agents

People who use e-mail already use one or more mail user agents. A mail user agent (UA) is a program, or a set of programs, used to send and read e-mail. UAs may allow the user to invoke an editor, file mail in folders, sort, and otherwise manipulate e-mail, but their basic jobs are sending and reading it. Descriptions of some common UAs follow:

`Mail`

> Standard with all BSD based UNIX systems and is similar to `mailx` on System V systems (which got its functionality from `Mail`). It is a line based mail interface and is widely used because of its broad availability. `Mail` allows reading, sending, forwarding, and editing of e-mail messages.

`elm`

> A public domain, screen based mail UA, which provides a full screen user interface for sending and reading e-mail, maintaining folders of received e-mail, and maintaining personal aliases and mailing lists.

`emacs`

> An editor, many implementations of which contain "modes" for filing, searching, sending, and reading e-mail; the best of these are based on `mh`.

MH

> The Rand message handler, a publicly available suite of programs for reading, sending, forwarding, sorting, filing, and removing mail. It supports mail folders and mail messages, all using commands that work from the UNIX command line, allowing for the creation of customized mail tools and shortcuts through the pipe and filter features of the UNIX shells.

2.7. Mail Protocols

A *protocol* is more or less the format of the data stream between two cooperating processes in a network of some kind. All data streams have some kind of format, even when it's so transparent that it becomes hard to pin down. A printer, for example, might require that only fixed length lines be sent to it, or it might require that lines end with an ASCII CR, or it might require that lines end with an ASCII CR-LF. In each case a certain protocol must be observed if correct output is to be produced. E-mail tends to use "heavier" protocols, involving a lot of *query/response* operations on both sides.

We do not intend to present a detailed view of any particular protocol; there are references available for any given protocol, and if you care about the details, you will need the official reference in any case. However, it is important to the operation of Sendmail that you understand the nature of protocols in general, since often a Postmaster is left staring at the *protocol trace* from some failed e-mail transaction, asking herself, "So what happened here?"

2.7.1. SMTP

The protocol Sendmail handles the most, and handles the best, is the one built into it: SMTP, the "Simple Mail Transport Protocol." The official reference for this protocol is RFC 821, as modified by RFC 1123 and others. Note that SMTP is evolving to handle so called "8 bit data" even as this book is going to the printer; read Usenet to learn more (for example, comp.mail.sendmail).

If you run Sendmail in *verbose* (-v) mode, especially when trying out a failing address or when draining the queue, you will see a lot of SMTP *protocol traces*. The one in Figure 2-9 is an example. The words MAIL, RCPT, DATA, QUIT, and "." are called *verbs* in SMTP's terminology. You can see, deep in the heart of this example, that a normal RFC 822 format e-mail message is being sent. All the other stuff is *meta* data, used to control delivery but not actually part of the message being sent.

The RCPT command shown in the trace happen to specify the same addresses as are shown in the To: header inside the DATA section. However, had the message been sent to an *alias* which happened to contain the two addresses shown, magic would happen. The RCPT command would still be exactly as shown, but the To: header would show the name of the alias, as qualified by the sending host's name or *mail domain*. This is another example of how the envelope recipient addresses can differ from the header recipients. Since *mailing lists* are implemented most often via aliases, this difference between envelope and header recipients is quite common.

2.7.2. UUCP

The UUCP protocol's ability to carry e-mail comes from its more general facility, uux, which allows processes on a host to execute commands on its neighbor hosts and to send a *standard input* file to those commands over the network. The remote

```
220 gw.home.vix.com KJS 5.65/08May93 ready to 1-1-lose at \
        Mon, 9 Aug 93 01:00:22 -0700
MAIL From:<vix@al.org>
250 <vix@al.org>... Sender ok
RCPT To:<fma@al.org>
250 <fma@al.org>... Recipient ok
RCPT To:<vix@al.org>
250 <vix@al.org>... Recipient ok
DATA
354 Enter mail, end with "." on a line by itself
From: vix@al.org (Paul Vixie)
To: fma@al.org (Fred), vix@al.org (Paul)
Subject: testing

foo!

250 Ok
QUIT
221 gw.home.vix.com closing connection
```

Figure 2-9. SMTP Protocol Trace

command used for UUCP mail is rmail, and from this we derive the common terminology, "I sent it to her with a uux rmail."

The actual protocol of uux rmail is rather hard to pin down. Some of the *meta* data is sent on the rmail *command line* (most notably the envelope recipient list); some is prepended to the data stream (that being the so called "UUCP From_ line"); some is set aside in UUCP's internal *control files* (which are where the sending process' credentials are stored, for transport layer backpropagation of delivery failures). UUCP is quite a mess, and we're not even talking about its channel level protocols. However, it is probably the second most common mail transport protocol after SMTP, and you would do well to poke around a running system's spool directories and log files some time when things are going well, since things can get pretty badly scrambled when things are *not* going well and it helps to have a perceptual baseline.

Our example for UUCP is harder to follow, but give it a try. Here's what it looked like to send a test message:

```
% Mail -v -s foo frbzwrl!vix
bar
^D
frbzwrl!vix... Connecting to frbzwrl (uux-rmail)...
frbzwrl!vix... Sent
```

Now, here's what it looked like in the *spool directory*, and note that your mileage will probably vary since every UUCP version is different:

```
# head /var/spool/uucp/frbzwrl/D.*
==> /var/spool/uucp/frbzwrl/D.alB7Vs2 <==
From vixie  Mon Aug  9 01:16:00 1993 remote from al
Received: by gw id AA20630; Mon, 9 Aug 93 01:16:00 -0700
Date: Mon, 9 Aug 93 01:16:00 -0700
From: al!paul (Paul Vixie)
Message-Id: <9308090816.AA20630@gw>
To: frbzwrl!vix
Subject: foo

bar

==> /var/spool/uucp/frbzwrl/D.alX7Vs0 <==
U vixie al
R vixie
F D.alS7Vs3
I D.alS7Vs3
C rmail vix
```

Here you can see that the envelope information is spread out all over the place. UUCP can decode it all, and so must you from time to time. The sender's UUCP *node name* was al, and his login name was vixie. Sending to user vix on neighbor node frbzwrl produced the files you see in the example.

The envelope recipients are specified in the D.*X (pronounced "dee dot ex") file, on the C (for "command") line, which specifies that a program called rmail will be run on the remote computer, with the arguments as shown. The envelope sender is present in the D.*X file on the U line and also the R line, and in the D.* ("dee dot") file on the From_ pseudoheader (note the lack of a : after the word From). These envelope senders will not always be the same, depending on whether the sender's Sendmail had to queue the message, and on the phase of the moon at the time the message was sent. The files could as easily be D.*, C.* and X.*, and they could be in different subdirectories per remote host, or different subdirectories per file name prefix, or they could be in one giant /var/spool/uucp directory. The details depend upon the artistic preferences of your UUCP implementation.

2.8. Summary

We've examined — virtually dissected — RFC 822 conformant e-mail addresses and identified the parts of an e-mail message. More ground needs to be covered before we jump into Sendmail configuration.

3

Addressing and Delivery

We now examine some common e-mail address formats and discuss how they are used. Three of the most common formats are featured: Internet, UUCP, and DECnet.

3.1. Sendmail and the Domain Name System

The Internet domain name system (DNS) is a distributed, replicated, consistent database that maps domain names to Internet resources. A domain name is a dotted concatenation of tokens (words), such as nic.ddn.mil, uunet.uu.net, or 1.1.45.128.in-addr.arpa. An Internet resource could be a host's list of network addresses or names, or a domain's list of mail exchanges or name servers, or a variety of other increasingly obscure things that don't concern the average Postmaster. We will present a brief overview of the DNS as it is viewed by Sendmail and its Postmasters.

The Internet DNS is described by Internet RFCs, a relevant subset of which are shown in Table 3-1. These RFCs are all of the readable variety; every Postmaster should have them on hand and should have at least glanced through them. Be aware

RFC 974	Mail routing and the domain system
RFC 1034	Domain Names — Concepts and Facilities
RFC 1035	Domain Names — Implementation and Specification
RFC 1123	Requirements for Internet Hosts — Application and Support

Table 3-1. Internet RFCs

that the use of the Well Known Service Resource Record (WKS RR) for detecting SMTP capable hosts, that was encouraged in RFC 974, was later deprecated in RFC 1123. RFC 974 is very short and very useful; section 5 of RFC 1123, that deals with e-mail and SMTP, is very interesting reading — careful readers will note that several paragraphs of RFC 1123 appear to have been written with Sendmail in mind, and that's exactly what happened.

BIND, that we will sometimes refer to, is the Berkeley Internet Name Domain — the BSD UNIX implementation of the DNS.

3.1.1. Domain Names

A domain name has some number of *label*s in it, separated by dots. These labels name branches of the domain *tree*, with the rightmost label representing the first branch off the *root*; this rightmost label is called the *top level domain* (sometimes "TLD") of a domain name.[1] Thus, the top level domain of `uunet.uu.net` is `net`, and the top level domain of `nic.ddn.mil` is `mil`.

3.1.1.1. Top Level Domain Names

Top level domains were chosen to represent different kinds of entities; however, no real thought was given to international use until after the United States began to use its set of top level domains.[2] Thus, there are two sets of top level domains: those representing countries and those representing the United States' preinternational conventions. Note that there is a top level US domain, but it is only used by individuals — organizations such as schools and businesses use the older, preinternational top level domains. Note also that organizations outside the United States are free to join the preinternational top level domains. Therefore, you cannot assume from a domain's preinternational top level that it is registered to an organization in the United States.

---

[1] Note that in the U. K., domains drive on the other side of the road, and the top level domain is on the lefthand side. Configuring Sendmail in that environment is left as an exercise for the reader.

[2] In case this is not clear from the context: We wish to express our sincere displeasure with the provincial, narrow-minded planning that polluted the top level domain name space with things that should have been under US from the very beginning. Leaving off TERRA and SOL is forgivable; leaving off US is not — at least for MIL and GOV.

One assumes that government and military organizations belonging to organizations other than the U. S. government would not be welcome in GOV and MIL, but we won't know until someone tries to do it. The other top level domains shown are all in active use, inside and outside of the United States. The rest of the top level domains are ISO standard two letter country codes such as US, JP and DE. It is not entirely clear from year to year whether new domains should be registered in the preinternational domains (e.g., COM and EDU) or in the appropriate international domain (e.g., UK or DE). If you have an opinion when you register a new domain, you will probably get your way.

Preinternational top level domains are shown below.

Top Level Domain	Purpose
EDU	Educational
COM	Commercial
MIL	Military
GOV	Government
NET	Network (infrastructure)
ORG	Organizations (things that don't fit elsewhere)
INT	International entities
NATO	North Atlantic Treaty Organization
ARPA	DNS internal data structures

3.1.1.2. Domains and Subdomains

Any registered name in the DNS tree is a domain, even if it is a host name with no other names "under" it. Every subdomain is also a domain, with the difference being that when one speaks of a "subdomain," one makes an implicit reference to the parent domain — that is, "of what domain are we a subdomain?" Look at it another way: Every domain is either a top level domain or a subdomain. We admit that this terminology can be confusing, but understanding these subtleties is crucial to success with the DNS.

Thus, uunet.uu.net is a domain even though there is no domain that ends in .uunet.uu.net. Likewise, uunet.uu.net is a subdomain, whose parent is the uu.net domain, which is a subdomain of net, which is a top level domain.

Figure 3-1 should help demonstrate why the DNS is thought of as a "tree." Note that this is a tree in the computer science sense of that word, and the domains are often called "nodes" or perhaps "leaf nodes" or "leaf domains."

3.1.1.3. The Resolver and DNSRCH

The software used by Sendmail to look up domains in the DNS is called the *resolver*.
The resolver is built into modern C Libraries, both as directly callable functions (e.g.,
res_search) and as stubs hidden behind the gethostbyname and gethostbyaddr functions. The resolver has many options, most of them turned "on" by
default; one of them is called DNSRCH.

DNSRCH tells the resolver to try partial name matches by adding the local domain
to the requested name, in bits and pieces. If your local domain is cs.suny.edu and
you ask for foo.cs, the resolver will search first for foo.cs.cs.suny.edu (which
will not be found, obviously), then for foo.cs.suny.edu, which is presumably
what you are looking for. But if you were hoping to get to the foo subdomain of the
top level CS domain (which is Czechoslovakia), you would have to add a trailing dot
to the name, which turns off DNSRCH processing for the current search. (More on
this later; you're not out of the woods yet.)

Some Sendmail variants turn DNSRCH off entirely. Partially qualified domain
matching should be done in the Sendmail configuration file or, preferably, not at all.

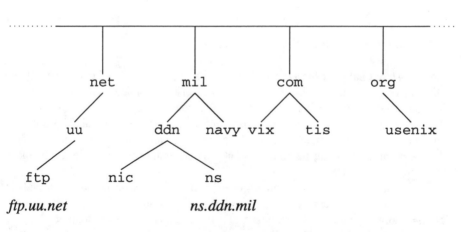

Figure 3-1. DNS Tree

3.1.2. Resource Records (RRs)

Each "node" of the DNS "tree" is populated by zero or more *resource records*, usually referred to as RRs. Each RR has a type and some type-specific data (see Table 3-2). Some RR types permit more than one RR of that type to exist at a given node; other types permit only one RR of that type to exist at a given mode. All RR types permit zero RRs of that type to exist at a given node.

3.1.2.1. CNAME RRs

A CNAME RR is an alias that tells you that the real name of the domain you are looking up is something different from what you've looked up. It is illegal to have a CNAME (or any other RR) refer to a CNAME.

A CNAME RR is often used when some well known domain changes its name, and you need to support mail to the old address for the indefinite future. CNAME RRs are also used for host nicknames.

It is illegal to put domain names that have CNAME RRs into the SMTP envelope, which is one good reason to resolve domain names in S0 or S2 and in S1; this will replace any CNAMEs with the actual name of the A RR or MX RR that mail can be sent to. (This discussion will make more sense later.)

Note that if a domain name has a CNAME RR, no other RRs can be present. A domain name is either an alias, or not.

RR Type	Number Permitted	Description
CNAME	One	Canonical *NAME*; this name is an alias pointing at the true or *canonical* name for this domain.
MX	Many	*M*ail e*X*changer; this domain's mail is handled by the host designated by this RR's data field.
A	Many	*A*ddress; this domain is a host, and this RR's data field contains one of its addresses.
PTR	Many	*P*oin*T*e*R*; this domain is a host address, and this RR's data field is the canonical ("true") name of the host.

Table 3-2. Resource Records

3.1.2.2. MX RRs

An MX RR designates a *mail exchange*. Each MX RR has two data fields: *priority* and *host*. The *priority* field is an unsigned 16 bit number (from 0 to 65535) that specifies the priority of this mail exchange; lower numbers are said to have a higher *priority*. The *host* field is the name of the mail exchange host; it must be a DNS name that has at least one A (Internet address) RR. An MX *host* cannot refer to a CNAME RR, and any MX RRs at the name it points to will be ignored — MX RRs cannot point to other MX RRs.

MX RRs can be either *specific* or *wildcard*. A *specific* MX RR has the same name as the domain name Sendmail is searching for. A *wildcard* MX RR has a similar name, except that some number of initial labels of the domain name are replaced by an asterisk (*). Thus,

```
decpa.enet.frobozz.com. IN MX 0 enet-gw.pa.frobozz.com.
```

is a *specific* MX RR, while

```
*.enet.frobozz.com. IN MX 0 enet-gw.pa.frobozz.com.
```

is a *wildcard* MX RR. Either one would be found if Sendmail searched for `decpa.enet.frobozz.com`; if both were present, the *specific* MX RR would take precedence.

Wildcard MX RRs are in general a bad idea, since most Sendmails are compiled with the DNSRCH option turned on. This means that partial name matches can occur; an MX RR at `*.frobozz.com` would match against any MX RR lookup anywhere under `frobozz.com`, even one down in a subdomain. If that subdomain does not have its own MX RR, the wildcard at the parent domain will match, which is almost never what you want because nonexistent names will seem to exist when you use the $[...$:...$] notation in `sendmail.cf`. If you want to make delivery decisions based on the existence of a name in the DNS, wildcard MX RRs are going to stand in your way.

3.1.2.3. A RRs

An A RR is a numeric Internet address (such as `192.112.36.5`, which is one of the addresses given for the `nic.ddn.mil` name). There can be many addresses for a name; Sendmail tries them all, if necessary, until it finds one that works. Note that both RFC 974 and RFC 1123 specify that the SMTP sender try these addresses in the order returned by the DNS, and Sendmail does this. However, the order is essentially random, so you can't reliably dictate the order in which addresses will be tried.

3.1.2.4. PTR RRs

Strictly speaking, Sendmail doesn't use PTR RRs. However, they are the cause of confusion at times. A PTR RR is a pointer from an IP address back to a domain name. Since the precedence of IP addresses is left to right and the precedence of domain names is right to left, the Internet address is reversed when entered into the DNS; it is also pushed back into a dimly lit corner so as not to offend anybody. The 192.112.36.5 address keeps its PTR RRs at 5.36.112.192.in-addr.arpa.

When Sendmail receives an incoming SMTP connection, it learns from the UNIX kernel the Internet address of the initiating host. When this host sends its HELO command (which identifies the sending SMTP client to the receiving SMTP server), Sendmail does a gethostbyaddr on the sender's Internet address and compares the result to the value received in the HELO command. If the names differ, Sendmail figures that something is broken and answers the sending SMTP client with the helpful question

Hello *gethostbyaddr-result*, why do you call yourself *HELO-host-name*?[3]

Note that no error has occurred; mail will still be delivered. However, the name Sendmail will log in its Received: header and in its syslog messages is the one returned by gethostbyname, since this name is derived from known facts whereas the HELO command can contain pretty much any old garbage.

When you see this message while cleaning out your Sendmail queue, it means that some remote Sendmail is running on a network whose PTR RRs are broken. But that's not what will happen; usually, if a name server is broken, it is *your* name server. So what will happen is that several remote Postmasters will simultaneously send you mail telling you that your PTR RRs are broken. Chances are good that as the Postmaster, you are also in charge of the name servers for your domain; if not, there's still a better than even chance that you eat lunch several times a week with the person who is in charge of the name servers for your domain. Either way, you should probably try to fix your PTR RRs and keep them fixed. Having them wrong won't keep things from working, but it will keep things from working *well*, and it will definitely cause more static to arrive in your mailbox from other well-meaning-we're-sure Postmasters.

---

[3] Note that this example violates RFC 821, as do all IDA variants, since the first word of this response *should* be a canonical host name.

3.1.3. Delivery Using the DNS

When Sendmail tries to deliver mail to a domain, it first searches for MX RRs for that domain's name. If none are found, Sendmail searches for A RRs for that name. In either case, if a CNAME RR is encountered, the query will be repeated using the canonical name.

If Sendmail cannot find an MX RR for a domain, but can find an A RR, it acts as if there were a single MX RR for the domain, pointing at the domain itself (which is quite legal), at priority zero (0); it then proceeds as if this MX RR had actually been found in the DNS.

Once Sendmail has a pile of MX RRs (or one fake one, as explained above) for a domain, it sorts them by priority (lowest numbers first). It then scans the list looking for its own name ($w; also $=w in *KJS*). If it finds any MX host that matches its own name, it removes this MX RR and all others with an equal or lower MX priority (equal or higher number). This is how Sendmail can achieve mail routing through MX RRs — it simply never sees itself in an MX RR list. If it did, as you can imagine, mail transport could get into loops as a system tried to deliver mail, handing the message off to itself over and over again.

Given a sorted, self-excluded MX RR list, Sendmail tries to deliver the mail using the highest priority (lowest numbered) MX RR and then working its way down the list. If several MX RRs have the same priority, Sendmail reorders them randomly. This is called "load balancing," since it has the effect that all same-cost MX RRs have an equal chance of being used for any given mail delivery. For each MX RR it tries, Sendmail looks for A RRs for the MX host; each of these A RRs is tried.

If Sendmail gets an SMTP connection out of this web of CNAMEs and MXs and As, it tries to deliver the mail. If it succeeds, then all recipients of the current delivery — remember, the SMTP protocol permits multiple recipients per transaction — are crossed off the envelope recipient list. If an error occurs, Sendmail either sends a bounced mail notification to the sender (if the error was of the permanent, nonretriable variety) or requeues the recipient for retry during some later queue run. The processing continues with the next envelope recipient. When the envelope recipient list is finally empty, the message is removed from the queue.

These are the steps Sendmail goes through in determining delivery.

(1) Check for specific MX record(s) for the host. If at least one exists, try to reach them, one at a time, in precedence order.

(2) If no specific MX record exists, check for A record(s) for the host. If any exist, try to connect to them.

(3) If no A record and no specific MX record exist, try for a wildcard MX record. If one or more exist, try to reach the mail exchanges in precedence order.

The actual steps taken are more subtle than this, due to DNS details, but you can proceed as though it were as simple as we're making it look. We do.

3.2. Non-Internet Addressing

Either a UUCP path or a DECnet address looks to the Internet standards as if it were one big happy *local part*, and if that *local part* contains no special characters, it is probably a *user*. There are, however, certain de facto standard ways to interpret certain special characters in a *local part*. While *local part* interpretation is allowed to vary on a host-by-host basis, you can pretty much count on the rules described below.

3.2.1. The Percent ("%") Hack

The percent hack is a dirty trick (which is now an Internet standard: RFC 1123) that lets you delay evaluation of more than one "@" in an address, which, as we've pointed out, are not allowed. The rule for this is that if you encounter an address containing no "@" in it but which does contain at least one "%", then you turn the rightmost "%" into an "@" and start over. This hack is very simple and amazingly effective. Consider

user%domain%dom2@dom1

This recipient is reached by sending the mail to *dom1*'s mail exchange, which removes its name, sees the lack of any "@" and the presence of one or more "%", turns the rightmost "%" into an "@", and retries. This process continues until the mail exchange for *domain* has received the message from the mail exchange for *dom2* and delivers it to *user* (or to *user*'s alias, if any).

The percent hack is possibly the most standard of all nonstandardized interpretations of the *local part*. In the above example, *domain* might actually be something that will be interpreted in some known way by the mail exchange for *dom2*. For example, you might see

```
paul%vixie.uucp@pa.frobozz.com
```

From the Internet's point of view, this is a valid address, since the thing to the right of the "@" is a registered domain name, and the thing to the left of the "@" is a *local part* that happens to contain a "%". However, "%" is "just another text character," the Internet standards don't care about it. When the mail reaches any of the mail exchanges for the `pa.frobozz.com` domain, they will perform the percent hack rule and turn the address into `paul@vixie.uucp`, which will then be seen as a local pseudodomain, forwarded first to `pa.frobozz.com`'s UUCP gateway and then to the UUCP neighbor called `vixie` via `rmail` to user `paul`. There are other ways to handle it than with a local `.uucp` pseudodomain, but they all boil down to the same thing.

For another example, let's look at the address

```
<maddog%shaman%xirtlu.uucp@gw.frobozz.com>
```

and see what address parts are relevant as the message moves closer to final delivery.

Address	Host
`<maddog%shaman%xirtlu.uucp@gw.frobozz.com>`	`localhost`
`<maddog%shaman@xirtlu.uucp>`	`gw.frobozz.com`
`<maddog@shaman>`	`xirtlu`
`<maddog>`	`shaman`

Like many of the outlands of e-mail addressing, this is somewhat subtle and convoluted and depends on local interpretation and side effects and a lot of other fairly dangerous things — all of which makes it more like real life than most other parts of the computing industry.

3.2.2. UUCP Paths

A UUCP mail address is written as a "UUCP Path" or in "bang notation" (the " ! " being pronounced "bang"). It is called a path because the address notation explicitly indicates the "path" the mail should take through a network of hosts, as in

host1 ! host2 ! host3 ! user

This recipient is reached by sending the mail to *host1*, which removes its own name and forwards it to *host2*, which removes its own name and forwards it to *host3*, which removes its own name and delivers the message to the local *user*.

Address	Host
host1!host2!host3!user	*localhost*
host2!host3!user	*host1*
host3!user	*host2*
user	*host3*

There is no requirement that these UUCP "hosts" be actual UUCP neighbors of each other; they can be Internet domains, as in

```
uunet!pa.frobozz.com!vixie
```

which relies on private knowledge that the UUCP host called uunet will accept a leading term that is a domain name and forward message this using the Internet, rather than assuming that the leading term must be one of its own UUCP neighbors. Private knowledge can also tell you that a given UUCP host will process certain pseudodomains, as in

```
frbzwrl!decpa.enet!vixie
```

which relies on the fact that `frbzwrl` is the UUCP gateway into a network called Easynet whose nodes are reached with the pseudodomain qualifier `.enet`, even though these pseudodomains are not registered with the Internet DNS.

Address	Host
`frbzwrl!decpa.enet!vixie`	`localhost`
`decpa.enet!vixie`	`frbzwrl`
`vixie`	`decpa`

3.2.2.1. So-Called "Smart Hosts"

Hybrid addresses which depend on private knowledge are fairly safe until you try to forward your mail through a so-called "smart host," which looks ahead in the UUCP path for the last thing it recognizes and creates a new route to that place. One assumption often made by these so-called "smart hosts" is that if a UUCP path term has a dot (.) in it, it must be a fully qualified, registered name in the Internet DNS. Such a host will not be able to find pseudodomains, since these only make sense to the UUCP node to their left in the path. Mysterious mail bounces will ensue, then major flame wars on Usenet will ensue. "Smart hosts" are becoming less popular as the years go by. But then, so is long haul UUCP.

While we're on the subject of so-called "smart hosts," we should mention that this kind of UUCP path shortcutting is also often done even for UUCP path terms that contain no dots. If such a so-called "smart host" sees a term way down the path that it thinks it recognizes, and it believes it knows a shorter route to that place than the one given in the path, it will cheerfully rewrite the path with the supposedly "better" route. Given that the UUCP map data used to do this "optimization" is almost always out of date and that a user may be specifying an apparently "suboptimal" path purposely — for example, to route around a down or congested host, to test a path, or to send commercial or otherwise proprietary data through a particular string of hosts known to be "safe" for such traffic — we believe that this so-called path optimization is *always* the wrong thing to do. While it is true that many working and oft used UUCP paths are suboptimal, the fact remains that they *work*. No problem solved by path optimization cannot be solved by other means; moreover, there are problems *caused* by path optimization that cannot be solved by *any* means.

Note that the most benign possible "smart" UUCP host is actually quite useful. This kind of truly smart host will search for a UUCP path to the "next hop" of a given recipient path if and only if the next hop is not a registered neighbor of the smart host. The effect of this is that if someone uses a path that you advertised as working, that path will work exactly as specified, with no shortcutting or other unpredictable behaviour. If someone tries to use a path that you did *not* advertise as working, then you are free to search for a route to the next hop since the alternative is to bounce the mail back to the sender.

As an example, consider a UUCP node named `vixie` with registered neighbors `frbzwrl` and `tcomeng`. If some remote user sends mail via a UUCP path of `...!vixie!tcomeng!uunet!frbzwrl!...`, then the first hop, as seen on `vixie`, will be `tcomeng`, and since this is a direct connection, the mail is submitted (via `uux rmail`) to UUCP node `tcomeng` with a forward path of `uunet!frbzwrl!...`. It's true that another direct neighbor (`frbzwrl`) can be seen later on in the path; we have no way of knowing if our `frbzwrl` neighbor is actually the same host as `tcomeng`'s `frbzwrl` neighbor. Even if we assume that it is the same host, it is possible that our UUCP connection to `frbzwrl` is working poorly or not at all, and that the sender of the mail message knows that and is deliberately using a suboptimal path. We can *always* get the mail through if we honor any registered next hop information presented to us in the path, but we will often fail to get the mail through if we attempt to second guess a sender.

3.2.2.2. Hybrid, or Mixed-Mode, UUCP Addresses

There can be and often are a lot more than three hosts in a UUCP path; it's safe to say that UUCP paths get ugly fast. Since there are many places a UUCP connected host will want to send mail to that are not on the directly connected UUCP network, it is becoming common to emit "hybrid" addresses. A hybrid address is one that has more than one kind of addressing character in it. An example is

host!user@domain

which is reached by forwarding the mail to *domain*'s mail exchange. At that point, the @*domain* part is removed and the UUCP path is processed as above. These addresses are common for Internet hosts that act as UUCP gateways. Note that it is possible, and preferred, for UUCP-only hosts to have and use domain names, since a UUCP-only domain can then have a mail exchange registered for it that points back to the UUCP host's Internet gateway host. Registering a domain is preferred mostly because so many hosts are so badly misconfigured with respect to hybrid addresses.

Some hybrid addresses are more likely to be creatively misinterpreted than others. It is, for example, "safer" to generate hybrid UUCP-style addresses using the percent hack than to mix "`!`" and "`@`" in the same address. A UUCP user `avolio` on a nonregistered node `farm` behind a UUCP-to-Internet gateway `vix.com` could be represented as

`farm!avolio@vix.com`

if you are willing to bet that most Internet hosts will see the `@vix.com` before the `farm!` — but it's a bet you would probably lose. An address of

`avolio%farm.uucp@vix.com`

is much less likely to be damaged or misinterpreted by other mail gateways. If `vix.com`'s mailer were willing to give up some flexibility in its address interpretation, it could even emit mixed-mode addresses of the form

`avolio%farm@vix.com`

This depends on not caring that it's no longer possible to have a local Ethernet host `farm` *and* a UUCP neighbor `farm`. It's better, and more common, to use the `.uucp` pseudodomain in there.

3.2.3. DECnet Paths

DECnet is fundamentally like UUCP in its semantics; only the syntax differs. A DECnet Phase IV path uses "`::`" instead of "`!`", as in

node1::*node2*::*user*[4]

This recipient is reached by opening a DECnet/MAIL11 connection to *node1* which will remove its own name from the path and open a connection to *node2*. *node2* will remove its own name from the path and deliver to the local address *user*. This sounds very simple, but it turns out that DECnet has a lot of surprises in store for us.

If *node1* in the previous example is a VMS host running standard MAIL11 software, then it will synchronously (that is, at the time your host is forwarding the mail to *node1*) open a connection to *node2*. If you have a long path full of VMS nodes, delivering this mail will be a synchronous operation involving all of those nodes. The likelihood of any given mail message getting through this synchronous mesh is somewhere between low and nil, and even if it works, your mailer will have to keep its connection to *node1* open until the last node in the chain has accepted the message and closed the connection. This increases the occupancy time of process table

---

[4] This address would have to be "quoted" if it were to appear inside a mail header, according to RFC 822. Note that some vendor-provided MAIL11 gateways get this wrong.

slots on your host, even though those processes are spending a lot of time waiting (using no CPU time). On a busy MAIL11 host, you will run out of process table slots, file table slots, and virtual memory, unless you carefully limit the number of outbound connections you have running at any given time. This is very difficult, and will probably require custom programming to fix.

If any of the nodes in the path is running a modified MAIL11 package that queues incoming mail and forwards it asynchronously, your host's involvement ends as soon as that node has received your message. A node running Sendmail will work this way — it fully receives and acknowledges an incoming message before it tries to forward it to the "next hop."

As with UUCP paths or invocations of the percent hack, you can hide all kinds of things in a DECnet path if you know that the previous node in the path will interpret its next hop information in a particular way. For example, if you are on a DECnet network that has a node on it called DECWRL, and you know this node is running Sendmail and accepts a variety of hybrid Internet or UUCP addresses, then you can confidently send to addresses like those shown below.

Example Address	Actual Destination
`DECWRL::"vixie!paul"`[5]	user on DECWRL's UUCP neighbor
`DECWRL::"paul@vixie.uucp"`	same but using a pseudodomain
`DECWRL::"paul@vix.com"`	user at an Internet domain

3.3. Pseudodomains, Foreign Addresses, and Encapsulation

Not all mail-carrying networks use the Internet's *user@domain* syntax to specify senders and recipients. Some use an "@" to separate the user name from the host name, but the thing to the right of the "@" is still not a *domain*. More commonly, networks invent their own syntax using creative punctuation characters like "::" or "!". Sendmail can deal with all of this, but it takes some creativity on the part of a sendmail.cf programmer to get all the addresses in and out without damage or misinterpretation.

Since Sendmail is often a *gateway* between incompatible mail domains (usually the Internet and a small number of non-Internet networks), it has to be able to *rewrite* addresses into a format that is both syntactically valid and semantically meaningful for the network into which the mail is being forwarded. In its near infinite flexibility,

---

[5] The quotes are used in DECnet mail to protect the mail system from "foreign" address syntax.

Sendmail has all the tools you need to do this rewrite operation, but first you have to know what you want to do, and then you have to program Sendmail to do it.

The act of rewriting addresses into a different mail protocol's syntax is called *encapsulation*. Getting them back out again is sometimes called *decapsulation*.

3.3.1. Pseudodomains

Most `sendmail.cf` files, including the one described here, use an internal form for non-Internet addresses that looks as if there is an actual domain named after the transport to be used. So, mail destined for some UUCP neighbor might be sent as

`decuac!avolio`

Internally, with the configuration file we'll look at later, Sendmail will convert this to

`avolio@decuac.UUCP`

This is more convenient for `sendmail.cf` programmers, since this is close to the *canonical form* of such an address, which is

`avolio<@decuac.UUCP>`

Because the canonical form is used internally, it is possible for users to actually specify foreign-protocol addresses using the *user@address.pseudodomain* notation, meaning that a user can actually send mail to the

`avolio@decuac.UUCP`

address. Sendmail will convert this address during the delivery process to the

`decuac!avolio`

syntax needed by the UUCP transport. This would have been necessary anyway, given that `avolio<@decuac.UUCP>` would have been the canonical form even if `decuac!avolio` had been the address.

Assuming that you choose a pseudodomain that users will enjoy typing, users may actually prefer the pseudodomain syntax to the native syntax of the foreign protocol (since *user@node*.UUCP rolls off the fingertips so much more easily than *node!user*).

If you are going to accept such pseudodomains on input, it is very tempting to emit them as well, so that a user who receives a gatewayed message that came from a foreign protocol will see *user@domain* in the `From:` header rather than the uglier and comparatively rarer *node::user* or *node!user* or whatever. However, it is vitally important that you not export foreign addresses in *user@pseudodomain* format without taking special care not to violate the Internet standards. For example, if you emit a message with the header

```
From: avolio@decuac.UUCP
```

you had better have total control over all the mailers in the domain to which you are sending the message, since you are depending on their interpretation of this meaningless address being the same as your interpretation of it — which is not a safe bet at all. You might get away with this inside your local domain, if you control the `sendmail.cf` files on all hosts that might see this address. In this way, you can guarantee that each host will understand it as a pseudodomain, about which the domain name servers will be clueless, and will send any user or transport generated replies back to the foreign protocol's gateway, circumventing the name servers. But beware! You are taking your life in your hands if you send this address outside your domain — the address will not be repliable and you *will* hear complaints about it.

One thing you can do to make this process less tricky is to qualify the pseudodomain with your own domain name, and then put a "wildcard MX" record into the domain name system under that name. For example, you can arrange for mail from any instance of *node::user* to be rewritten as

user@node.enet.frobozz.com

and then create an MX record such as

```
*.ENET.FROBOZZ.COM    IN    MX 50 enet-gw.pa.frobozz.com.
```

Given such an MX, the address you rewrote into will be valid no matter what mail transport sees it, inside or outside your local domain. Replies will go back to your gateway (`enet-gw.pa.frobozz.com` in this example), which will recognize the *qualified pseudodomain* and forward the mail through the foreign protocol agent (which is DECnet MAIL11 in this example).

The key here is to qualify the pseudodomain. If you don't, the address is officially nonexistent, and you will have to be terribly careful about which mailers see it and will have to ensure that those mailers qualify or rewrite the address into an officially recognized form before passing the message outside your domain of control. This is harder than it may seem. Users might include such messages inside other messages (where Sendmail can't see them), and recipients outside your domain of control might see the addresses and try to send to them, which will not work. This will mean an extra pile of complaints for you to deal with on Monday morning. Be careful out there.

3.3.2. Foreign Addresses

The more common way to encapsulate a foreign address is simply to add your externally visible @*domain* to it. For example, if `frbzwrl.frobozz.com` receives mail from user `avolio` on UUCP neighbor `decuac`, it could forward the message into the

Internet with the header

```
From: decuac!avolio@frbzwrl.frobozz.com
```

Since the Internet defines "@" but not "!", the official (and, thankfully, common) interpretation of this address is

decuac!*avolio*`@frbzwrl.frobozz.com`

which treats `decuac!avolio` as the *local part*, even though it contains a "!" character.

Of course, if another UUCP-speaking mailer sees this, it may look at such a *mixed-mode* address differently than your mailer did, and if it gives (for example) higher precedence to "!" than to "@", it will treat the address as

`decuac`!*avolio@frbzwrl.frobozz.com*

which probably will not work. Generate mixed mode addresses at your own discretion; we do it on our own gateways since we believe that the mail universe is really an Internet with outlands. When we get letter bombs from people who think the universe is really a UUCP web with outlands or a DECnet with outlands, we engage in "hearty debate."

The proper scheme is to treat such mail according to which transport you receive it from; if it comes in over UUCP, then you should ideally give "!" highest precedence; likewise, if it comes in over DECnet, you should ideally give ":: " highest precedence, and so on for any other non-Internet protocols you support. However, we don't do this on our mail gateways, or recommend in this book that you do it. Though it would be ideal, it happens to be *impossible* given Sendmail's design. There is just no clean way to rewrite addresses based on their incoming transport. This sort of thing is better done in the transport agent that calls Sendmail (for example, `rmail` or `mail111d`), and some of the newer agents are starting to do this.

In the absence of the ability to implement this ideal, many non-Internet transports have moved away from this problem area by just using Internet domain names and "@" notation. As Internet centrists, we applaud this trend.

Meanwhile, it's a messy situation. You have not seen gore until you've witnessed a flame fest between "@"-ists and "!"-ists. You should generate mixed mode addresses according to your interest in publicly defending your position.

3.3.3. Choosing an Encapsulation Approach

Some protocols lend themselves well to pseudodomain encapsulation, and some do not. DECnet networks, for example, are usually *fully connected*, which means that any DECnet node can reach any other DECnet node in what appears to the application program to be "one hop," even though there may be several bridges and/or routers between "here" and "there." This sort of foreign network lends itself quite well to a qualified pseudodomain, since if you ever want to list multiple gateways on the wild-card MX record, all such gateways will at least appear to "directly" reach all nodes of the foreign network, even though one gateway may be in California and another in Massachusetts.

On the other hand, protocols like UUCP that are not fully connected but instead require a full hop-by-hop path to be specified between any given values of "here" and "there," are very awkward to encapsulate inside a *qualified pseudodomain*. Consider the case of mail coming to `frbzwrl.frobozz.com` via UUCP from `vixie!amber!ken`. We can't just turn this into

`ken@vixie!amber.uucp.frobozz.com`

since such an address makes no sense. It will be interpreted either as

ken@vixie!amber.uucp.frobozz.com

or as

ken@vixie!amber.uucp.frobozz.com

neither of which is correct. We could have rewritten that address to

`ken@amber.vixie.uucp.frobozz.com`

but this just creates a different problem, which is that, given that `frbzwrl.frobozz.com` is not the only UUCP gateway in the `frobozz.com` domain, how can we ensure that mail sent to this address reaches the right UUCP gateway? We can't. To make this sort of thing work you have to guarantee that the names to the left of the pseudodomain are globally unique across all UUCP gateways in your domain and teach the gateways how to recognize (and forward) each other's mail; or you have to limit yourself to one UUCP gateway per domain. You could qualify the pseudodomain with your entire host name, but this makes it pretty ugly even before you consider long UUCP paths.

For example,

`olivea!veritas!amdcad!weitek!ram`

becomes:

`ram@weitek.amdcad.veritas.olivea.uucp.uucp-gw-1.pa.frobozz.com`

This is only a small example; common pathnames are 10 to 20 nodes long. All in all, we recommend against this approach, since it does not scale well. We are not, there-fore, going to tell you how to implement it.

If your foreign mail network is fully connected, a pseudodomain under the highest domain for which you are authoritative (and can therefore control the actions of all gateways therein) is the best approach. For a network that is not fully connected where the hop-by-hop path is necessary, we recommend that you consider emitting mixed mode addresses or using the percent hack.

To see all this in action, consider a mail message that came from user jhc on a DECnet node called ESSEX and was sent to some alias that caused it to be sent first to another DECnet node FASTBX and from there via Internet to gw.al.org. From there it was sent to a UUCP node called vixie and then to a user named paul. The envelope sender's address might grow as follows:

Address	Received via	On host
jhc	local	ESSEX::
ESSEX::jhc	DECnet	FASTBX::
jhc@ESSEX.enet.frobozz.com	Internet	gw.al.org
al!ESSEX.enet!jhc	UUCP	vixie!

3.4. Host Name Abbreviation

As we previously presented, the DNS supports domain name abbreviation through its *search list* facility, whereby a *default domain* (or several) will be added to domain names during the query process. This feature will be critically important to the success of your network, since without it your users would always have to type *fully qualified* domain names even when referring to "local" hosts and other network objects.

This feature is not without pitfalls, however, as we will now demonstrate.

3.4.1. Relative Addresses Change with Location

Let's assume that we are on gildor.dco.frobozz.com and the following other hosts exist.

```
jove.pa.frobozz.com
gatekeeper.dco.frobozz.com
gatekeeper.frobozz.com
```

Our DNS *search list* contains the following elements:

```
dco.frobozz.com
frobozz.com
```

If we refer to host names jove.pa or gatekeeper the DNS will go through the following tests.

Try	Result
`jove.pa`	FAIL
`jove.pa.dco.frobozz.com`	FAIL
`jove.pa.frobozz.com`	SUCCEED
`gatekeeper`	FAIL
`gatekeeper.dco.frobozz.com`	SUCCEED

Isn't this handy? Well, maybe not. If we move to Detroit and are sitting on `gildor.det.frobozz.com`. Notice the domain name change; our DNS *search list* is now

```
det.frobozz.com
frobozz.com
```

DNS queries behave slightly differently.

Try	Result
`jove.pa`	FAIL
`jove.pa.det.frobozz.com`	FAIL
`jove.pa.frobozz.com`	SUCCEED
`gatekeeper`	FAIL
`gatekeeper.det.frobozz.com`	FAIL
`gatekeeper.frobozz.com`	SUCCEED

Notice that referring to `gatekeeper` got us to a different host, depending on where we were sitting. The results were

Location	Host name	Resolved to
`det.frobozz.com`	`gatekeeper`	`gatekeeper.frobozz.com`
`dco.frobozz.com`	`gatekeeper`	`gatekeeper.dco.frobozz.com`

This is because we used a *relative* rather than an *absolute* host name. We cannot determine what will happen when we use *relative* names.

We should not use abbreviated host names in addresses. With the previous example in mind, consider that mail to `joe@gatekeeper` might get to the right person *today*, but you have no control over where it will go tomorrow.

If we create a mail message such as in Figure 3-2, `vixie` will get a mail message with the address headers

```
From: Frederick M Avolio <avolio@dco.frobozz.com>
To: vixie@cognition.pa, fma@al.org
```

```
From: Frederick M Avolio <avolio>
To: vixie@cognition.pa, fma@al.org
Subject: Test Mail

This is a test. Please ignore.
```

Figure 3-2

---

which makes sense to him and would work fine if he wanted to reply to the message. However, fma would get mail with the *same* address header lines. The problem is that on fma's machine in the al.org domain, cognition.pa makes no sense, and he is left to ponder what to do with it. He could decide it must mean cognition.pa.frobozz.com, but he could just as easily decide on cognition.pa.dco.frobozz.com, which would not work. This is an example of undefined input leading to arbitrary results.

But wait. It gets worse.

3.4.2. Relative Addresses May Become Ambiguous

Nondeterministic addresses are bad enough. Ambiguous ones are worse. Let's suppose that these two hosts exist:

```
alpha.cs.pimento.edu
beta.ee.pimento.edu
```

Both are at Pimento University, Joe in Computer Science (.cs) and Mary in Electrical Engineering (.ee). Mail could be addressed as in Figure 3-3

The mail addressing makes sense to both Joe and Mary. If Mary wants to send mail to Joe, she can continue to use this addressing. But what is unclear here is the mechanism that decides on the mail routing. If it is the DNS itself, you are counting on permanence in a changing system. If it is built into a local MTA, then someone has made some assumptions about the world that could be erroneous.

In the example, suppose that someone on beta.ee.pimento.edu decided that she needed to send an e-mail message to a user on a system in Czechoslovakia. The top level country domain for Czechoslovakia is .cs.

You should begin to see the problem. An assumption was made, either by the sender or the implementer of the MTA configuration, about the meaning of the characters .cs, unqualified, on the righthand side of an address. The DNS will send mail addressed to, for example, root@alpha.cs to the user root on

---

```
From: joe@alpha.cs
To: mary@beta.ee
Subject: Test mail with abbreviated host names
```

This is a test.

Figure 3-3

---

alpha.cs.pimento.edu, even if the intended recipient is a system administrator on a system in Prague.

As we pointed out earlier, you can get around this by addressing the mail to root@alpha.cs., which *will* direct it to the proper destination. But alpha.cs. (note the trailing dot) is not a proper address, and any system along the way can helpfully remove the trailing dot. Also, when root@alpha.cs writes back and the recipient decides to reply, the problems start all over again. Finally, "alpha.cs." might not be recognized as the same mail location as "alpha.cs".

CS has been used as an easy example. This is not a red herring, though. Many other collisions are possible if people depend on abbreviating host names. This quote appeared in an article posted to comp.mail.sendmail:

> "I experienced a somewhat graphic and tragic example of 'smart'
> name completion ... A fully qualified and correct address in Siberia
> (*.su) was magically transformed into an unknown and unrepliable
> Sydney University site-name (*.su.oz.au) :-(".

A similar experience was reported by a friend at a college in London, England, which shall go nameless (but its initials are "IC"), where they use domain names based on department names. Similar to the .cs problem above, this problem happened with the Chemistry department. At this college, they have "hardcoded" the root domains into their Sendmail configuration files. So what happens to mail when someone tries to abbreviate mail addresses for, let's say, the Chemistry department? Why, it goes to Switzerland (.CH), of course!

3.4.3. Relative Addressing Does Not Carry to the Top Level

The hierarchical nature of the DNS leads one to think that every level is treated equally. This, however, is not the case. Let's suppose we have two individuals with these mail addresses:

```
jimbo@east.sun.com
avolio@fma.frobozz.com
```

If we carry our address abbreviation assumptions to their logical ends, `avolio` should be able to send mail to `jimbo` as `jimbo@east.sun` and `jimbo` will send mail to `avolio` as `avolio@fma.dec`.

We might assume that the DNS will dutifully go through the following steps:

Try	Result
`east.sun`	FAIL
`east.sun.fma.frobozz.com`	FAIL
`east.sun.frobozz.com`	FAIL
`east.sun.com`	SUCCEED

But we would be wrong. The top level domains are treated specially by the DNS. For all purposes, the software behaves as if `sun.com` and `frobozz.com` were both root level names. This bit of sanity should have been carried to a greater extreme.

3.4.4. What We Support

Because of these problems, we do not believe that host name abbreviations should be supported. The risks of misdelivered or unrepliable messages are too great to be considered "worth it." We believe only wholly unqualified host names, fully qualified host names, and domain names should be supported for mail addresses in a Sendmail configuration. Thus, the rules we follow are simple:

(1) If the canonicalized address has no host part, it is meant for delivery by the local user agent.

(2) If the right hand side of an address (to the right of an "@") has a simple token (no dots) as the host part, we tack on our local domain. So

```
vixie@cognition
```

(in the Palo Alto office of our organization) is assumed to mean

```
vixie@cognition.pa.frobozz.com
```

This means that even on incoming mail we will tack on our domain if none is present. This is what we do, and this is what the configuration file we present in this book will do. Our approach has been the cause of some arguments with people who erroneously sent out unqualified host names on e-mail. There is no alternative. The *only* defined meaning for

user@simplename

is

user@simplename . our-domain

No other meaning is possible. If you take the side of the angels, you will also receive flames. Take comfort in the knowledge that you are *right*.

(3)   If the domain part of an address has at least one dot in it, we assume it is fully qualified and it is sent "as is" through the DNS. Note that this could mean that abbreviations could be used unless DNSRCH was turned off when your Sendmail binary was built. We do not disable DNSRCH, we simply discourage it. As should you.

4

Aliases and Local Delivery

Every mail message has a set of destinations, called recipients or recipient addresses. At some point during the processing, handling, and forwarding of each recipient's copy of a message, the message will undergo final or *local* delivery. This cannot happen until the message reaches the host where the recipient actually reads her mail; one of sendmail.cf's principle functions is the recognition of *local* recipients and the *local delivery* of mail to them. If a recipient address is not found to be *local*, Sendmail sends it out via some network ("nonlocal") mailer in its role as a *gateway* or *relay*. This chapter describes *local delivery*.

Often a user will be known by some set of names other than (or in addition to) her login name. Sendmail's aliases database is a way to funnel mail from all of these names into a single mailbox. Likewise, a user will probably read her mail on some particular host, but it is inconvenient for other users to have to know which host that is, since a user might move her mailbox to a different host, or the host's name might be difficult to spell or to remember. The aliases database can direct a user's mail toward her *mail host* no matter which host in the local domain first receives any given message. This is particularly useful because it allows a user to appear to be reachable at the border gateway or on the main mail hub.

4.1. Local Delivery Strategies

Given the flexibility allowed by sendmail.cf, it should come as no surprise that there are many different ways to identify mail as "local" so that it can be delivered to the local mail user agent.

Generally, Ruleset 0 will strip off the local domain(s) and host name(s) until the domain disappears from the address or cannot be stripped any further. When what remains of the address contains no domain or only some domain for which the local Sendmail is *authoritative*, this is given to the local mail user agent.

4.1.1. Multiple Local User Agents

It is entirely possible that different subsets of your user community will want to use different — and incompatible — local user agents. While most of the user agents in use in your environment will employ a common system mailbox location and format, there will be other user agents that use their own custom databases for storage of delivered but as yet unread mail.

4.1.1.1. /bin/mail

Most user agents will happily share a common system mailbox; MH, UCB Mail, Elm, and others share /var/spool/mail/*user-name* without interference, and users can switch between these user agents at will. These files contain potentially many messages, catenated together with separators called "UNIX From_ lines" which are of the form

```
From rich@ai.wossamotta.edu Sun Aug 23 14:31:09 1992
```

The /bin/mail program, which appends messages to these files, will modify any line of a message if it begins with the string "From " to make it begin instead with ">From ": This ensures that no line of the message is accidentally interpreted as a message separator later on when the user agent reads this mailbox file.

4.1.1.2. POP

The post office protocol (POP) agent keeps a user's unread mail in files named /var/spool/pop/*user-name*, whose format is different from that used by /bin/mail. The messages are catenated together as before, but the separator is a line consisting of four ASCII SOH (*control-A*) characters (MMDF format). Because this file is in a different location and has a different format from the one used by /bin/mail, users cannot switch between POP and other user agents without help from their system administrator, who must arrange for their mail to be delivered through the appropriate local user agent's delivery mechanism. Some newer versions of POP store mail in the same place and in the same way as /bin/mail.

4.1.1.3. Other Local Transports

There are nearly as many user agents as there are UNIX programmers. While most UAs tend to use only the most common existing environment as a way to make life easier for their users, several have attempted to redefine the environment in ways that are probably "better" in some technical sense but which, in our opinion are not "better enough" to justify the cost to users and system administrators in maintaining multiple environments.

One example of this is MMDF, which is a message transfer agent in competition with Sendmail, but which includes its own set of user agents. These user agents store incoming mail in files called .mailbox in the recipients' home directories, and they use the "four SOH" message separator described above for POP. While the format is the same as POP's, the location is different. Unless the user agents know to look in both places, the fact that the format happens to be the same gains absolutely nothing in terms of interoperability.

4.1.2. Per-User Local Agent Selection

Since some of your users may want to employ a user agent that requires an unusual and incompatible local user delivery agent, care should be taken to ensure that you can provide this flexibility — even if you don't need it at the outset — without breaking your whole model. We will use POP as an example.

If your default local delivery agent is /bin/mail and you call this mailer from Ruleset 0 when no other action seems appropriate, adding a rule just before this "default" is taken will allow you to support POP users. This relies on the local aliases database having something "special" for each POP user, such as

```
vixie: vixie.pop
```

We will discuss aliases in detail in a bit, but for now it is sufficient to understand that this example says that any mail for local address vixie will be sent, instead, to local address vixie.pop. In the presence of this alias, if you arranged for mail to *user*.pop to resolve to the POP mailer rather than the local mailer, mail sent to vixie would end up being delivered through the POP transport rather than through the /bin/mail program. Once you have this working, you can switch a user from /bin/mail to POP just by editing the aliases database, with no per-user changes needed in sendmail.cf or anywhere else.

As you read through the documentation for POP and in particular popd, you will encounter several examples of proposed modifications to sendmail.cf. Take them with a kilogram of salt and think it through for yourself, since only you know your local environment and it is very likely that sendmail.cf snippets written by someone else will not apply to your configuration. We note with particular concern that the recommended syntax for POP aliases is

```
vixie: vixie@pop
```

and this is the syntax supported by most `sendmail.cf` snippets that claim to support POP. This syntax will work, but woe be unto thee if you support it and also have a host named `pop` on your local network. Do not build your `sendmail.cf` file from an eclectic pile of bits and pieces, unless you carefully examine each change. If you don't understand your `sendmail.cf`, then it is most probably wrong in detail and it is absolutely wrong in the abstract. *You* are the one who will have to fix your mailer if someone else's contribution to your `sendmail.cf` breaks it. Tread carefully — those toes you see before you are your own.

4.1.3. Local Agent Options

Sendmail has the ability to rewrite headers as they pass through, based on the mailer that is used for delivery. The `local` mailer (which is usually `/bin/mail`, but this discussion applies to POP as well) has its own mailer specific rewrite rulesets, which gives you the flexibility to decide how you want addresses to look when users see them in incoming mail.

Consider mail sent from outside the local domain. If it arrives in one of your users' mailboxes, you can safely assume that it was sent to that user's address at some domain or subdomain for which you are *authoritative*. When your user sees this mail, do you want her to see a `To:` or `Cc:` header that contains the full original domain to which the mail was sent? For example,

```
From: win@lcs.wossamotta.edu
To: vixie@frbzwrl.frobozz.com
```

The alternative is to have the user see only the *local part*, with the domain removed:

```
From: win@lcs.wossamotta.edu
To: vixie
```

Beware. The second choice is attractive because it is shorter and contains less potentially redundant information. However, at least one user agent — UCB Mail — does the wrong thing in this scenario. If UCB Mail sees a `To:` header without a domain and a `From:` header *with* a domain, it assumes that some transport is misconfigured and aggressively seeks to rectify the "error" by appending the sender's domain to the unqualified recipient addresses. Your headers, in other words, might show up as

```
From: win@lcs.wossamotta.edu
To: vixie@lcs.wossamotta.edu
```

even though user `vixie` does not have an account in the `lcs.wossamotta.edu` domain and this mail was actually sent to and received by

```
<vixie@frbzwrl.frobozz.com>
```

UCB Mail considers this a feature, and it is not an option — you can't turn this "feature" off. You may find yourself gravitating toward some user agent other than UCB Mail for reasons unrelated to this, but rest assured — at least one and probably many of your users will want to use UCB Mail and you *will* end up supporting it sooner or later.

Placating UCB Mail on this point is not necessarily a bad thing to do. Though seeing one's own domain on incoming mail may seem redundant, if there are multiple domains for which you are authoritative (for example, `pa.frobozz.com`, `frbzwrl.frobozz.com`, and `wrl.frobozz.com` are all handled by the same mail gateway, which has only one `aliases` database), it can be useful or at least amusing to see which addresses your various correspondents are using to reach you.

But what about local mail? If someone on your own host (or, in the case of a shared `aliases` database, someone else in your mail cluster) sends you mail, do you want or need to see the full domain in the `From:` and `To:` headers? We think not. Our rule is not "The domain shall always be specified," but instead "Whatever the original `To:` and `Cc:` headers said is what the recipient ought to see." If user `reid` sends mail, while logged into host `torrey.pa.frobozz.com`, to address `<vixie@acetes>`, and `acetes`' `aliases` database, shared with all `pa.frobozz.com` hosts, says

```
vixie: vixie@cognition
```

then the mail will ultimately be delivered to the recipient's mailbox with the headers

```
From: reid
To: vixie@acetes
```

We chose the value shown for the `From:` header, since it is almost never useful to know what host a user was logged in to when the mail was sent, if all hosts in your subdomain share a common `aliases` database. If you really want to know which local host a message was sent from, you can always check the `Received:` headers.

We chose the value shown for the `To:` header, since this was the address to which the mail was sent, and the message transfer agent that rewrites least, rewrites best. The only penalty in this design is that if this mail is `Cc:`'d to some other user and that user does a "reply all" operation in her user agent, recipient `vixie`'s copy of the reply will be unnecessarily sent by way of host `acetes`, which has to forward the message to `vixie`'s mail host after consulting its `aliases` database.

We believe it is better to retain information that cannot be recovered than to delete information that is, in the grand scheme of things, not really harmful. In an alias equivalenced subdomain, users will eventually tend to send to a *user-name* rather than to a *user-name@host*, so most of the time local mail will be delivered with no domain on either the `From:` or `To:` headers.

4.2. Aliases

If a mailer is called `local`, (in the Sendmail configuration file), Sendmail knows that any address delivered via that mailer is considered *local* and it will therefore attempt to *alias* it. To *alias* an address means to search for it in the local `aliases` database, and if it is found, to replace the address with the alias value (called the *expansion* for reasons that will become clear shortly). If there is no alias for this address in the `aliases` database, Sendmail will search for a file called `.forward` in the recipient's home directory; if found, `.forward`'s contents become the alias expansion. Note that the system's `aliases` database overrides a user's `.forward` file if the `aliases` database contains an entry for this user. Conversely, if the *user-name* does not correspond to a local account, then no `.forward` file is possible.

In practice, the `aliases` database is edited only by the system administrator and `.forward` files are edited only by users; it is somewhat natural that the system administrator's aliases should take precedence if overlaps occur. In the case of a shared, transport level alias meant to direct a user's mail to some specific *mail host*, that mail host will strip its own name out of the transport level alias, and on that (and *only* that) host, the user's `.forward` file will be used.

4.2.1. Details

Let's have a look at some examples to see how this logic applies. Assume the existence of an alias such as

```
vix: vixie
```

This would tell Sendmail that if the `local` mailer is called with the address <vix>, replace the address with <vixie> and start all over with Ruleset 3 and Ruleset 0. The reason for starting over is that the expansion may well contain routing characters, as in

```
vixie: vixie@cognition.pa.frobozz.com
```

Mail sent to <vixie> in the presence of that alias ends up being delivered to <vixie@cognition.pa.frobozz.com>, which is not a local name. If aliasing only expanded local names into other local names, then expansions such as the above would not be possible. Thus, whenever an alias "match" occurs, the expansion is passed back through Ruleset 3 and Ruleset 0 to give it a chance to be evaluated to some other mailer.

Given these two aliases on a host that calls itself `frbzwrl.frobozz.com`,

```
vix: vixie
vixie: vixie@cognition
```

mail sent to <vix@frbzwrl.frobozz.com> will be handled as shown in Table 4-1. This looks convoluted, and it is, but such is the price of generality. It all happens very quickly; lookups in the aliases database are particularly fast. The root concept behind all of this is that only mailers marked *local* in their Flags= clause will cause aliasing to be performed.

4.2.2. Distribution Lists

Aliases need not expand to a single address. Subject to the restrictions explained later, an alias can expand to any number of addresses, some of which can be other aliases in the local transport or in some other transport. Mail that is sent to such an alias will be received by all the addresses that alias expands to. Because of the "fan out" nature of this kind of alias, we sometimes call them *distribution lists*.

Distribution lists can become the lifeblood of an organization's information flow, if they are implemented reliably. A group of users who are on one distribution list can hold extended "conferences" just by reading and replying to messages from other users. This is especially wonderful when not all of the users sleep in the same time zone.

Address	After
<vix@frbzwrl.frobozz.com>	(input)
vix<@frbzwrl.frobozz.com>	(Ruleset 3)
vix	(Ruleset 0 or a utility called thereby)
$#local $:vix	(Ruleset 0 hands it to the local mailer)
vixie	(local mailer causes aliasing)
vixie	(Ruleset 3 has no rewriting to do)
$#local $:vixie	(Ruleset 0 hands it to the local mailer again)
vixie@cognition	(local mailer causes aliasing)
vixie<@cognition>	(Ruleset 3)
$#smtp $@cognition $:vixie	(Ruleset 0 resolves to the SMTP mailer)

Table 4-1. Ruleset Calling Example

The downside of distribution lists is that since they are fairly easy to join and *very* easy to send mail to, a user will often find her mailbox overrun by messages she considers to be noise, static, drivel, or some combination thereof. As a distribution list grows, the likelihood increases that its original charter will not apply to all the discussions that take place therein; Therefore, it is important for distribution list maintainers to be on the lists they maintain so that they can recognize this trend and suggest splitting the list when the appropriate time comes.

4.2.3. Transport Level vs. User Level Aliases

Many user agents have their own alias mechanisms. An example of an alias mechanism is the private (per-user) `.mailrc` file used by UCB Mail. This file permits a user to create aliases similar in appearance and function to sendmail's aliases, in that mail could be addressed by a user to the `<vix>` address and end up being sent to `<vix@cognition.pa.frobozz.com>`. MH, Elm, and others, also provide this feature, though, of course, using files whose names and formats are completely different from UCB Mail's.

There are two important differences among a transport level mechanism (like sendmail's `aliases` database) and any user level mechanism.

First, user level aliases are usually not shared between multiple users; Transport level aliases are shared among all users on a particular host (and perhaps on all hosts in a domain, as well). Therefore, each user's private alias database might contain aliases that have the same names as but very different expansions from aliases in other users' private alias databases or the transport level `aliases` database. There are no actual collisions from this, but it can be confusing for users who set up private aliases, forget about them, and then try to use them from some other user's account, which results in what appears to that user to be a mysterious failure.

Second, user level aliases are expanded into the headers of outgoing mail, whereas transport level aliases go out in their unexpanded form. This means that mail sent to `<avolio>` in the presence of user level alias

```
avolio: avolio@dco.frobozz.com
```

results in the header

```
To: avolio@dco.frobozz.com
```

Mail sent to `<avolio>` with no such user level alias but with transport level alias

```
avolio: avolio@dco.frobozz.com
```

results in the header

```
To: avolio
```

If this transport alias is present in the `pa.frobozz.com` domain and mail is sent to it, Fred will be in the odd position of receiving mail that claims to be

```
To: avolio@pa.frobozz.com
```

even if his mail host is in some completely different domain. Head scratching confusion aside, this has an evil side effect: All the `Cc:` recipients will see that same `To:` header, and if they reply to "all recipients," Fred's copy of their reply will be sent back to `<avolio@pa.frobozz.com>`, where it will be forwarded to `<avolio@dco.frobozz.com>` and ultimately end up in his mailbox on host `gildor.dco.frobozz.com` after taking an extra roundtrip from Washington, D.C. (`dco.frobozz.com`), to Palo Alto, California (`pa.frobozz.com`).

We therefore recommend against transport level "convenience" aliases because of the performance penalty on all replies. Mail sent to a distribution list that happens to contain a remote user is a different matter — replies *must* go back through the original transport, since only it knows what the distribution list's alias expands to. A transport level alias with only one name on it should only be added if the destination host is in the local domain. Therefore,

```
vixie: vixie@cognition
```

is acceptable, since it is used only to funnel the mail to the user's local mail host, whereas

```
vixie: vixie@cognition.pa.frobozz.com
```

in some transport level `aliases` database outside the `pa.frobozz.com` domain is probably (rather, almost certainly) a bad idea. While this rule applies more to large organizations than to average size organizations, the principle still applies, and besides that, you never know which organizations are going to be large later — they all seem small or average sized at first.

One exception to this rule is if a user has held an account in some domain and then moves to a different domain. It is reasonable to want to forward that user's mail to her new address, at least until all of her correspondents update their alias files (which means "forever," since aliases that continue to work will never be changed). In most such cases, the performance penalty will be paid continuously until some Postmaster decides that the price is too high and deletes the old alias.

There are domains that export mail with a `From:` address that makes it look as though all users had an account on the gateway host itself or that all users are reachable at the top level domain itself. For example, the address

```
Hayes.Pa@Xerox.COM
```

puts a site identifier at the end of the *local part* rather than using a subdomain. The penalties for doing it this way are that all internal sites must be reached through the same gateway (which is not a problem if you don't anticipate ever having more than one gateway) and that your `sendmail.cf` needs some extra logic in it to detect these qualifiers in the *local part*. Another example is

```
Lenard_Lovestreet@Previous.COM
```

which does not even contain a site identifier and therefore makes the additional assumption that there will never be too many employees to list them all in the gateway's `aliases` database. Our advice: Use a subdomain unless you are sure that your domain will never grow. Since you can never be sure of this, and history indicates that the opposite is always true, our advice translates to: Use subdomains.

4.3. `aliases` Syntax

Sendmail's `aliases` database has a normal text file that you are expected to edit with some text editor (`vi` and `emacs` are examples). Because the file is "text," the format was optimized for ease of editing and is actually very pleasant to work with once you know about the various "gotchas."

  `aliases` consists of some number of aliases, blank lines, and comments. Blank lines and comment lines cannot appear inside an alias; they must appear (if at all) between aliases, where they will be ignored by Sendmail. A comment is any line that begins with a pound sign (#).

  Each alias consists of the name being aliased, a colon (:), and the expansion, which usually consists of one address or several addresses separated by commas (,). Blanks and tabs (ASCII HT or *control-I*) surrounding addresses in the expansion will be ignored. Aliases can continue across multiple lines if the continuation lines are begun with blanks and/or tabs.

  Comments cannot appear on the same line with alias text — that is, the following is illegal:

```
avolio: avolio@dco.frobozz.com      # fred in washington
```

That sort of comment would have to be written as

```
# fred in washington
avolio: avolio@dco.frobozz.com
```

To put comments on the same line as alias text, use RFC 822 comment format. This looks something like

```
avolio: avolio@dco.frobozz.com (Fred in Washington)
```

or

```
avolio: Fred in Washington <avolio@dco.frobozz.com>
```

Note that this type of comment works quite well in the presence of commas:

```
sendmail-hackers: avolio@dco.frobozz.com (fred),
                  vixie@pa.frobozz.com (paul)
```

If the same name is aliased more than once, the last one in `aliases` is the one that is used. This fact is important to the *local override* discussion later on.

4.4. `:include:` **Files**

We've discussed many of the issues that might come up in your use of `:include:` files, so we will close this chapter by explaining what they are, what your motivations might be for using them, and how to get them set up.

If you have a large distribution list, it is possible that you will not want the entire alias expansion to be present in the system wide (or network wide) `aliases` database. Reasons for this might be among the following:

- It would be convenient for the list maintainer (`owner-*`) to be a different person or group of people from the `aliases` database maintainer, and neither would necessarily be able to edit both the list *and* the database because of security concerns or other administrative boundaries.

- The list is *very* large and makes sharing the `aliases` database across many hosts an overly resource consuming (that is, slow) process.

- The list changes a lot, and running `newaliases` on all your hosts takes a long time and isn't really necessary, since you could be expanding the alias on only one host.

We strongly encourage the use of `:include:` files whenever you have a list that will not fit on four or fewer lines in an `aliases` file. Use of `:include:` tends to force us to expand all of our aliases on the same host, which is a good thing in itself. This expansion, in turn, makes it easier for you to add *double queuing* in the future, as you will certainly do if your list is popular or large.

To use an `:include:` file, you replace the alias expansion as follows:

```
kjs-workers: :include: /udir/vixie/Mail/.lists/kjs-workers
```

The effect of this is that when mail is delivered to the `kjs-workers` alias, the expansion is from the contents of the file

```
/udir/vixie/Mail/.lists/kjs-workers
```

This file contains one address per line, with or without RFC 822 style comments.

For example:

```
Paul Vixie              <vixie@vix.com>
Lenard Lövestreet       <lenard_lovestreet@previous.com>
Paul Apple              <Paul-Apple@pimento.edu>
Neil Rickly             <rickly@cs.mulligan.edu>
```

We recommend that you follow this example. Use the same kind of comments on all addresses and use ASCII HT (*tab*) characters to keep things neat. When a distribution list grows longer than a handful of addresses, your neatness will be paid back many times over from ease of maintainence.

4.5. `aliases` Database Issues

Note that the text version of the `aliases` database (`/etc/aliases`) must be translated into the binary "fast access" version (`/etc/aliases.(dir,pag)` or `/etc/aliases.db`) using the `newaliases` or `sendmail -bi` commands. This must be done whenever the text version is edited or replaced. There is a `sendmail.cf` option that automates this operation, but we recommend against using it because its exclusive locking mechanism (necessary to prevent several autorebuilds from happening simultaneously) is failure prone.

Because of limitations of the underlying database library, alias expansions cannot be longer than 1,024 characters. Most versions of Sendmail do not check for this condition, and the database library does not report any kind of error message. This means that alias expansions longer than 1,024 characters will probably be silently truncated, and the only way you will ever find out about it is when addresses toward the end of the expansion never get any mail, or, if you get lucky, the truncation will appear mid-address and the distribution list will generate errors because of the truncated address.

The customary way around this problem is to use `:include:` files or to break up your expansion across several aliases, so that each expansion is less than 1,024 characters. In the actual distribution list alias, reference each of these *subaliases*. This ends up looking something like:

```
list: list-a, list-b, list-c
list-a: long, list, of, names, 1K, characters, or, so
list-b: another, long, list, of, names, of, about, 1K
list-c: smaller, list, with, newest, additions, on, it
```

In this example, when `list-c` looks like it's getting pretty long, you change the list alias to include `list-d` as well, and then create `list-d` and add your new names to that. Of course, as addresses are removed from the list, the size of the different *subaliases* will get out of balance and you will probably want to smash them all together with your text editor and then break them apart into *subaliases* again.

4.6. Sharing and Distributing Aliases

An alias that directs a user's mail at some specific mail host is going to be most useful if it is visible on all hosts in the local domain. It is not reasonable to expect the system administrator to manually update the `aliases` database on every host on her network; issues of scale and error probabilities as well as boredom make that impossible.

Clearly, if the `aliases` database is to be shared across all or most hosts in a domain, some kind of automation is called for. As with all such problems, there are many different solutions available, all incompatible with each other. You can use `rdist`, `sup`, NIS, Hesiod, or NFS. Each has technical strengths and weaknesses, though the technology that wins in any given domain is probably going to be the one that came with your operating system.

`rdist` and `sup` are tools that let you replicate files across some set of hosts. They are sometimes used to keep operating system files (including binary files, commands, and even kernels) up to date with respect to some central server. The use of these tools for configuration files like the `aliases` database is probably overkill, but when all you have is a hammer, everything looks like a nail. `rdist` is available free from U.C. Berkeley and is shipped as part of most modern "open" operating systems. `sup` is available free from Carnegie Mellon University and is part of most Mach-derived operating systems. Each has a configuration file with a relatively obscure syntax and will take some time to learn. We use (and recommend) `rdist` because it is more widely available and its bugs are better understood. A simple `Distfile` (used by `rdist`) would be

```
/etc/aliases -> ( cognition volition efficacy )
        install;
        special /etc/aliases "newaliases";
```

NIS is the Network Information Service that is present on most modern, so called "open," operating systems. NIS is licensed by Sun Microsystems and if you have it you may already be using it. NIS capable operating systems normally include a version of Sendmail that is capable of retrieving aliases from the NIS server rather than requiring a local `aliases` database on each host. This has some advantages to the system administrator, since she need only update the `aliases` database on the NIS server and her changes will be transparently and quickly visible on all the hosts in the NIS domain.

We recommend against using NIS, partly out of religious zealotry regarding UDP based protocols with bone jarringly short, nonadaptive timeouts and partly because it is unlikely that you will have the libraries needed to build an NIS capable version of Sendmail (note that IDA Sendmail contains code to access NIS, but can only be compiled on systems that contain the Sun NIS libraries). We recommend using NIS for your aliases distribution only if you are already using it for your other administrative databases.

Hesiod is the extended name service created by MIT Project Athena. It uses the DNS (Domain Name Service) to provide network wide access to a copy of the `aliases` database. We recommend it in preference to NIS, since it is based on the more open DNS protocol and since the name space follows the hierarchy of the DNS, which you should already be using for your host address database. However, Hesiod is not widely available on commercial platforms and, as with NIS, it is unlikely that your Hesiod vendor gave you source code to the Hesiod capable version of Sendmail you will need to use. Again, we recommend using Hesiod for your `aliases` distribution only if you are already using it for your other administrative databases.

Finally we come to NFS, the Network File System, which like NIS is licensed by Sun Microsystems and is shipped with many modern operating systems. Assuming that all your hosts mount at least one domain wide file system, you need only make `/etc/aliases` (and `/etc/aliases.dir` and `/etc/aliases.pag`) symbolic links to those files in the domain wide file system or change the OA option in `sendmail.cf` to directly specify the NFS path to these files.

For example, if your domain wide file system is called `/org`, you could have symbolic links on all your MIPS based hosts such as

```
/etc/aliases       →    /org/share/etc/aliases
/etc/aliases.dir   →    /org/mips/etc/aliases.dir
/etc/aliases.pag   →    /org/mips/etc/aliases.pag
```

while on your SPARC based hosts you could use

```
/etc/aliases       →    /org/share/etc/aliases
/etc/aliases.dir   →    /org/sparc/etc/aliases.dir
/etc/aliases.pag   →    /org/sparc/etc/aliases.pag
```

The reason for using different `.dir` and `.pag` files for different architectures is that the binary database format is highly architecture dependent; the byte order and possibly the alignment will be different depending on the kind of computer you are using. If you go this route, you will need to build the binary databases on a native server for each architecture. We generally recommend against using NFS for `aliases` distribution, since a minor blip in the NFS server will either result in hundreds of hung Sendmail daemons or in hundreds of bounced mail messages, depending on what mount options you use. Traditional NFS does not have a "hot fallback" mechanism, and there is a relatively tight binding between a client and its servers.

The other approaches described above all permit multiple servers or, in the case of `rdist` and `sup`, require no server at all except during updates.

It would be impolite to close this section without at least mentioning NeXT Computer's NetInfo system. NetInfo is rather like NIS in that it has servers and clients, and the clients can have local `aliases` databases. Nevertheless, few other vendors have adopted the NetInfo system — if you have a NeXT computer, you have NetInfo; otherwise, you probably don't. We do not feel that NetInfo is going to take the world by storm in quite the same way that NIS has — it's sad, but true. NetInfo does permit local overrides with no special hacking required, but since you will ideally pick a single alias distribution mechanism for your entire network, NetInfo is attractive only if all of your computers run operating systems licensed from NeXT Computers, Inc.

4.7. Local Overrides

One problem with all of these approaches is that aliases *must* be the same on all computers. You can't have a name aliased differently on one host than on all other hosts. This facility, if you had it, would be called a *local override*. According to the above survey of different mechanisms for sharing the `aliases` database, you probably do not have this facility.

The lack of local overrides presents problems for `:include:` alias expansions (described later), since the file referenced by the `:include:` directive is likely to be present on only one host, while every other host will also see the `:include:` but be unable to read the file. Making the `:include:` files reachable via NFS solves this problem but at the expense of having all your mail bounce — or all your Sendmail daemons wedge — during server reboots. We consider this unacceptable; your sensitivities may be different from ours.

Lack of local overrides also makes it difficult for large domains that share most aliases but have a few aliases that differ for each local subset of hosts. The `pa.frobozz.com` domain is an example of this: Most aliases are the same on all hosts, but administrative aliases such as `postmaster` and `root` depend on which building the host is located in, and they can therefore point to the local support staff. If you don't need this feature yet, be cautious because you will need it soon enough — all campus networks get there sooner or later.

Of all the mechanisms we've surveyed, only NIS and NetInfo have the inherent ability to have a subset of names aliased from local data and use the domain wide alias database only as a "fallback." However, there are ways to add this feature to several of the other mechanisms. You can also learn to live without it.

To add this feature to `rdist`, you can make the tool that distributes new `/etc/aliases` files a little more complex than a single `Distfile`. What we do in `pa.frobozz.com` is put all the "user home mail server" aliases into a file called homes, put all the distribution lists into a file called `groups`, and then, for each host, permit a file called `local.`*host-name* that, if present, is appended to the other two when forming the `aliases` file that is sent to the host whose name is *host-name*. This depends on the fact that the last alias for a name is the one that is used. Briefly, a tool that implements local overrides in `rdist` would look like

```
#!/bin/sh
HOSTS="cognition volition efficacy"
for HOST in $HOSTS; do
    FILES="groups homes"
    [ -s local.$HOST ] && FILES="$FILES local.$HOST"
    cat $FILES > aliases
    rdist -f - <<EOF
    aliases -> ( $HOST )
        install -B /etc;
        special aliases "newaliases";
EOF
done
exit
```

The salient differences between this example and the previous `rdist` example are that the `Distfile` is included as a shell "here document" rather than being in a separate file, and that the `-B` option is given so that only if there is a "binary difference" between the old and new files will the file be copied — which is necessary since the default is to compare modification times, and these will always be different because we are rebuilding the server's file for each `rdist`. This is approximately the mechanism we use for `pa.frobozz.com`, and though it won't win any awards for elegance, it is simple and reliable.

In practice, such an update mechanism should get its list of hosts from some other registry (such as `/etc/hosts`). In large organizations, the main administrative server for each subdomain would run such an update mechanism, but would only `rdist` to a few large servers in each building, which would then update their local clients with a similar or perhaps very different mechanism. If you are not doing something like this now, you should consider it. If you are already doing it, you need only integrate our "override" semantics into your existing `aliases` update mechanism.

One way to live without "local overrides" is to give up on having your administrative aliases be different for different collections of hosts. To force your distribution lists to be expanded on some specific computer, use two aliases:

```
list: list-real@mailhost
list-real: :include: /var/local/adm/maillists/list
```

The first one is the one everyone will send to; it will forward the mail to host `mailhost` which will see its own name, strip it off, alias that result, see the `:include:`, read the designated file, and ain't life grand. This is the next best thing after a modified rdist, and we recommend that you use it rather than switching to NIS (unless you are already using NIS in spite of our warnings).

4.8. Other Syntactic Trivia

If an entry in an alias expansion is preceded by a backslash (\), it will not be subject to further alias expansion. For example,

```
vixie: vixie@acetes, \vixie
```

Mail sent to vixie in the presence of this alias is expanded to vixie@acetes and \vixie in the normal way; vixie@acetes gets a copy, and local user vixie gets a copy. Without the backslash in front of vixie in the expansion, this becomes an alias loop.

If an entry in an alias expansion begins with a vertical bar (|), often called a *pipe*, it represents a /bin/sh command to be executed, with the message as its standard input. For example,

```
msgs: "|/usr/ucb/msgs -s"
```

Mail sent to msgs in the presence of this alias is *piped* to the /usr/ucb/msgs program whose argument is -s. Aliases of this form should be enclosed in double quotes (").

Note that you will want to make sure that the command is textually unique for each user who might pipe her mail through it, since only one copy will be sent to each unique address. For example,

```
avolio: "|/usr/local/etc/user-has-left"
vixie:  "|/usr/local/etc/user-has-left"
```

In the presence of these two aliases and a program or script called user-has-left that might send back a message explaining that the recipient has left the domain, any mail sent

```
To: vixie, avolio
```

will cause only one invocation of the user-has-left script. Sendmail deletes duplicate addresses when building recipient lists. So, even though the script might be prepared to parse the mail headers to identify the recipient, you code these aliases with user names on the command lines just to force the expansions to be unique. For example:

```
avolio: "|/usr/local/etc/user-has-left avolio"
vixie:  "|/usr/local/etc/user-has-left vixie"
```

This is probably the right way to design your `user-has-left` script in any case, since if mail is sent to a distribution list that happens to contain these two users, the mail headers will not include their names as recipients. It is better to propagate the envelope recipient information on the command line and use that information to identify the recipient user.

Programs that Sendmail pipes to in this way will run as the recipient user if the pipe syntax was used in a recipient's `.forward` file. If the pipe syntax was used in the `aliases` database, the piped program will run as the sender if the sender is a local user; otherwise, the piped program will run as the user and group identified in `sendmail.cf` with Ou*uid* and Og*gid*. The defaults for both Ou and Og are configurable when building the Sendmail binary, but are usually 1, which is user `daemon` and group `daemon` on most systems.

If an alias expansion begins with a slash (`/`), it represents the name of a file to which the message should be appended. This file must already exist. While opening this file, Sendmail will run as the recipient or the sender, or as the default user and group specified in `sendmail.cf`. This is just as for piped programs as explained above. Since Sendmail runs as a user and group for incoming network mail that is different from those for locally originated mail, the file must in practice be world writable if this feature is used from the `aliases` database. Using it from a `.forward` file lets you predict that it will always open the file as the recipient user (and her default group from the `passwd` database). A system administrator would have to create a dummy account for each alias just to use this feature. It is probably because of all these security related limitations that we have never seen this feature used in a production mail system. It's just not worth it.

The expansion prevention and pipe to program features are often used together in `.forward` files, where, when a user goes on vacation, you might find something like this:

```
\eric,  "|/usr/ucb/vacation -a allman eric"
```

Here, the user wants to receive a copy of all incoming mail and also to pipe a copy through the `vacation` program — that sends back mail of the form "I am on vacation," but only one time per sender per week. This transmission quickly informs your correspondents that you are on vacation, but does not answer every message they send you; A reminder is sent out each week if you are still on vacation and still getting mail from that sender. The `vacation` program is freely available; try `Archie` (see Appendix K). Note that since this is a `.forward` file, the aliases could have been entered on two lines, without the comma, as in

```
\eric
"|/usr/ucb/vacation -a allman eric"
```

Sendmail will not permit these special syntaxes to be used in a message envelope; they *must* come either from the `aliases` database or from a user's `.forward` file.

The :include: syntax is even more restrictive; it can only come from the aliases database. The reason for this is security: Only a local user should be able to select the programs that are executed (piped to) on the local host. Only a system administrator should be able to select the files that are opened because of :include: directives or append to file directives.

Historically, nearly all of Sendmail's well publicized security problems occur via bugs or deliberate back doors in these special features in the alias mechanism. If the security looks tight, relax and enjoy it — it wasn't always so. If it looks inconvenient, well, inconvenience is the root of all security. Look closely: There's probably a way to do whatever you want. You just have to be careful.

4.9. Predefined Aliases

There are several aliases that Sendmail expects you to define, and it looks for a *derived* alias name in support of each distribution list. The predefined aliases are MAILER-DAEMON and Postmaster. Note that case is not significant in alias names; we show MAILER-DAEMON in ALL UPPER CASE, since that's how the Internet literature talks about it, not because mailer-daemon won't work equally well. Note that these names are *conventions* that every sendmail.cf and aliases file must work to uphold; the MAILER-DAEMON name is set in sendmail.cf with a

DnMAILER-DAEMON

definition; you could certainly define a different name there, but please *don't!* — you will only cause strife and confusion for yourself and other system administrators who follow in your path.

MAILER-DAEMON (really $n) is where mail goes if it can't be delivered to a recipient and cannot be sent back to the sender. The way it works is tricky but worth knowing about. Any mail message that cannot be delivered to any recipient can cause a nondelivery notification to be sent back to the sender, telling her which recipients were unreachable and which bad things happened during delivery. These nondelivery notifications originate from the MAILER-DAEMON address. If one of these nondelivery notifications is itself undeliverable, it causes a second nondelivery notification to be sent back to the sender of the first nondelivery notification — which is to say, MAILER-DAEMON. Woe be unto thee if MAILER-DAEMON does not expand to a valid address! Depending on which version of Sendmail you are running, Sendmail can get into an infinite loop bouncing mail to a MAILER-DAEMON alias that is invalid. Many sites use the alias

MAILER-DAEMON: /dev/null

on the premise that if mail is not deliverable or returnable, it should be sent to the great bit bucket in the sky. We don't recommend this practice, since about a third of the MAILER-DAEMON mail sent by any given message transfer agent will point up a real problem somewhere in the transport system. You are better off learning about such things before remote Postmasters start sending you hate mail about your broken MTA.

Postmaster is where users are encouraged to send complaints about the mail service. This alias also tends to receive a lot of questions of the form "How can I send mail to John Q. Public who works in your Widget division?" The Postmaster alias ought to resolve to the address of some real person, probably a system administrator capable of solving Sendmail related problems. Directing Postmaster's mail to /dev/null is considered impolite (and, it violates RFC 822).

4.10. owner-* Aliases

Each alias has a potential owner-* alias. For example, the alias

```
sendmail-workers: vixie, avolio
```

could have an owner-* alias of the form

```
owner-sendmail-workers: vixie
```

The effect of this form is that if Sendmail has trouble delivering mail through the sendmail-workers alias, the nondelivery notification will be sent to owner-sendmail-workers rather than to the sender. This is helpful if not every person who sends mail to this alias is capable of editing the aliases database to fix or remove broken addresses.

However, this feature is not as helpful as it could be, since only a delivery problem that occurs on the host whose Sendmail expanded the alias can be affected by the presence of an owner-* alias. For example, if the above aliases are instead written as

```
sendmail-workers: vixie, avolio@dco.frobozz.com
owner-sendmail-workers: vixie
```

a user who sends to this alias will be exempt from any errors that occur during the alias expansion and initial forwarding. However, if a problem occurs over in the dco.frobozz.com domain, the Sendmail running on the server for dco.frobozz.com will have no knowledge of the owner-* alias in the originating host's aliases database; it will therefore send all nondelivery notifications back to the sender rather than to the owner of the alias. Of course, there is a solution to this problem, called "double queuing."

4.11. Double Queuing

The usual solution to reliably getting delivery errors back to the list maintainer is called *double queuing*. Double queuing has become extremely popular in the last few years, and it's safe to say that all large public distribution lists are handled this way. The idea is to have the "visible" alias be a pipe to another Sendmail with some command line arguments that make the *envelope sender* be the owner-* alias. This sounds resource intensive, and it can be, unless you are very careful. It also sounds complicated, but is not. Here's an example:

```
kjs: "| sendmail -fowner-kjs -oi -odq kjs-real"
owner-kjs: vixie
kjs-real: vixie, lenard_lovestret@previous.com,
        apples@pimento.edu, rickly@cs.mulligan.edu
```

The effect of this is that when a mail message is delivered to the kjs alias, another Sendmail process is created with the mail message as its standard input. Three things happen in this *subsendmail*: (1) the envelope sender address is set unconditionally to owner-kjs; (2) lines consisting only of a dot (.) are not treated as end of message markers; and (3) the *envelope recipient* is set to kjs-real, which, as an alias, will be expanded in the obvious way.

You can include other command line arguments if you want. Sometimes it is useful to set the delivery method (-od?) if the default in sendmail.cf (Od?) is not what you want for this distribution list. (Typically the sendmail.cf file specifies Odb, and you override it on large distributions to be -odq). You might also want the message to be queued up in a different queue directory (-oQ*pathname*) than the normal one specified in sendmail.cf (OQ*pathname*); this would be helpful if you wanted to "run the queue" with different parameters for messages going out to your large distribution lists. In that case you would start queue daemons in your system startup script in addition to the normal sendmail -bd -q30m; something like

```
sendmail -oQ/var/mq-kjs -q10m -oY
```

Don't worry too much if none of this makes sense. When you need to know it you will know that you need to know it, and you will remember having read it here.

Double queuing can be combined with the other tricks we've mentioned. For example, if you have a distribution list that is longer than the internal database limit of 1,024 characters, and you are using something like

```
list: list-a, list-b, list-c
list-a: long, list, of, names, 1K, characters, or, so
list-b: another, long, list, of, names, of, about, 1K
list-c: smaller, list, with, newest, additions, on, it
```

then you can use instead

```
list: "| sendmail -fowner-list -oi list-a list-b list-c"
list-a: long, list, of, names, 1K, characters, or, so
list-b: another, long, list, of, names, of, about, 1K
list-c: smaller, list, with, newest, additions, on, it
```

However, if you are using :include: files and you need to force the mail over to some specific host where the mail can be expanded, you probably can't get much help from this intuitive combination:

```
list: "| sendmail -fowner-list -oi list-real@mailhost"
list-real: :include: /var/local/adm/maillists/list
```

Though this lets you change the *envelope sender* before sending the message to the host that can expand the :include: file, it is likely that you will want to control the delivery (-od?) or queue directory (-oQ*pathname*) *after* the alias expansion, since the processing required just to forward the message to the expansion host is trivial, while the processing required to actually expand the :include: file and deliver the message to potentially hundreds of recipients is exactly what you would be hoping to manage with the additional command line arguments. The answer to this one is to *double-queue* on both systems, but with different incantations for the different needs.

With Sendmail there is rarely a single right way to do things. You will develop your own habits after you figure out what works best for you. You will get the most mileage out of these tricks if you make them as simple as possible while still getting the mail delivered. Be careful not to melt down your computer while experimenting to find the simplest working solution.

4.12. Aliases and Security

Some distribution lists are sufficiently sensitive or even controversial to cause their members to prefer that their membership remain a secret. Though it is possible for a user agent to "hide" the members of a user level alias by submitting a message to the transport with a normal envelope but with an empty or meaningless header, this only works for distribution lists that are "moderated" by some user (where a user "manually" forwards e-mail submissions to the list). If the distribution function is to be automatic (meaning that mail arrives for a given distribution list name and is automatically sent to the members of that list with no user intervention), the distribution list will usually be in the transport level aliases database.

As we explained earlier, transport level aliases are not expanded in the headers, and so at first glance a transport level distribution list appears to be "secure," in that members will not see each other's addresses on mail they receive through the distribution list. The To: or Cc: header will contain the address of the distribution list rather than the address of any particular user (unless addresses other than the distribution list were explicitly included by the sender, which is not a separate problem.)

However, there are ways to learn the membership of a distribution list other than by having the list appear in the headers of a mail message. If a list is to be "secure," care must be taken to avoid the list's membership being visible to anyone but the maintainer of the list.

4.12.1. Grepping for Aliases

Obviously one can search the local `aliases` file with a text editor or a text searching tool out of the `grep` family. The `aliases` file need not be world readable, since Sendmail runs as `root` or `daemon` whenever it is looking up an alias; however, it *tends to be* world readable, and this is a battle you would lose if you fought it.

4.12.2. `telnet` to the SMTP Port

`telnet` is an IP/TCP client capable of connecting to a server port on some specified host. Consider the following session transcript:

```
% telnet frbzwrl.frobozz.com smtp
Trying 16.1.0.1...
Connected to frbzwrl.frobozz.com.
Escape character is '^]'.
220-frbzwrl.frobozz.com Sendmail 5.65/30may91
220 ready at Sun, 23 Aug 92 20:52:42 -0700
expn admin
250-<reid@torrey>
250 <vixie@cognition>
quit
221 frbzwrl.frobozz.com closing connection
Connection closed by foreign host.
%
```

This shows a user learning the contents of the `<admin@frbzwrl.frobozz.com>` alias, which reads

```
admin: vixie, reid
reid: reid@torrey
vixie: vixie@cognition
```

It would have made no difference had this alias been a `:include:` expansion; Sendmail will cheerfully expand any alias this way, to the extent that it knows the answer (and if it doesn't know the answer, the alias is not going to work).

Note that a `:include:` file, or the `aliases` file itself, could be made non-world-readable (readable by user `daemon` is enough to let Sendmail do what it needs to do).

This would keep `grep` from working, but would not deter `telnet` in the least, since `telnet` uses Sendmail itself to expand any working alias.

4.12.3. What Can Be Done?

One thing a lot of system administrators do is recompile Sendmail without support for the `expn` command (or the `vrfy` command, which is similar). This is a trivial modification to Sendmail; so trivial that there is no compile time option for it. If you want to make this change, go ahead and make it. Then make sure that every workstation that has your site wide `aliases` file (or has access to it through one of the distribution and sharing schemes mentioned earlier) is running your lobotomized Sendmail binary. If you think this is going to be a lot of work, you're right. If you think it will probably still not be secure, you're right again. If you want to see another way to get some security, keep reading.

The right solution is to let some or even most of your workstations run with the vendor's standard Sendmail binary and participate fully in the domain wide `aliases` distribution, but then to make sure that the information a user can glean with `grep` or `telnet` does not include full expansions of your more sensitive distribution lists. Note that this is a bit of work and will cost some performance — so don't do it with every distribution list, just the ones you want to keep secure. Consider this alias:

```
sendmail-haters: sendmail-haters@cognition
```

This is a small step toward security; a `telnet` user who sees this will have to disconnect from whatever host she connected to and reconnect to the Sendmail daemon (really: "SMTP server") on `cognition`. Once having done that, she ordinarily sees the full expansion, since `cognition` ordinarily has a normal, working alias for this distribution list.

However, in this (contrived) example, the alias on `cognition` uses a modified version of double queuing:

```
sendmail-haters:
    "|sendmail -f sendmail-haters-request
                    -oQ/var/spool/mq/sendmail-haters
                    -oA/var/spool/mq/sendmail-haters/aliases
                    -oi sendmail-haters"
```

which causes Sendmail to run with an alternate queue directory and to attempt delivery using an alternate (and *private*) `aliases` database. You *must* also use the `-f` command line argument to Sendmail to change the envelope sender, since if this string matches the user name of some user on your system, many versions of Sendmail will "run as that user" when delivering from the secondary queue. This should not be a hardship, since you'll want to set `-f` to the list request address, anyway.

Note that the directory (/var/spool/mq/sendmail-haters in this example) should be owned and writable by user daemon. There must be a private aliases database located at the path shown (or at some other path if you so choose; putting the private aliases file inside the private queue directory is a matter of personal taste). Create or edit this file normally and then run

```
newaliases -oA/var/spool/mq/sendmail-haters/aliases
```

This will create aliases.dir and aliases.pag files in the same directory specified for aliases with the -oA option. Note that the aliases* files don't get in Sendmail's way even if you put them into the queue directory, since they do not have names similar to those Sendmail uses for its queue files.

You can put anything you want in this aliases database, but only Sendmails run with the above -oA option will ever use this file, and therefore only MAILER-DAEMON and the distribution alias itself (sendmail-haters in this example) need be present. You could share such a private aliases database among all of your "secure" distribution lists; just set the -oA option appropriately in the double queuing aliases.

This private aliases file should not be world readable, lest it become readable to users of grep. It can be writable by the list maintainer so long as it is readable by Sendmail, which will be running as user daemon and perhaps group daemon at the time of delivery. You could use a :include: directive in the private aliases database, but this file would be subject to exactly the same security requirements as the private aliases database itself, so :include: doesn't really help secure you against grep users unless you make it as inconvenient to edit as the private aliases database itself.

Since there is no sendmail -bd process running in this private queue directory, you are safe from telnet users. However, this means that any messages that are temporarily unforwardable at the time they are received in the alternate queue directory will not be retried later unless you start up a queue daemon for this directory, as in:

```
sendmail -oQ/var/spool/mq/sendmail-haters -q30m
```

Without a -bd option, this daemon will not listen for incoming SMTP connections (which it can't do in any case since there is presumably already a sendmail -bd daemon running in the main queue directory). But the -q30m option works even for daemons running without -bd; it will cause a sendmail -q to be run every 30 minutes.

If you have a large number of sensitive lists, you will not want to start a separate sendmail -q30m process for each one, since this will create a lot of junk in your process table. In this case you can run a succession of sendmail -q processes from an every-15-minute Cron entry, or you can share a single private queue directory (and its associated private aliases database) among all of your sensitive distribution lists. If you are willing to share the sensitive information among all of the maintainers of your sensitive lists, this is clearly the low overhead way to handle sensitive lists.

The important security tricks for sensitive distribution lists are

- make sure that the addresses you want kept secret are not present in any `aliases` database or `:include:` file which is normally read by the `sendmail -bd` process;

- make sure that the files which contain sensitive addresses are readable to Sendmail but not by unauthorized users.

All that said, it remains that the only secure computers in the world are not connected to networks at all and are installed in locked rooms with armed guards at the doors and windows.

5

Configuration Design

Sendmail is made to be configurable because there is no single configuration that will satisfy the needs of every host, site, or network. Network connectivity, mail protocols, error handling, and administration are among the issues that come into play when planning a Sendmail configuration.

5.1. Why Design?

In designing a Sendmail configuration, we must take into account the overall design or philosophy behind our company's, campus's, or facility's e-mail system. So, before we can design and build our Sendmail configuration here (and we hope to do much of this from already existing bits and pieces), we will discuss the design issues associated with mail distribution systems on a network within an organization.

5.2. Mail Distribution Systems

The simplest way of designing your mail distribution system is for each host — each discrete computer node — to make a connection to any other host for which it has mail. Thus, if Anne on host cognition.frobozz.com wants to send mail to Eric on grizzly.wossamotta.edu, Anne's host establishes a connection to Eric's host and the mail is transferred (see Figure 5-1). This works well, but not in all cases.

What if Anne's machine and Eric's machine speak different network protocols (e.g., IP/TCP vs. DECnet)? What if Anne's machine expects RFC 822 mail headers and Eric's expects X.400 headers? Or what if Eric's machine isn't often connected; say it's a notebook personal computer he carries around from place to place? Or what if either or both of Anne's and Eric's machines sit behind a screening gateway of some kind for security reasons?

Of course, these are all real, everyday examples and so are part of what we consider when designing a mail distribution system. Should a user who wants to send e-mail to people on hosts on the Internet, on a UUCP-only machine, and on a DECnet-only node be required to run IP and DECnet and have a dial-out port on her machine? Certainly not. From the user's perspective, the best thing would be for her to send mail, addressing each person as he or she needs mail addressed, and having her mail system do the rest without any special knowledge or work on her part.

What we would like is for the world to *look like* Figure 5-1 to the end e-mail users — at least as much as is possible. One way to do this, as we said, is to make every end-node (Anne's or Eric's machines) very smart and very well equipped and connect it to every network possible. Or we can employ intermediary hosts. This is what we will discuss here.

5.3. Design Components

In this discussion, we go back to the model of p-mail and how it is delivered, for the problem is the same (and was the same when postal services were being designed way back when people first started to communicate via the written word). If we write a letter in Maryland, one way to get it to California is to put it in an envelope, jump into a car, hit the highways, and arrive bright tailed and bushy tailed at the destination to hand it over. This is a drag, what with having to work, pay the bills (and driving all over the country to deliver the payments), and so on.

We could hire a messenger who has the job of delivery, but if we only hire one person, mail delivery will drag on for weeks, and if we hire many messengers, mail delivery will become prohibitively expensive. So we "post" the mail. We deliver it to the local post office, which takes it from there to the destination.

Of course, the post office has the same decision to make, and what most postal systems in most countries have decided on is some model of end post offices (which are

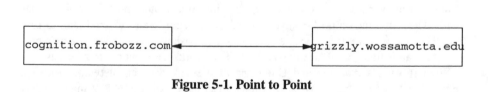

Figure 5-1. Point to Point

responsible for the final delivery to a mailbox) linked to larger hub post offices, which are in turn linked together. To simplify things a bit, many letters destined for Palo Alto, California, from Glenwood, Maryland, can be bundled together and carried off by one messenger, thereby saving money. In fact, there are many messengers and many bundles going to intermediate cities, and much bundling and unbundling along the way, but you get the idea. This is what we do with e-mail.

We will discuss four different types of mail configurations: the *mail gateway*, the *mail hub*, the *smart client*, and the *simple client*. We will see that the mail gateway is a special case of the mail hub, and the simple client is a special case of the smart client. We also will present our definition of a *mail cluster* and how it fits in to mail system design. First, a few brief definitions:

Mail gateway

> a host or a process that sits between one environment and at least one other and handles the relay of mail. It can, and often does, more than this, but relaying mail is its primary job. (See Figure 5-2.)

Mail hub

> a host that acts as a relay site between gateway hosts and other mail hubs. This may also be a gateway, but it doesn't have to be. (See Figure 5-3.)

Simple client

> a client that handles only local mail delivery. All other mail gets sent, without any processing, to a mail hub. Incoming mail tends to be received by a hub which then offers mail to the simple client hosts via NFS or POP.

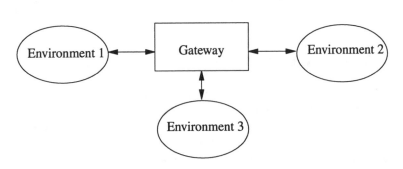

Figure 5-2. Mail Gateway

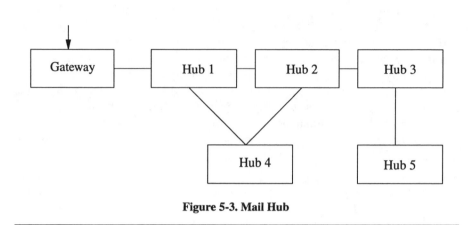

Figure 5-3. Mail Hub

Smart client
> an end host that can send mail directly to some, but not all, other hosts. It must be able to speak at least one network protocol and one mail protocol, and be connected to at least one physical network. It might handle some mail delivery itself and may hand off others to a Mail Hub.

Mail cluster
> a group of mail hosts that share a common *user name space* (user `allen` on one host is the same person as user `allen` on another host) and a common `aliases` database (more on mail aliases later).

5.3.1. The Mail Gateway

As described earlier, the environments could differ as to network protocol and mail protocol, or they could simply be physically isolated from each other such that the gateway must be involved in any mail transaction. However, mail gateways usually do much more than just connect different environments.

Mail gateway hosts are used, in some cases, because of security firewalls being in place between networks. In such a case, it is impossible for a client on one side to connect to a client on the other. So, the gateway receives the mail and passes it on.

Another use for a mail gateway is header translation. In the following example, mail is being sent using DECnet. Notice that the headers do not conform to RFC 822.

```
From: ufp::munar
To: frbzwrl::mudsters
Subject: New version of MUDlocate

Blah Blah Blah
```

If this mail goes through the gateway destined for someone on, say, the Internet, those addresses are going to make replying to the sender or the others on the distribution list difficult. The :: construction of MAIL11 addresses is not defined outside of the DECnet arena. The gateway machine must fix this up. There are a number of things it can do, but the way we do it is shown here:

```
From: munar@ufp.enet.frobozz.com
To: mudsters@frbzwrl.pa.frobozz.com
Subject: New version of MUDlocate

Blah Blah Blah
```

We made up a zone under FROBOZZ.COM called ENET, and when mail comes in for ufp.ENET.FROBOZZ.COM, our gateway will know to send it via DECnet to node ufp. The outside world is protected from the undefined addressing, mail coming in gets properly delivered, and the addresses get properly modified. The internal DECnet machine might see mail come in from someone such as

```
frbzwrl::"mike@netwolf.bigred.edu"
```

which is an example of the format that DECnet user is probably used to seeing and typing Internet e-mail addresses in.

Another service a gateway *must* provide, if a "private" network is isolated from the Internet, is *mail exchange* service for hosts in its domain. Since internal machines cannot be reached directly, the gateway on the outside must get the mail from the outside destined for inside clients.

Another service it *might* provide is uniformity of addressing, as perceived by people on the outside. Since this is more generally the job of a mail hub, of which the mail gateway is a special case, we will discuss it later in that context.

A mail gateway must be well connected and highly reliable, since, in many instances, it is a major bottleneck — meaning that many other hosts' communications rely on it. A gateway must also have the most up-to-date information possible about internal as well as external connectivity, host names, protocols, and the like.

5.3.2. The Mail Hub

Mail hubs are concentration points in the flow of e-mail. Often distributed based on geography and network population, they move the load off other hubs and off the gateways. They gather mail from client hosts (usually local ones) and pass it on to other hubs closer to the intended destination. If the e-mail is destined to go off the internal network, the goal is one of the mail gateways.

Again, thinking of the p-mail analogy, if we mail a letter in Glenwood, we don't expect that someone will pick it up, jump on a plane, and fly it all the way to its destination. We expect the mail to be sorted, bundled, and sent off to another, closer hub, where it will be resorted, rebundled, and sent on its way, getting closer (at least conceptually) to the final destination. If we think of this in terms of a *hierarchy*, we see that eventually we start moving in a "downward" direction on our way to the addressee, as illustrated in Figure 5-4.

For e-mail, the hub might also give the mail a uniformity of addressing, taking addresses in the form

user@host.domain

and turning them into

user@domain

For example,

```
vixie@cognition.pa.frobozz.com
```

becomes

```
vixie@pa.frobozz.com
```

to people on the outside of FROBOZZ.COM.

There are many reasons to make addresses uniform. One reason is *security*. The fewer people on the outside of a network who know about what is inside, the better. Two other reasons are *reliability* and long-term stability. The hub machine might have a staff of people keeping it going, while a particular user's machine (and so her mailbox) might be down for days if she happens to be out of town. Remember, our goal — as either the sender or receiver of mail — is to get the mail as close to the final mailbox as possible. Finally, *aesthetics* or concern for other people's typing fingers might move us to want addresses such as

```
roj@dc.frobozz.com
```

over

```
roj@gandalf.sws.dc.frobozz.com
```

This brings up one other service of the hub. It not only can show a cleaner, more uniform addressing scheme to the outside world (outside of the hub's domain — again, in both senses of the word), but if it does, it *must* be able to deliver mail that

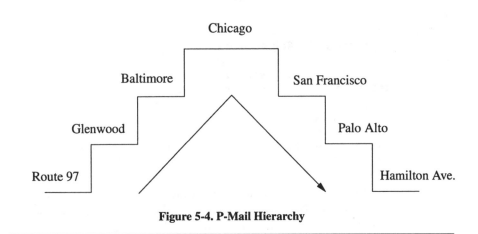

Figure 5-4. P-Mail Hierarchy

comes to it with such addressing. In the above example, even though `roj` might not be a local user on the hub for `dc.frobozz.com`, it had better know how to deliver mail for user `roj`. Consequently, the hub can act as a mail directory and distribution system (an alias system). Perhaps mail for `roj`, `messy`, and `roger.messy` will all get to the same person.

It could also give people *hints* about mail if it wants to, such that if the hub got mail for `smith@dc.frobozz.com` (continuing to use this example) and there were multiple users with `smith` as part of their name, mail could be returned to the sender indicating this and listing the alternatives for disambiguation. (See Figure 5-5.) You can, no doubt, now think of other services similar to this one. If the hub gets mail for a user no longer with the firm, it can send out a reply to that effect without having to do this on the departed individual's workstation (which has since been given to someone else and, of course, renamed for that user's favorite hobbit or beer or whatever).

In a large network, the hubs play the important role of moving mail closer to the intended recipient and getting it off other hubs or the gateways. In a network where all mail goes from the gateways directly to the machines holding the addressees' mailboxes, network outages lead to terrible queue jams on the gateways. Also, changes of naming (hosts and mailboxes) must then be propagated to the gateways.

The larger the network and the associated number of possible mailboxes, the more important the role of mail hubs for the smooth flow of e-mail.

```
To: vixie@al.org
From: Mailer-Daemon@dc.frobozz.com
Subject: Mail for smith@dc.frobozz.com

Hello.  You sent mail to the address "smith."  There are
multiple users we could send this to.

              Jane Smith          isjane.smith@dc.frobozz.com
              Peter Smith         ispeter.smith@dc.frobozz.com
              Lynne Smith         islynne@dc.frobozz.com

Thank you.
```

Figure 5-5. E-Mail Address Disambiguation Example

5.3.3. The Smart Client

A client host can handle most mail through its mail hub, but may choose not to in some instances. A smart client usually can handle mail to a subset of the e-mail world. It probably always chooses to handle mail for delivery to local mailboxes — mailboxes on the client itself. It may send mail directly to all mailboxes on machines within its local area, but it may choose to use the hub for all external mail and all mail for addresses in other mail domains or hosts.

For example, we may create mail intended for a mail user on a personal computer. We might know the host that provides mail service for PC users, and so we can send it directly there, but we may choose to send it to the mail hub to handle. Things change, and this means we won't have to keep the smart clients up to date on all servers and all addresses. The people running the hub have to worry about it. People sending e-mail do not.

Smart clients almost always do some but not all mail delivery. The majority of mail hosts in the world are to some degree smart clients. At one site we know of, all IP hosts are configured to send IP mail directly to any host with an address record or an MX record on the Internet. But any mail for a UUCP host, such as

```
sushi!ruthel
```

goes to a hub with UUCP connections. At another site, say Digital in Palo Alto, hosts are configured to send mail for IP hosts in DEC.COM *directly*, while mail for DECnet hosts goes to a DECnet mail hub and "outside" mail goes to a hub that then sends it on to the appropriate gateway.

In Figure 5-6 we see that mail from `gildor.dco.frobozz.com` gets handed to a local hub, which passes it on to the "best reachable" gateway which in turn sends it to the gateway for Pimento University's mail network. Finally, the mail gets to the mailbox `louie` on his host `borabora`. All of this is, of course, transparent to the mail user who uses the simple mail address, which is, in this example:

`louie@borabora.pimento.edu`

How does someone decide what will and what will not be handled by the local machine? It varies. Going back to our p-mail example, we would probably deliver mail to the person in the next office personally, but not to a person in an office across town or around the globe.

Some smart clients may rely on mail hubs more than others. Just because a client is smart does not mean it has to do all the "direct" delivery it can. Perhaps the mail hub has some special handing built in, some specialized software that must remain up to date in order to be effective. Perhaps the smart client is not connected all the time. It can choose to send out mail directly but to rely on the hub for incoming mail delivery. Perhaps a client does not want to do any mail handling at all except mail for local delivery.

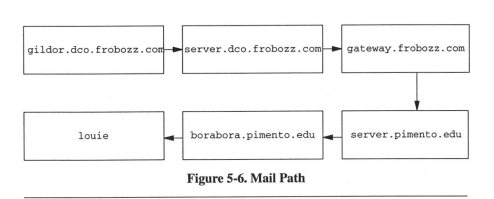

Figure 5-6. Mail Path

5.3.4. The Simple Client

A simple client asks the question "Is this mail for a mailbox on this machine?" If the answer is "Yes," the mail is given to the local mailer program (such as

/usr/libexec/mail.local) and the mail is delivered. If the answer is "No," the mail is given to the local mail hub. Period. This makes for a fairly simple send-mail.cf file (see Appendix E).

Simple clients also have very low administrative overhead. Outgoing mail connections are only made to a small subset of mail hubs, perhaps only one. The send-mail.cf file for this kind of host is simple and, believe it or not, easy to understand.

5.3.5. The Mail Cluster

As stated, members of a Mail Cluster share a common name space, including system mail aliases. Mail sent to a user on any one of the hosts in the cluster will get to the proper mailbox. Let's suppose, for example, that we have two users, each a different host, with their respective mailboxes located on their own host. (See Figure 5-7.)

If murphy on burfle sends mail to mail address rjl, in a Mail Cluster, mail gets delivered to rjl on host sushi. The mail looks to rjl as if it came from a local user murphy. Replying works correctly because mail to murphy from host sushi, similarly, gets to the proper mailbox on burfle.

In a mail cluster, provision can be made for special — nonglobal — mail addresses. For example, root might be aliased to a different user on each host in a mail cluster. Such a user name cannot be treated uniformly across all hosts. In Chapter 8, we show how to implement a local mail cluster and handle this and other possibilities.

In function, if not necessarily in name, most groups of hosts these days are aggregated together into mail clusters. The days of treating workstations as first class hosts whose names matter are finally waning, since there are a whole lot more of them (workstations) than most people expected. Managing a workstation as other than a satellite of a large server is just too hard when you have hundreds or thousands of them.

5.4. The Checklist

Before sitting down to write or modify a sendmail.cf file, we have to ask ourselves some questions and gather some data, including but not necessarily limited to the following:

(1)   We usually need to know our *parent domain name* for our Sendmail configuration. This is usually everything following the first dot (.) in our own fully qualified host name. The parent domain name will usually be the same for

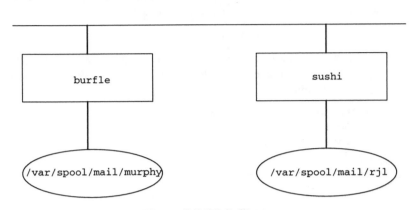

Figure 5-7. Mail Cluster

most of our hosts, or at least most hosts of a given mail hub. For example, the `.dco.frobozz.com` in `vanidor.dco.frobozz.com`.

(2)   If this host is known by any other names or if this host should treat any other host names as local, these names are our *pseudonyms* and we need to take them into account as we configure Sendmail. We might have pseudonyms because we are consolidating hosts and we need old addresses to continue to work; or, we could be a mail hub, needing to accept mail addressed to the mail hub's generic domain name(s).

(3)   We decide what kinds of mail we wish to handle. UUCP? TCP/IP? DECnet? Handle doesn't mean *directly deliver*. It means we will decide what kinds of mail our Sendmail should recognize and dispatch.

(4)   For each type of mail we decide to handle, we decide how we will handle it. This may require us deciding on what kinds of mail goes to which relays.[1]

---

[1] Ooops. We forgot to tell you, didn't we, that hubs, gateways, smart clients, and any other Sendmail host running a nonsimple `sendmail.cf` is generically referred to as a *relay*. Sorry, it won't happen again.

(5)   The format of addresses on outgoing mail is something we think about at this
time. In the situation where user `cathy` is on node

```
talos.dc.frobozz.com
```

which is on a "screened network" such that mail goes through gateway
`gatekeeper.frobozz.com`, the following are some possible choices for
cathy's mail address:

```
cathy@talos.dc.frobozz.com
cathy@dc.frobozz.com
cathy@gatekeeper.frobozz.com
cathy@frobozz.com
cathy%talos.dc@frobozz.com
cathy%talos.dc.frobozz.com@frobozz.com
```

When these questions are dealt with, and some more we shall see as we delve into a
`sendmail.cf` file line by line, we are ready to design our mail configuration. So
now we look at the components of a `sendmail.cf` file to get enough information
under our belts to go on to some real examples.

6

Configuration Basics

The Sendmail configuration file is called `sendmail.cf`. It tells Sendmail how to parse and rewrite mail addresses, what MTAs it should know about, how to route mail, and to set options and other values. `sendmail.cf` is designed to be easily parsed by the Sendmail program, and as a result is not optimized for parsing by human brains. Some people find it obtuse and hard to read and understand, but we trust that if you take the time to study Sendmail configuration with our help, after a while you will see that it really *is* obtuse and hard to read and understand. ("Ha Ha," as Dave Barry would say, "Just kidding.")

6.1. Basic Format, Variables, and Classes

The `sendmail.cf` is best understood if looked at a section at a time. To do that we will explain how to recognize each section and, in the telling, describe the job or function of each section. We'll also help you understand the configuration file's characters and symbols. (A frosted mocha would be a good thing to have in your hand about now.)

As stated, the `sendmail.cf` was designed to be easy to parse by Sendmail. It is made up of different types of lines, and a line's *type* is determined by its first character. Blank lines are ignored and should be used whenever they add readability. Lines beginning with a tab (ASCII HT) character are treated as continuations of the previous line.

The other types of lines we will discuss are:

#	comments
D	macro definitions
C	class definitions
F	file class definitions
O	options to Sendmail (like those passed on the command line)
S	rulesets; sets of rules — sort of like subroutines
R	rules; the executable statements of rulesets

6.1.1. Comments

Any line with a pound sign (#) in the first column is treated as a comment line and ignored by Sendmail. As with good software coding, you should sprinkle your configuration file liberally with comments. Correction — make that "with clear and concise comments." Old `sendmail.cf` files never die. They just get edited.

6.1.2. Macro Definitions (Variables)

Variables, when defined and later used, are treated just like string constants. The form of a macro definition is

`DXvalue`

where X is a single character and `value` is a character string (no blanks or tabs allowed). When defining your own macros, stick with upper-case letters, since many lower-case letters are already defined internally by Sendmail. So, if you define macro D to be `dco.frobozz.com`,

`DDdco.frobozz.com`

later, $D used in a rule gets replaced with the string `dco.frobozz.com`.

Though we will look at rules in detail shortly, we should mention that a Sendmail rule is made up of three parts: a pattern to match, called the lefthand side or LHS; a transformation to apply, called the RHS; and a comment area.

The following macros are defined internally by Sendmail:

a	The Date: in Arpanet format (e.g., "Tue, 14 Jan 92 10:39:35 -0500").
b	The current date in Arpanet format.
c	The hop count. Essentially the number of Received: headers.
d	The time in ctime format (e.g., "Tue Jan 14 10:39:35 1992").
f	The sender (from) address.
g	The sender address relative to the recipient (a *path*).
h	The recipient host.
i	The queue identifier (usually built from the *pid*).
p	The Sendmail *pid*.
r	The protocol used.
s	The sender's host name.
t	The current time (e.g., "920114103935").
u	The recipient user.
v	The version number of the compiled Sendmail.
w	The name of this host (might be fully qualified, or not).[1]
x	The full name of the sender (e.g., "Bullwinkle T. Moose").
y	The name of the sender's tty port (e.g., 09 for /dev/tty09).
z	The home directory of the recipient.

The following macros *must be* defined by you in sendmail.cf. (Sample definitions are shown in Figure 6-1.)

e	The SMTP login message.
j	The fully qualified name of this host.
l	The format for a UNIX From_[2] line.
n	Sendmail's own e-mail address, for sending error notifications.
o	The set of operators (delimiters).
q	The default format for sender addresses.

Consider Figure 6-1. Did you catch that we slipped something in on you in that definition for q? That is a Sendmail "If" statement. It reads "define q to be the value of g and if macro x is defined ($?x), then follow it by a blank and then follow it with the value of macro x in parenthesis. Otherwise, don't follow the value of g with anything." The $. is the "End-If"; $|, by the way, is an "Else".

---

[1] You can override this in sendmail.cf if your host doesn't know the value you want to use.

[2] We use the notation "From_" to show the word From when it must be followed by a blank.

Macros must be defined before they are used. Macros may be used in defining other macros, as we see in Figure 6-1.

6.1.3. Classes

Classes are sets of tokens to be used for matching in the pattern side (LHS) of a rule. Using classes, you can test to see if part of an address matches one of a set of words or tokens. Classes can be defined directly using C lines or indirectly in an outside file using F lines. For example,

```
Ccword1 word2 word3
```

where C is the class name. Lower case class names are reserved for Sendmail, so, as with macro names, you should only use upper case letters when selecting a new class name. So,

```
CDdnet decnet uucp
```

defines class D to be made up of dnet, decnet, and uucp. There may be more than one of these lines, and they aggregate naturally. So, the following three lines are equivalent to the above single line:

```
CDdnet
CDdecnet
CDuucp
```

Similarly, classes can have their definitions read in from files. The form of the statement is

```
FB/etc/bogus-domains
```

When using the F statement to define classes, you may add an optional format to be used by scanf (see *scanf*(3)) when reading from the file, as in

```
FZ/etc/uucp/L.sys %[0-9a-ZA-Z_-]
```

```
De$j Sendmail $v ready at $b.   Talk to me, Goose.
DnMAILER-DAEMON
DlFrom $g $d
Do.:%@!=/
Dq$g$?x ($x)$.
Dj$w.$D
```

Figure 6-1. Sample Definitions

This reads strings from the file /etc/uucp/L.sys. According to the format (which begins with percent sign "%") the class tokens are made up of any number of digits, letters (upper or lower case), underscores, or hyphens. So in the above example, only the first word of each line from the /etc/uucp/L.sys file will be put into the class definition. This facility is almost never useful, since it does not provide any way to skip "comment" lines of the source file.

Note that classes in Classic Sendmail (up through release 5, non-IDA) can only usefully contain single token elements. So while it is very convenient to be able to put multitoken elements such as domains, subdomains, or fully qualified host names into a class, you can only do this in IDA or R8 Sendmail.

6.2. Rules

Rules are the "executable" lines of the configuration files and do the most work. They are also what gives Sendmail its well deserved reputation for being obscure (but then it also provides income for people willing and able to write about and talk about Sendmail configurations).

If you have ever programmed in the SNOBOL computer language (and understood what you did), you already have the background for understanding Sendmail rules. Don't worry if you haven't — though you have missed the experience of a lifetime — because we look at pattern matching in a few pages. Sendmail rules, and SNOBOL statements, are pattern matching and transformation rules.

Rules start with the letter R and have a *lefthand side* (LHS), a *righthand side* (RHS), and an optional comment field. Each section of the line is separated by one or more tab characters (not blanks, tabs!). If you use blanks, Sendmail will complain bitterly about them when it reads your sendmail.cf file. Blanks sometimes sneak in if you use xterm's *cut and paste* facility to copy text around while editing sendmail.cf (the *paste* command converts tabs to spaces).

The rules are applied to each address in the mail (we will talk about how, when, and why later). The application goes this way: If the address matches the pattern of the LHS, it is transformed according to the RHS. Unless the RHS contains a control command indicating otherwise (again, more later), the address again tries to match the LHS, and the transformation, if it matches, is again carried out. When it fails to match, the next rule is used. In this way a set of rules, a ruleset, is "executed," one rule at a time, top to bottom, for each address in the mail. The following is an example of a rule:

```
R$-@$w          $1                      Example
```

To understand rules, we need to understand the special symbols used in them and we must define some terms.

Delimiter:
> A character considered to be *place indicators* or operators. The @ and .s in vixie@pa.frobozz.com are delimiters. The set of delimiters often includes ".:%@!=/][".

Token:
> Think of it as a word, or as a string of characters that are not delimiters. In the previous example, vixie, @, pa, frobozz, and com are the tokens. Every delimiter is a token.

6.2.1. Special Symbols Used on the LHS

As with many other recent programming languages, the "$" character is used to introduce special symbols that are to be treated differently than literal text would be. While literal text in the LHS must match exactly, symbols preceded by "$" can match in most inexact ways, as shown below:

$*	Zero or more tokens.
$+	One or more tokens.
$-	Exactly one token.
$=X	Any token (or group of tokens in IDA or R8) in Class X.
$~X	Any token *not* in class X.
$X	The exact string defined by macro X (see section on Macros).

For example, the pattern

```
$-@$*
```

applied to the address

```
vixie@pa.frobozz.com
```

has vixie match $-, the @ match @, and pa.frobozz.com match $*. More on this later.

6.2.2. Special Symbols Used on the RHS

The RHS also uses "$" to introduce special, nonliteral text. Literal text is copied into the result, um, literally, but special symbols cause special things to be copied into the result instead. Naturally, the set of RHS special symbols is disjoint from the LHS's, but this is honestly due to their context and is not meant solely to confuse you.

Well, maybe it's at least partly to confuse you. Two special symbols are even more special than the others, since they work differently (or not at all) depending on whether they are the first symbol on the RHS, or are used later on in the middle of it. Let's get these over with first. Recall that the default action of a rule is "iterate until match fails," or, to express it in pseudocode,

```
while LHS matches do
    rewrite address using RHS
done
```

The special symbols (which we'll refer to as RHS *introducers* since we know of no better term) modify this behaviour as follows:

$:   Apply this transformation exactly once, then go to the next rule. That is,

```
if LHS matches then
    rewrite address using RHS
endif
```

The difference from the default behaviour is that a `while` construct has become an `if`.

$@   After applying this transformation, exit from the ruleset. So:

```
if LHS matches then
    rewrite address using RHS
    return
endif
```

The difference from $: is that a `return` occurs after the `rewrite`.

Any RHS that could generate a result that matches its own LHS is a candidate for a $: or $@ introducer, since otherwise, Sendmail will just sit there and spin on that rule until something goes "boom."

The other special RHS symbols are straightforward in that their meaning does not depend on their location:

$n   token number n matched on the LHS by a pattern variable. Given the LHS $-@$+ and the address vixie@pa.frobozz.com, $1 on the RHS is vixie and $2 is pa.frobozz.com. @ matches @, since it is literal.

$>m   Call ruleset number m. This is like a function call. It is a more elaborate way of doing a transformation. For example, the rule

```
R$+                 $>8$1
```

says that if the address has one or more tokens (is nonempty), send the entire string to Ruleset 8. Whatever Ruleset 8 does to the address is carried back to this rule.

$[Send everything before the next $] to the DNS resolver, and use result of that lookup as the transformation.

$]   See $[. For example,

```
R$+<@[$+]>                    $:$1<@$[$2$]>
```

If we have an address for mail such as B1FF@[192.5.214.100] (which is valid — the numbers in the square brackets are evaluated as an IP address), this rule sends the IP address to the DNS. If the DNS comes up with a host name for the address, the IP address is replaced with the host name. This allows MX records to be used in this case.

$:   (IDA only.) This introduces an "Else" if used between a $[and $]. For example,

```
R$*<@$+>$*                    $:$1<@$[$2$:$2.BOGUS$]>$3
```

would change the host name to the value returned by the DNS, or would append .BOGUS to it if the DNS did not recognize it. This kind of appendix is very useful for making later decisions about this address.

6.3. Pattern Matching — A Brief Interlude

We now take a break to make sure that we have the pattern-matching basics down at this point, since to understand the sendmail.cf, file you will need to understand rulesets. To understand rulesets, you must understand the rules they contain, and to understand rules, you need to understand pattern matching and transformations. So, before we get any further into rulesets, let's look at some examples.

First, we need to keep in mind that Sendmail applies the rulesets and their rules to individual addresses. It isn't important at this point to worry about which ones, when, why, and so on. Let's just concentrate on the mechanics of it for now.

Consider the following *patterns*:

1)	$-@$-
2)	$+@$+.FROBOZZ.COM
3)	$*@$+.FROBOZZ.COM
4)	$+@$-.$+.FROBOZZ.COM
5)	$+@$+
6)	$-.$+@$-.MTS$*

Now, given the address

frederick.avolio@cop.mts.frobozz.com

which of the examples will match against it? Not pattern 1, which says "a single token followed by an (@) followed by a single token." The address doesn't match that pattern, since there isn't a single token before the @. There are three tokens: frederick, a dot (.), and avolio.

If pattern 2 is applied to the address, the first element of the pattern, $+, matches frederick.avolio (it matches one *or more* tokens). The next is a literal @ that matches the @ in the address. The next, $+ (match one or more tokens), matches cop.mts. The rest of the address matches exactly — a ., the word FROBOZZ, another ., and the word COM. Notice that *case* (upper or lower) doesn't matter in Sendmail pattern matching.

Pattern 3 is a more general case of pattern 2, with the first element of the pattern saying "zero or more" instead of "one or more," so pattern 3 works.

Pattern 4 works also. The $+ matches frederick.avolio, @ matches @, $- (one token) matches cop; . matches .; $+ matches mts; . matches .; and so on.

With pattern 5, the $+ matches all of frederick.avolio; the @ matches the @; and $+ matches the rest (cop.mts.frobozz.com).

Finally, pattern 6 works also. Element $- matches frederick, . matches .; $+ matches avolio; @ matches @; $- matches cop; . matches .; MTS matches mts; and $* (zero or more tokens) matches .frobozz.com.

Now let's look at another example from the other angle.

1)	avolio@dco.frobozz.com
2)	avolio@gildor.dco.frobozz.com
3)	vixie@gildor.cop8.frobozz.com
4)	vixie@gildor.frobozz.com

If macro w is set to gildor and class C is dco, cop8, enet, which of these addresses will be matched by the pattern $+@$w.$=C.$+?

Remember what $=C means? It is the pattern, in this case, "dco OR cop8 OR enet." So this pattern will match addresses 2 and 3. The first part, $+, matches avolio in the first two and vixie in the last two. The @ matches the @ in all. The $w acts as if we had typed gildor in its place (that's what macros do). So $w, which is gildor, matches gildor in 2, 3, and 4 (and this is where we fail to match address 1). Next, the . matches the . after gildor in all, and the pattern $=C — that matches any of the three strings dco, cop8, and enet — matches dco in address 2 and cop8 in 3, but fails to match dec in address 4. Finally, the . matches the .s in 2 and 3, and $+ matches the "One or more tokens" frobozz.com in both.

How about this pattern?

$-@$+.FROBOZZ.COM

They all match.

What's the simplest pattern you can write that will match all four addresses?[3]

As Sendmail applies patterns to character strings — addresses — parts of the address that match patterns in the LHS of the rule are assigned numbers so that that can be referred to in the RHS transformation, as we have seen. Parts of the address that match constants in the string or macros are *not* assigned numbers, however.

Given the definitions

```
DPFROBOZZ.COM
CDdco cop8
```

and the pattern

```
$+<@$=D.$P>$*
```

we see in Figure 6-2 how the address

```
cathy<@cop8.frobozz.com>
```

is parsed. (The angle brackets < and > are used inside the configuration file to isolate the domain part of an address, as we'll discuss later.)

The first pattern (`$+`) matches `cathy`, which gets assigned to `$1`. The < and @ match each other, but get no numeric place value because they are string constants. Next, `$=D` matches `cop8`, since `$=D` is a pattern (that says "dco *or* cop8"). `cop8` becomes `$2` on the RHS. The `.` matches the `.`, and `$P`, which is a macro that expands to `FROBOZZ.COM`, matches the `frobozz.com`, but because it is treated as a string constant (remember, this is how macros work — they are expanded in place as if the values assigned to them were typed in their place), no numeric value is linked

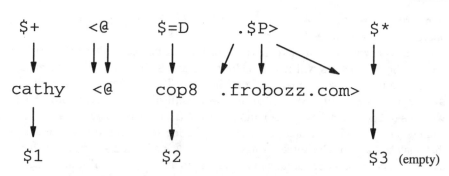

Figure 6-2. Address Decomposition Example

---

[3] Either the pattern `$*` or `$+` will match all of these addresses.

to it. The closing >s match, and the final $* matches nothing, but since it means "zero or more tokens" it matches the empty string, which becomes the value of $3 on the RHS.

6.4. Rulesets

A *ruleset* in sendmail.cf is the equivalent of a *subroutine* in other programming languages. It takes an address as input and returns an address as output, and its job is usually to do something to that address, such as change frbzwrl!vixie into vixie<@frbzwrl.UUCP> (or vice versa). A ruleset is made up of *rules*. It starts with a ruleset start line (an S followed by a positive integer) and ends when Sendmail encounters anything except a rule, continuation, blank, or comment line. Thus, Ruleset 3 starts with the line

S3

Ruleset numbers in pre-R8 Sendmail versions are in the range 0 through 30.

Some rulesets are automatically used for certain internal tasks. While you may define your own rulesets, there are certain rulesets coded into Sendmail to be used for particular purposes.

6.4.1. Predefined Rulesets

Rulesets 0 through 4 are predefined. (Also 5 and 6 if you are using IDA; see discussion of the O/ option, below.) Briefly, these are

S0	Makes the delivery decision on each envelope address
S1	Called on sender addresses before the mailer-specific S= ruleset
S2	Called on recipient addresses before the mailer-specific R= ruleset
S3	Preprocesses an address to turn it into internal ("canonical") form
S4	Postprocesses an address to get it back to external form
S5	(IDA only) like S1 but for header addresses; depends on O/
S6	(IDA only) like S2 but for header addresses; depends on O/

If the IDA O/ option is used, S1 and S2 process only the envelope addresses, and the header addresses go through S5 and S6.

So, in what order are these rulesets called? We are going to have to explain Sendmail's internals somewhat before you will be able to grasp the internal ruleset calling scheme. Understanding this is crucial to any successful sendmail.cf programmer.

6.4.2. When Are They Called?

Sendmail has two main phases when trying to deliver a message: the *routing* phase and the *delivery* phase. To *route* a message, Sendmail puts all of the envelope recipient addresses on a list, and then, for each address, calls S3 and S0. S0 returns some extra stuff that no other ruleset has reason to return; rather than an address, S0 returns a "tuple" of [*mailer, host, address*]. When Sendmail has tuples for all envelope recipient addresses, it groups them together by [*mailer, host*] combinations and starts calling mailers.

Let's demonstrate this with an example. Say there are five envelope recipients:

```
frbzwrl!vixie
farm!avolio
vixie@pa.frobozz.com
avolio@dco.frobozz.com
paul@vixie.sf.ca.us
```

Without explaining why or how, for now let's say that the tuples come back from S0 as:

Envelope Recipients	S3/S0 Tuple
frbzwrl!vixie	[uucp, frbzwrl, vixie]
frbzwrl!farm!avolio	[uucp, frbzwrl, farm!avolio]
vixie@pa.frobozz.com	[smtp, pa.frobozz.com, vixie]
avolio@dco.frobozz.com	[smtp, dco.frobozz.com, avolio]
paul@vixie.sf.ca.us	[smtp, vixie.sf.ca.us, paul]

Sendmail is going to end up making mailer calls: one to the uucp mailer and three to the smtp mailer, as follows:

Mailer	Host	Users
uucp	frbzwrl	vixie, farm!avolio
smtp	pa.frobozz.com	vixie
smtp	dco.frobozz.com	avolio
smtp	vixie.sf.ca.us	vixie

Note that because it called S0 on all addresses before calling any mailers, Sendmail was able to determine that two of the five envelope recipients had the same [*mailer, host*] and is therefore able to send just one copy of the message to the UUCP neighbor called frbzwrl. The envelope we hand to frbzwrl will have two addresses in it, and frbzwrl is responsible for sending one copy to its vixie user and one to `avolio` on UUCP neighbor `farm`. But since the other addresses are going to different SMTP hosts, Sendmail is going to have to call mailer `smtp` three times and send out three copies of the mail.

A more common example is something like this:

Envelope Recipients	S3/S0 Tuple
`postmaster@dco.frobozz.com`	[smtp, dco.frobozz.com, postmaster]
`root@dco.frobozz.com`	[smtp, dco.frobozz.com, root]
`usenet@dco.frobozz.com`	[smtp, dco.frobozz.com, usenet]
`avolio@dco.frobozz.com`	[smtp, dco.frobozz.com, avolio]

After grouping together by [*mailer, host*], we have

Mailer	Host (`$h`)	Users (`$u`)
smtp	dco.frobozz.com	postmaster, root, usenet, avolio

Here, Sendmail learned from S0 that all four envelope addresses are headed for the same [*mailer, host*], so it can just call mailer `smtp` one time, tell it to contact `dco.frobozz.com`, and hand it all four user names.

6.4.3. Rulesets Called During the Delivery Phase

Once Sendmail is done *routing*, it knows what mailers it has to call. Now it can start *delivering*, which means calling each mailer and *munging*[4] the envelope addresses and the header into the form needed by that mailer. The reason that the mailer-specific munging is saved for this phase is that different mailers have different

---

[4] "*mung*: /muhng/ alt. 'munge' /muhnj/ [in 1960 at MIT, 'Mash Until No Good'; sometime after that the derivation from the {recursive acronym} 'Mung Until No Good' became standard] vt. 1. To make changes to a file, esp. large-scale and irrevocable changes. 2. To destroy, usually accidentally, occasionally maliciously. The system only mungs things maliciously; this is a consequence of Finagle's Law. See *scribble, mangle, trash, nuke*. Reports from Usenet suggest that the pronunciation /muhnj/ is now usual in speech, but the spelling 'mung' is still common in program comments (compare the widespread confusion over the proper spelling of kluge). 3. The kind of beans of which the sprouts are used in Chinese food..." From *The Hackers' Dictionary* compiled by Guy L. Steele, Jr., et al., available on various and sundry Internet Anonymous FTP sites.

requirements; when you have a piece of mail from `vixie@pa.frobozz.com` and you want to hand it to an SMTP neighbor, there is little or nothing to be done to the sender's address. But if you're going to send it to a UUCP neighbor, you may (or may not!) have to translate it into `pa.frobozz.com!vixie`, and if you do this, you almost certainly want to add your own UUCP host name as well, making something like `frbzwrl!pa.frobozz.com!vixie`.

When Sendmail is calling a mailer, it knows the mailer name, the host name it is going to give to that mailer, and the list of envelope recipient addresses that host will have to deal with. We'll talk more about mailers later in this chapter; all we are concerned about here are the `S=` and `R=` values of each mailer. These specify the rulesets that we want to call in order to munge the sender (`S=`) and recipient (`R=`) addresses. In normal Sendmail (or IDA without `O/` specified), the envelope sender address and all header sender addresses (`From:`, `Sender:`, and so on) are sent through the `S=` ruleset; likewise, the envelope recipient addresses and the header recipient addresses are passed through `R=`. This can be inconvenient if you want to do slightly different things to the envelope addresses than what you do to the header addresses. We'll explain IDA's solution to this in a bit.

For each sender address (for example, `From:`), Sendmail calls the following rulesets:

```
S3
S1
S=  (from mailer)
S4
```

For each recipient address (for example, `To:`, `Cc:`), Sendmail calls the following rulesets.

```
S3
S2
R=  (from mailer)
S4
```

The envelope sender is treated slightly differently. Sendmail wants to verify that it can return mail to the envelope sender address if an error occurs during delivery, so it calls S3 and S0 on the envelope sender before attempting delivery. If this step fails, Sendmail will try S3 and S0 on the name defined in the configuration file as the mail user address of Sendmail (usually `mailer-daemon`); if this also fails, Sendmail will try one last time with the `Postmaster` address and then punt the mail after logging messages to `syslog` to the effect that the `sendmail.cf` file is so broken that it can't even parse `Postmaster`. Once Sendmail knows which mailer it will use to send mail back to the envelope sender, it makes believe that it knows which mailer the message is "from." Knowing this, Sendmail can look at that mailer's `C` flag to determine whether partially qualified or unqualified header addresses should have the sending host's parent domain name tacked on. We recommend against use of the C mailer flag; the time to properly qualify a host name is *before* it escapes a domain.

If running IDA with O/ turned on, the S= and R= fields of the mailer can specify two ruleset numbers (separated by a slash (/), hence O/'s name). The first ruleset number specifies the ruleset to be used to mung the envelope addresses; the second ruleset number specifies the ruleset to be used to mung the header addresses. Thus, instead of S=10, R=20,, you might use S=10/11, R=20/21. In the latter example we call 10 the Se= and 11 the Sh=; likewise we call 20 the Re= and 21 the Rh=. Please note that the actual syntax is S=w/x and R=y/z and that Se/Sh/Re/Rh is just a way of describing the effects here.

So with all that said, IDA with O/ turned on calls the following rulesets for senders:

Envelope	Header
S3	S3
S1	S5
Se= (from mailer)	Sh= (from mailer)
S4	S4

Whereas for recipients:

Envelope	Header
S3	S3
S2	S6
Re= (from mailer)	Rh= (from mailer)
S4	S4

6.4.4. Rulesets That Are Not Predefined

Other than S0/S1/S2/S3/S4 (and sometimes S5/S6), all the other ruleset numbers are left for you, the sendmail.cf programmer, to choose. You will choose the numbers for S= and R= in the mailers; you will choose random numbers when you need a "utility ruleset" that you plan to call from somewhere else. Usually the layout of the programmer chosen ruleset numbers is S=10 and R=20 for the first mailer, S=11 and R=21 for the second mailer, and so on. This makes it hard to build boilerplate sendmail.cf packages, since not all the possible mailers will be boiled into every generated sendmail.cf file. But assuming that you have no more than 10 mailers, you probably won't get beyond S29, which is the compiled in limit in many Sendmail versions. Utility rulesets should be in the s7/s8/s9 range; if you need more than three, start at s29 and work your way downward — just make sure you don't collide with your mailers. Sendmail's error reporting isn't very good, and if you use the same ruleset more than once, it may not tell you and it may just dump core. We use the "grep ^S sendmail.cf" command quite often.

If you use IDA with o/, you have a potentially bigger problem, since each mailer can take up four ruleset numbers rather than just two. There is no good solution to this if you want to regularize your ruleset-number space, other than to use S=10/15, R=20/25, and then S=11/16, R=21/26, and so on. Probably what you will end up doing is using numbers from the utility numbering space, and only using the "/" feature on mailers that really need it. The "/" is optional; IDA with o/ treats S=10 as S=10/10; likewise, R=20 is treated as R=20/20. This lets you run the envelope and header addresses through the same ruleset, which is what you want to do most often.

Note that you can recompile Sendmail to support more than 30 rulesets if you want to get ambitious. This will make your sendmail.cf files less portable, of course.

6.4.5. Summary

In summary, different rulesets are called for different kinds of addresses (sender vs. recipient and, if running IDA with o/, envelope vs. header); further, the actual list of called rulesets depends on what S3 and S0 say.

6.5. And All the Other Lines

The other kinds of lines in a sendmail.cf file are mostly obscure paraphenalia that you almost never think about and hardly ever modify. The ones likely to be a source of trouble (or opportunity) are discussed below.

6.5.1. Options

Options for Sendmail execution, often used on the command line, may be put directly into the sendmail.cf file. This is especially useful for options that rarely if ever change, such as the location of Sendmail help and status files, the delivery mode to use, the location of the aliases file, the level to use for logging information, etc. See Appendix B for all options.

The format for the option line is the letter O, in the first column, followed by the option letter, optionally (no, really!) followed by a value. Some examples of options specified in the configuration file, which we will explain in the next chapter, are

```
OL9
Om
Oo
OQ/var/spool/mqueue
```

For boolean options, no value is needed. The default in those cases is TRUE. Options specified in the configuration file may be overridden on the Sendmail command line.

6.5.2. Header Definition

Lines beginning with H define the format for header lines that Sendmail will add to mail, if needed. The format of this line is

```
H?flag?name:format
```

which says that if flag is set in the mailer definition, the header name should be inserted with the indicated format. The ?flag? is optional. If it doesn't appear, the header is always used.

```
H?R?Received: by $j ($v/$V);
        id $i; $b
```

might add the following lines to a mail message

```
Received: by gildor.dco.frobozz.com (KJS3.4/st+p1.1);
        id AA01958; Fri, 29 Nov 91 18:40:17 EST
```

We'll see more examples of header definition lines later.

6.5.3. Trusted Users

Lines that begin with T define "trusted" users. Normally, the sender of a mail message is found by examining the ownership of the process that is running the Sendmail process on the mail being handled. Since, in many instances, the owner of the process is not the sender (when mail is from a user on another machine, for example), a means of overriding this sender address is required. Otherwise, Sendmail might indicate that the mail was from user daemon or uucp. Trusted users can override the sender information using the -f argument to Sendmail. Trusted users on many distributed sendmail.cf files include root, daemon, uucp, network (a nonexistent user on most machines), and often user eric. Unless Eric Allman, the author of Sendmail, has an account on your machine, this is probably not needed (and you may be giving a different user eric more privileges than you intend).

The line is in the form

```
Tuser1 user2 user3
```

and there may be multiple T lines, so the following lines are often found in configuration files:

```
Troot
Tdaemon
Tuucp
```

You should add a line for the login name of your system or mail administrator. This will allow the system manager to resend mail, if needed, without having her name appear in the headers. Note that this is a very valuable privilege, since if a user's login name does not appear on the T list, they will have to telnet to the host's smtp port in order to forge mail. Using telnet adds almost an entire minute of work for each forged mail message, and so T is considered an effective deterrent against forgery.[5]

6.5.4. Precedence

Sendmail prioritizes the processing of queued mail according to various criteria, including its size, the number of recipients, the time it was submitted, and its precedence. If no Precedence: header is present, the default is 0. The P line has the form

```
Pname=num
```

When the name is found in the Precedence: header, the message priority is set to num. For example, the following lines may be in your sendmail.cf:

```
Pfirst-class=0
Pspecial-delivery=100
Pjunk=-100
```

Numbers less that zero indicate that nondelivery notifications should not be sent for this mail; if it is undeliverable, it is simply deleted.

6.5.5. Mailers and Mailer Definitions

M lines describe particular mailers. A mailer definition describes what program, flags, and other arguments to use and invoke for message transfer agents particular to a certain method or protocol of mail delivery. The format of this line is

---

[5] Not!

```
Mname, field1=value, ...
```

in which `name` is the name of the mailer definition (used in the `sendmail.cf` file) and fields can be any of the following:

Path	The full pathname of the mailer (e.g., `/usr/bin/uux`)
Flags	Flags for this mailer
Sender	The rewriting ruleset number for Sender addresses
Recipient	The rewriting ruleset for Recipient addresses
Argv	An argument vector to pass to the program
Eol	The end-of-line string for this mailer
Maxsize	The maximum size allowed for mail to pass through this mailer

Normally, only the first character of the field name is used. We will look more deeply into mailer definitions later, but here is an example of one for a mailer used for UUCP mail:

```
Muucp,  P=/usr/bin/uux, F=sDFhu, S=13, R=23, M=100000,
        A=uux - $h!rmail ($u)
```

We see that the name of this mailer is uucp (`Muucp`). The program can be found in `/usr/bin/uux` (`P=`) to be executed with the arguments `uux - $h!rmail ($u)`, where `$h` is the recipient's host and `$u` is the recipient (`A=`). The particular sender and recipient header rewriting rulesets for this mailer are 13 (`S=`) and 23 (`R=`). And any message larger than `100000` (`M=`) will be returned to the sender as being too large to send. The flags indicate that quotes should be stripped from addresses (`s`), `Date:` and `From:` headers should be in the mail message (and added if they are not) (`DF`), and uppercase should be preserved in host and user names (`hu`).

6.6. Command Line Arguments

A complete list for Sendmail command line arguments can be found on the Sendmail man page (and Appendix A), but some common ones will be shown briefly here.

```
sendmail -bd -q1h:
```
> run Sendmail as a daemon, listening on an IP socket for new work (`-bd`). Every hour it should try to run through the queue to deliver mail (`-q1h`).

```
sendmail -bz:
```
> freeze the configuration file. This takes the information in `sendmail.cf` and creates `sendmail.fc`, a "compiled" version of the configuration file.

```
sendmail -q -v:
```
> run through the queue, try to deliver everything, be verbose about it.

`sendmail -bi`:
   initialize the `aliases` database — synonym for the `newaliases` command.

`sendmail -bt -Ctry.cf`:
   runs Sendmail in interactive test mode using `try.cf` as the configuration file.

7

Using IDA "dbm" Tables

Sendmail, when extended with the IDA kit, allows much of the address rewriting policy, and in fact much of the routing policy, to be stored external to the `sendmail.cf` in "dbm" tables. These tables are actually hash keyed databases, but you don't have to know very much about that in order to use them. The IDA kit comes with a utility called dbm that translates ordinary text files into "dbm" tables or updates existing "dbm" tables. If you can express your table in terms of keys and values, the actual storage details will be handled for you by the utilities.

7.1. Syntax

The fundamental operator for using "dbm" tables is the $(..$) construct, which takes as arguments a "table name" (a single character, usually a letter), a "lookup key" (usually a user, host, or domain name), a "replacement string" (useful if you embed sprintf style "%s" strings in your table values), and a "default value," which is almost always used to control subsequent processing in case the table lookup fails. The full glory of this construct is usually shown as:

$(*table key* [$@ *sprintf-string*] [$: *default-value*] $)

The *table* is a single character that has been associated with some extant "dbm" database using the K option, à la OKP/var/db/uupaths or some similar option early on in the `sendmail.cf`.

The *sprintf-string* is used as the argument to a forced sprintf call, which is made if and only if the *sprintf-string* is given and the table lookup resulted in a successful fetch of a value that contains a "%s" sequence. See the sprintf man page for details.

The *default-value* of a failed lookup is the search key. This means that if a lookup fails, the entire $(..$) construct will expand to the search string itself, which is usually convenient since this construct is normally placed in the RHS in a spot where either the search key or its replacement is acceptable and sensible and even useful. You can override this default by specifying one explicitly; this feature is often used to provide some kind of exceptional syntax in failed searches, so as to "catch" on exception handling rules later in the ruleset.

You will find the "dbm" table lookup, or something like it, at the heart of every robust Sendmail configuration. It is true of the IDA kits (classic, UIUC, and *KJS* all have it), and of Berkeley R8. No one with a big mail problem solves it with hard-coded `sendmail.cf` rules any more.

7.2. Details

"dbm" is a very fast way to look things up; it never requires more than three disk references to succeed or fail, regardless of the number of keys in or the total size of the table. However, Sendmail's use of "dbm" has always been unique. Sendmail historically used "dbm" for its `aliases` database, but because of the robustness of the "dbm" interface, the ASCII NUL ("\0") byte that terminates the string key and the string value were unintentionally stored in the database, with no ill effects other than a requirement to keep doing this for ever after to maintain compatibility with old databases. IDA's use of "dbm" goes far beyond the `aliases` database, but it retains the need for the terminating NUL in the key and value of every database element.

As mentioned in Chapter 6, most older implementations of the "dbm" interface will silently enforce a 1,024 byte limit on database values. This places unfortunate constraints on the `aliases` database, since mailing lists are frequently longer than 1,024 bytes. This limit rarely causes trouble for the IDA extensions since its tables are usually lists of users or hosts or domains, which are almost never more than a few hundred bytes in size.

7.3. Routing Control

When a host is used as an MX target for some other domain, Sendmail must be trained to do something special when it receives mail for that domain. Usually the right thing to do is call a non-TCP mailer such as `uux-rmail` or `mail11`. These protocols require a link layer "node name" to be specified as the destination of the mail; this node name is not necessarily related to or derivable from the destination domain. Some means must be employed to cause the mail to be sent using a new protocol, and some way has to be found to specify the link layer node name to be used as the destination host of the non-TCP protocol. One common such means is to add many rules to Ruleset 0 of the form

```
R$*<@vix.com>$*          $#uux-rmail $@vixie $:$1<@vix.com>$2
```

As you might imagine, this gets hard to manage when you have several dozen or several hundred domains for which you are the target MX RR. Problems include efficiency (since Sendmail processes these rules in order), uniqueness (since your `sendmail.cf` file is no longer shareable among many hosts if it has a list of MX domains encoded in it), and manageability (let's face it, `sendmail.cf` is easy to make mistakes on while you are editing it, especially if editing one rule among hundreds of others that look just like it).

Consider this excerpt from a real `sendmail.cf` from an IDA enhanced site:

```
CA@
OKE/usr/local/adm/mail/exceptions

...

S0

...

###
### try exception (people we MX for)
###

R$*<@$+.$+>$*          $:@$2.$3@!$1<@$2.$3>$4          dup and isolate
R@$-$*@!$*<@$+>$*       $(E$1$2$:@$2$)@!$3<@$4>$5       search exceptions
R$~A@!$*<@$+>$*         $:$1@uux-rmail@!$2<@$3>$4       found, no mailer
R$~A$*@$-@!$*<@$+>$*    $#$3 $@$1$2 $:$4<@$5>$6         found, with mailer
R@@!$+                 $1                             forget it
```

We apologize for the density and opacity of this example, but nothing less will do. Here's what's going on. Token class A is made to include only the single token, @. This will be used later to effect an *if not* construct using LHS matching. Next, table E is associated with the "dbm" table `/usr/local/adm/mail/exceptions`, which usually means that the file `/usr/local/adm/mail/exceptions.db` is opened internally, though older systems might have two separate files (ending in `.dir` and `.pag`) instead of only one (ending in `.db`).

In Ruleset 0, for addresses that have at least one dot in their domains, we duplicate the domain at the front of the address and isolate this duplicate from the rest of the address using a special syntax — @! — which we know will never be present in any real address. This turns an address such as `paul<@vix.com>` into `@vix.com@!paul<@vix.com>`.

Note that the address, which now follows the @!, is complete including its focus characters (< and >) and its *route-addr* syntax, if any. This is necessary because we will need the original address, intact, once we are done with the table lookups. That leading @ is also known never to appear in a real address (a *route-addr* would have a leading focus indicator (<) at the front of the address). We will use this leading @ to indicate success or failure of the table lookup.

The second rule matches only addresses that have been modified to our special syntax (leading @, embedded @!). Note that this rule does not introduce the RHS with $:; thus, it will iterate until it fails to match. This is an important detail. On each iteration, the E table is searched for a key that is the isolated *search-domain*. The default value in case the search fails is @$2, which means that if the search fails, the next iteration will search for a domain with the leading token stripped off. Keep in mind that a dot (.) is a *token*, in the sense that it will match a $- (or $+ for that matter, though we don't use it that way here). Also focus your attention on the LHS match which was for $-$+ — this sets $1 to the *first* token and $2 to the *remaining* tokens. A successful search will find the entire search domain and replace it with the value retrieved from the table; a failed search will replace the entire $(..$) construct with the *remaining* tokens from the search domain, i.e., all but the first. The remainder of the RHS merely appends the special syntax (@!) and the original address. The rule will iterate until the search domain has fewer than one token or no longer contains a leading at sign (@). Since a successful search replaces the initial part of the address with a table value, and table values presumably do not contain leading @'s, this means that a successful table lookup will terminate this rule's iteration.

The third rule shown will only match if the first token is something other than an at sign (@). (Remember token class A set earlier, and that $~A means "if the address doesn't contain a substring from class A at this point.") Since a successful table lookup would have generated an address without a leading @, and since this rule still has the special syntax (@!) requirement in its LHS pattern, it is safe to say that this rule handles addresses for which matches *were* found. This rule gets trickier, though: A database value is a destination name with an optional mailer name; if present, the mailer name will be separated from the destination name by — you guessed it — an at sign (@). If the retrieved table value has no @, a default mailer name is applied here. One more subtle thing about this rule: $~@ must match any number of tokens at the beginning of the address, up to a mandatory @. Some older Sendmails only match single tokens on class lookups.

The fourth rule is where we recognize successful table lookups and hand off the address to the specified mailer (which might have been the default we would have applied in the previous rule). The $@ (*host*) is the destination name from the table lookup value. The $: (*address*) is the original, isolated, unmodified address we started the ruleset with, which we reconstitute from the four winds that blew the tokens into $1 et al during the LHS parsing phase. Note that we also reconstitute the delimiters.

The fifth rule will never be executed if a table match is found. It recognizes attempted (but failed) lookups and removes the special syntax, thus returning the address to its standard form so that the rest of Ruleset 0 can proceed normally.

With these rules in place, the previous `vix.com` example can be accomplished using a table that mapped a key `vixie` to a value `vix.com`. As a beneficial side effect, this approach also catches addresses in subdomains; any of the following will be sent to the UUCP node called `vixie`:

```
paul@vix.com
paul@gw.home.vix.com
postmaster@office.home.vix.com
```

This multilevel matching is almost always what you want, and to get it from hard-coded rules in Ruleset 0, you would need something like this:

```
R$*<@$*vix.com>$*    $#uux-rmail $@vixie $:$1<@$2vix.com>$3
```

If you cannot easily tell the difference between this example and the earlier one, you are a candidate for table driven MX forwarding.

A table could include a variety of elements, some more specific than others. Consider the following set of elements:

Key	Value
`pa.vix.com`	`vix-gw@smtp`
`vix.com`	`vixie@uux-rmail`

In the presence of this table, mail sent to addresses whose domains end in `pa.vix.com` are sent via the `smtp` mailer to a host called `vix-gw` (which might be fully qualified or not, depending on where it is and how explicit you want to be). Mail to other addresses, ending in `vix.com` but not `pa.vix.com`, is sent via the `uux-rmail` mailer to node `vixie`. This approach is almost infinitely scalable, since the number of lookups needed to discover the right route for an address is dependent on the number of tokens in the address rather than the number of alternatives in the routing database. Most domains have fewer than 10 tokens in their names, so the number of table lookups will be quite small even in the worst case.

7.4. UUCP Path Lookups

Since a vast number of addresses are still reachable only via UUCP at the time of this writing, it is still common for Sendmail to need to do so called "smart routing" to

UUCP hosts. The reason this "routing" is called "smart" is that Sendmail can be given a severely truncated path, and as long as the "first hop" is in the local pathalias database and the path as given is complete and correct, the mail can still be delivered. In practice this means that users at any UUCP site that employs "smart routing" can reach one of us by mailing to vixie!paul, even though they probably will not have a direct UUCP link to the vixie node.

Mail users who have only used the *user@domain* form of addressing may not even realize that the underlying network is discovering end-to-end routes automatically, since this happens out of sight and out of mind. UUCP mail users, especially from the early days, know that the worst-case scenario is having to remember not only which host talks to which other host but which advertised links do and do not work this week. "Smart routing," when first introduced, was a real boon. These days it is rare for a host to have UUCP connections at all unless they are used only to reach Internet service providers. But just in case you still care, or are curious, here's how to make Sendmail route your UUCP mail for you.

7.4.1. UUCP Routing Databases

Before we begin, note that the mechanics of getting a UUCP "map," the pathalias program, and glue to put the two together are beyond the scope of this section. Look around with Archie (see Appendix K) for tools like uuhosts and uumail, which among other things can automate your UUCP map processing.

As before, we must first declare the tables we intend to search. This can happen anywhere in the sendmail.cf, but it is customary to put such declarations near the top because they are the most likely to need changes when systems are upgraded or software is borrowed.

```
OKN/usr/local/adm/mail/uunames
OKP/usr/local/adm/mail/uupaths
OKF/usr/local/adm/mail/uufakes
```

The uunames table just maps UUCP node names to themselves. This sounds useless, but when searched with an *or else* option, it provides the means by which Sendmail can make a "use / don't use" decision about a path. The goal here is to head off any possible routing if the first hop of a path is actually a neighbor of the current host. This is necessary; otherwise, an error in the input to pathalias will cause you to reach your own neighbors via some remote, suboptimal paths. This is a disaster, and avoiding it is relatively cheap and easy to do. Elements in this table look like this:

Key	Value
uunet	uunet!%s

As you will see, this is the same format as a `uupaths` table element.

The `uupaths` table maps UUCP node names to relative paths. This table is traditionally produced using Peter Honeyman's excellent `pathalias` program (use Archie to locate a copy; see Appendix K). Though it is possible to create and maintain the table by hand, doing so is almost always a sign of trouble, and if you find yourself doing it, you should rethink your strategy very carefully. There are still tens of thousands of UUCP host registrations published in the Usenet `comp.mail.maps` newsgroup, and if you want to reach enough of them that you prefer "smart routing," you should use some smart software to generate your routing table. An element of the `uupaths` table looks like this:

Key	Value
zygot	decwrl!apple!zygot!%s

Note that the UUCP node name in the key is nearly always present in the value, and that the value always ends in the string "`!%s`". This string will be given by Sendmail to the library function `sprintf`, and "`%s`" is a magic cookie used by `sprintf` for token insertion in a template. This will make more sense later.

Finally, the `uufakes` table is used to map UUCP node names to direct SMTP gateways for them. `uufakes` can be handy if you wish to pretend for the purposes of mail routing that you have a UUCP connection to some other host, even though you will actually use SMTP to deliver the mail. A need for something like `uufakes` often occurs when you first turn off a long standing UUCP connection to some other site, and you don't want to bounce mail during the time it will take Usenet's `comp.mail.maps` to publish an update of your node registration. You might install `uufakes` in your Sendmail so that you can switch from UUCP/TCP to SMTP/TCP without breaking existing paths for the several years it might take the network to stop generating mail over the old path. Elements of this table are of the form

Key	Value
uunet	%s@uunet.uu.net

Again, we see the magic `sprintf` string, "`%s`". This is where the *local part* will be placed if a table match occurs. Careful readers will have noted that the substitution is absolutely arbitrary and potentially very complex. Beware — that way lies utter madness.

7.4.2. UUCP Routing Logic

Down in Ruleset 0, following the exceptions logic shown above, you could put code
like the following:

```
R$+<@$-.$=z>    $:$>3$(F$2$@$1$:$1<@$2.UUX>$)    try fakes

R$+<@$-.$=z>    $:$>17$1<@$2.UUX>                try neighbor
R@!$-!$+        $#uux-rmail $@$1 $:$2            found it

R$+<@$-.$=z>    $:$>18$1<@$2.UUX>                try path
R@!$-!$+        $#uux-rmail $@$1 $:$2            found it

R$+<@$-.$=z>    $#uux-rmail $@$2 $:$1            error message
```

This code should look fairly similar to the exceptions logic. Almost all table-driven
`sendmail.cf` code has this same style. In this case we can search the `uufakes`
table directly, but the searches of the other two tables are complicated enough to be
better off in their own rulesets, where they can exit back to the main line of Ruleset 0
with a `$@` whenever they decide that they are done.

In this code, you can see that any address that uses a pseudodomain from the z
class (usually this class has the tokens `uucp` and `uux` in it) will have its host name
($2) looked up. If there is a table match, the *local part* ($1) will be used by
`sprintf` to replace the first `%s` in the table value. If no match occurs, the address is
returned to its canonical form, with the pseudodomain still attached so that subsequent rules can match on it. In any event, the result is sent back through Ruleset 3
for canonicalization, since it will probably lack *focus* (the < and > characters that sur-
round the @*domain*). We would like to send the result back through Ruleset 3 only if
it matches, but this adds a lot of code. Note that this rule provides yet another good
reason why Ruleset 3 should be idempotent[1] — most UUCP nodes will not be found
in the table, and Ruleset 3 will most often be called here with the *or else* clause of
the table lookup, which is already going to be in canonical form.

If the address survives this and makes it to the second rule shown, it will again be
searched for the UUCP pseudodomains (`uucp` and `uux`), and if they are present, the
whole address will be sent down into Ruleset 17. We chose 17 because it was available, not because it is special in any way. Your own `sendmail.cf` may use 17 for
something else, and in that case you should pick another number. When Ruleset 17
returns, or if we don't call it, we look for a special pattern — one with a leading `@!`.
We chose `@!` because it was unlikely to appear in a real address. Ruleset 17 signals
success by wrapping the address in this special syntax; you can bet that the rule after

---

[1] That is, it does nothing if the address is already in canonical form.

the call to $>17 will never match anything but the successful returns from Ruleset 17. This seems complicated, and it is, but that's data driven programming for you.

Anyway, if Ruleset 17 wants us to resolve the address it will signal that fact by prepending a @! and then separating the "first hop" from "the rest" by another ! character. There may be more ! characters in "the rest," but we haven't asked Sendmail to look for any, so it will always just stop on the first one — Ruleset 17's. Let's have a look at 17:

```
S17
R$+<@$-.$=Z>   $:$(N$2$@$1$:@!$1<@$2.UUX>$)   try neighbor
R$=A!$+        $@$2                           found @!, strip it, ret
R$+<@$+>$*     $@$1<@$2>$3                     still focused, ret
R$+            $@@!$1                          return with @! prefix
```

What we're looking for here is a neighbor. If we find one, we give the *local part* ($1) to sprintf for its "%s," as before. If we don't find a neighbor, we put an @! on the front of the address. This pattern will match the next rule's $=A!$+ since class A contains only the single token @. The purpose of this rule is to catch the "not found" case and return immediately with the original address, still in canonical form, with no special characters prepended. We can now depend on the fact that in the next rule, we will not be there at all unless a match *did* occur. Given that prerequisite, we can expand our pattern and match on *any* canonical form address. We send these addresses back to Ruleset 0, too, on the assumption that neighbor database lookups that result in canonical form addresses should probably not be resolved to $#uux-rmail back in Ruleset 0, which, as you saw above, is what will happen if we return something with that @! marker prepended to it. The last rule in 17 returns what we assume is a UUCP path, prefixed with a @! marker. Now you can go back and look at the Ruleset 17 calling sequence in Ruleset 0 and it should make more sense.

Hard as it may be to believe, this is the *clean* way to do this job.

Ruleset 18 is identical to Ruleset 17 except that it uses a different table. This time we're looking for a path, not a neighbor. The tables are in the same format, and the actions on matching and not matching are all the same. We could have encoded the table name as a syntax separated parameter to the utility ruleset and thereby would have needed only one such ruleset rather than two; we felt that these rulesets were already too complicated and that more generality would have come at the expense of what little simplicity remains. Here's 18:

```
S18
R$+<@$-.$=Z>   $:$(P$2$@$1$:@!$1<@$2.UUX>$)   try path
R$=A!$+        $@$2                           found @!, strip it, ret
R$+<@$+>$*     $@$1<@$2>$3                     still focused, ret
R$+            $@@!$1                          return with @! prefix
```

7.4.3. UUCP Routing — Summary

One thing to keep in mind here is that if you don't have any Internet connectivity and your UUCP connections are all you have, you might want to use the *domain* entries from the uupaths table. These are similar but with an important difference: The keys all contain dots (.) and possibly even begin with a dot. These keys look like this:

Key	Value
.crl.dec.com	decwrl!deccrl!%s
.dco.dec.com	decwrl!uunet!aplcen!decuac!%s
.dec.com	decwrl!%s
.prl.dec.com	decwrl!uunet!mcsun!corton!decprl!%s
crl.dec.com	decwrl!deccrl!%s
dco.dec.com	decwrl!uunet!aplcen!decuac!%s

We don't use these table elements in our example because we assume the more common cases, which are either having Internet connectivity (in which case you reach these domains directly, via SMTP) or using some Internet service provider for all your nonlocal traffic (in which case the service provider will reach the destinations directly, via SMTP). However, if you want to use the pathalias software and Usenet comp.mail.maps data to reach all Internet domains, you can do that by copying the general form of the exceptions logic shown above. As you will recall, elements of the exceptions database are allowed to be partial domain names, with leading dots. This is not an accident; that logic was once used to search the uupaths table back before end-to-end SMTP became the dominant transport for mail. Revising these rules back to that form is a trivial exercise, which we leave to you.

7.5. Address Generification

Most Sendmail sites throughout history have used a UNIX "login name" as the unique *local part* identifier for a user's mailbox, and during the lengthy period when hosts were expensive, we used an Internet "host name" as the *domain* qualifier following the @. Thus, we see addresses of the form

login-name @ host-name

This form has often been found to be too *specific*, in that it restricts the possibility of a user changing her login name or the name of the host where she reads her mail. Thus, we have seen in recent years a trend toward *generic* identifiers in e-mail addresses, which more closely resemble the formal definition of an address, which is *mailbox-name @ domain-name*

The technology used for generic *domain name*s is based on the Internet DNS's MX RRs. These RRs permit mail to be sent to a domain name but delivered to any of several different hosts. The names of the domain and its MX RR hosts need not be similar in any way — the facility is completely general. The technology used to actually generate reply addresses that use the generic domain name is less well understood.

Likewise, the technology needed to accept mail for generic user names is well understood; you just put entries in the `aliases` database for so called "full names" and let Sendmail handle mapping these to some UNIX login name during local delivery. However, the technology for generating reply addresses using generic mailbox names is less widely known.

We use a two step process in our generification of addresses. First, we focus only on the *domain-part* (the part after the @) and search a table. If a match occurs, the *domain-part* is replaced by the value from the table. Note that appropriate MX RRs must exist in the DNS or this process will create unrepliable addresses. You will also need to add to class w all generic names a host has been mapped to, since otherwise mail to those names will not be delivered locally by the hosts that own those mailboxes. Likewise, the generic user names must appear in the `aliases` database of receiving hosts, so that they can be mapped back to the login names and thus can be delivered to local mailboxes. After this first stage, the address will have the following form:

login-name @ domain name

The second stage is to take the entire address and search a second table for it, replacing the entire address with the table value if a match occurs. Thus, the form of an address after the second stage of generification is

mailbox-name @ domain name

The reason for the two stage process is that hosts tend to cluster in logical groups, each of which has a common user community. If several hosts all map to the same domain name, the user name table can be expressed in terms of that domain name rather than having to list all the different hosts a user might send mail from or receive it at.

Consider an example generic host name table:

Key	Value
`morality.baloney.com`	`baloney.com`
`opt1.baloney.com`	`baloney.com`
`watchman.baloney.com`	`baloney.com`

These three host names will be turned into `baloney.com` if they appear in an address, assuming that the set of login names on the three hosts (plus any others that map to this same generic name) is coherent. If the same login name does not refer to the same mailbox on all hosts that map to a single generic domain name, chaos will erupt.

As an example of a generic address table, consider the following:

Key	Value
vixie<@baloney.com>	Paul_Vixie<@Baloney.COM>
jerry<@baloney.com>	Jerry_Scarcioni<@Baloney.COM>
jimmie<@baloney.com>	Jim_Whaler<@Baloney.COM>

The interesting fact about this table is that the *focus* characters (< and >) are present in both the key and the value. This saves us from having to pass successful lookup results through Ruleset 3 and gives us the flexibility to match unfocused names (simple local login names, for example). Note that if your sendmail.cf is configured to use a pseudodomain such as <@LOCAL> on local names, you will need to include this in your table keys and values. If you get it right once, you will be on track forever.

Classic IDA Sendmail has always had a feature for generification, but it works a little differently than what we're presenting here. R8 has a similar facility, but since its table lookup mechanism is very different from IDA's, we won't present the details here. Both IDA and R8 include ample documentation of their features, so we will stick to the fundamentals, using IDA's table lookups because they are older and more widely used than R8's as of the time of this writing.

Here's how it works:

```
OKD/usr/local/adm/mail/domains
OKU/usr/local/adm/mail/users

...

S5
R$-           $:$1<@LOCAL>           qualify local name
R$+<@$+>$*    $:$1<@$(D$2$)>$3       generify domain name
R$+<@$+>$*    $:$(U$1<@$2>$)$3       generify user name

S6
R$-           $:$1<@LOCAL>           qualify local name
R$+<@$+>$*    $:$1<@$(D$2$)>$3       generify domain name
R$+<@$+>$*    $:$(U$1<@$2>$)$3       generify user name
R$-<@LOCAL>   $:$1                   remove local name
```

You might recall that in IDA Sendmail, Rulesets 5 and 6 can be enabled (via the O/ option) for processing only the header addresses. We chose to use them rather than Rulesets 1 and 2 because we didn't want to generify envelope addresses. This decision is a matter of local preference when it comes to the envelope sender, but it is absolutely vital that you not generify the envelope recipient. If you do, probably no mail will get through at all. You'll note in our example that Ruleset 5, which handles header senders, does not remove its own <@LOCAL>, whereas Ruleset 6, which handles header recipients, does. This has to do with Ruleset 4 in the sendmail.cf this example came out of, and you should adjust these rules to suit your own needs.

The two table search rules are the same in both rulesets, which means we could have put them into a common utility ruleset which could be called from both Ruleset 5 and Ruleset 6; however, with only two common rules, it's not worth it. The first rule searches for just the *domain-part* in the domain table, and the second rule searches for the entire address, including focus characters, in the user name table. Both rules have a $: on the RHS, so they will exit after one iteration whether the match succeeds or not. This means that table entries can't be chained together — if one element's data matches another's key, the replacement will use the first match rather than any successive or final match. Again, this is a matter of local preference. We fear table element loops more than we need table indirection. Your needs, and concerns, may be different.

You should also note that since no $: is present inside the "dbm" lookup (which is the $(through the $)), there is no *or else* clause. Thus, if either table lookup fails, the replacement text will be the key itself. This implements a "change if you find it; leave it alone otherwise" semantic.

7.6. Tools

We have shown data driven mechanisms by which mail can be routed and by which addresses can be generified, using "dbm" tables. The technology is not useful until you have some data for it to operate with; generating and managing this data is actually the larger task overall.

Given the requirement that DNS MX RRs match the generic domain table, it is tempting to generate both databases (the DNS zones and the domain table) from the same input data — perhaps even with a single tool that reads a single input database and generates both output databases.

Moreover, since it is necessary to synchronize the aliases database with the generic user name table, it is tempting to try to generate both from a single set of input. This is an area where interested Perl or TCL programmers can exercise great creativity as they incrementally build their own ideal local solution.

7.7. dbm

IDA Sendmail comes with a utility called dbm that can be used to initialize tables; dump their contents; or add, delete, or fetch elements. The dbm utility is just a wrapper around the dbm *library*, which is the same library Sendmail uses to retrieve elements during its operation. A UNIX "man page" for dbm is included with the IDA kit, so we will not detail its operation here.

8

Configuration Details

> *"You are in a maze of twisty little*
> *Sendmail rules, all obscure."*

We culled the above quote from Mike Shaddock's Usenet signature, and we believe that it is the best possible explication of that "sinking feeling" folks get when they get lost in the labyrinthine depths of a `sendmail.cf` file.

We are about to take a (nearly) line-by-line stroll through a `sendmail.cf` file, in which groups of lines are presented with commentary separating them. This is basically the file we use on *our* mail hosts. Later we will discuss how to build and maintain `sendmail.cf` files, but for now, remembering what we covered in the previous chapters, let's get to it.

A double espresso would be good right about now.

8.1. The Sendmail Configuration Files

In looking at the configuration file, you will learn how it works and how to modify (or even write!) one yourself. To review, let's remember that a configuration file has comments, macro definitions, class definitions, configuration options, header definitions, rulesets made up of rules, and mailer definitions. Our `sendmail.cf` is set up so that everything is presented, mostly, in that order (we put mailer-specific rulesets with the mailer definitions).

8.2. Opening Comments

A `sendmail.cf` file usually has some historical comments at the top. For brevity, we have taken them out of our examination in this chapter. The configuration file in its entirety is presented in Appendix D.

8.3. Macros and Classes

We define P to be a variable (or macro) whose value is FROBOZZ.COM. This is our *parent domain* and will be treated specially. In particular, while we may utilize mail gateways to get to external hosts, we might send mail directly to other hosts under our parent domain.

```
# parent domain
DPFROBOZZ.COM
# my domain
DNDCO.$P
# name exported on external internet mail
DW$N
# my host's official DNS name
Dj$w.$N
```

Our local domain is plugged into variable N. Now, remember what this means. Later in this configuration file, anywhere we have the character string $P or $N it will behave exactly as if we typed in FROBOZZ.COM or DCO.FROBOZZ.COM.

W gets the value DCO.FROBOZZ.COM — our local domain. Mail from this host that goes outside our local domain will have this as the domain part. In other words, instead of mail with the sender address avolio@gildor.DCO.FROBOZZ.COM, the sender's address will be avolio@DCO.FROBOZZ.COM.

By the way, unless we state otherwise, in this context when we refer to *domain-part*, we mean either a fully qualified host name or an unqualified host name. If we mean one or the other in particular, we will be explicit. Sendmail sets the variable w to be our host name. We assume here that $w is *not* fully qualified (with a domain name), and so variable j is set to be our fully qualified domain name (FQDN).

```
CJDNET ENET
DJdecnet-relay.$N
DEENET
```

In this section we set up some classes and variables for DECnet MAIL11. Class J is set to be the pseudodomains that indicate mail needs to be sent via DECnet and MAIL11 — here, the set [DNET, ENET]. This means that later in this file anywhere we match against this set (this pattern), it says "match DNET or ENET." If macro J is defined, as it is here, we will be sending any such mail to $J — in this case DECnet-relay.DCO.FROBOZZ.COM, our DECnet mail relay. Macro (or variable) E is set to be ENET (which is the true pseudodomain name for DECnet Phase IV mail inside Digital). Since some hosts insist on using DNET, we catch it in class J. Again, we'll see later how this is used.

```
# aliases at the $P level -- we think we are authoritative for these
Cddco cop8
# names which will be @domain qual'd on outbound localdom mail
CNroot news uucp mailer-daemon rdist nobody daemon
# trash top level doms: don't use $[...$] if end w/these
CTUUCP USENET ENET
```

Class d is the set of local domains we treat as "one big happy family" — a Mail Cluster. In this case it is dco and cop8. Among other things, this means that mail to

```
center@cop8.frobozz.com
```

and to

```
center@dco.frobozz.com
```

will get to the same user's mailbox. Mail clusters can span DNS domains. We include these here because we are authoritative for these subdomains. In other words, this machine knows how to properly get mail to any user whose mailbox is in either of these subdomains.

However, as mentioned before in our short discussion of Mail Clusters, there are some user names that should not be treated as global names. While user layman might be the same across all systems in a mail cluster, user root or mailer-daemon should always be qualified with the local host's FQDN. Class N sets up the set of those names.

Finally, we list the set of pseudodomain names used internally in this configuration file, which should never escape into a mail message. If we ever have a host name with one of these as the top level — for example

```
king@talos.enet
```

this sendmail.cf will catch that and make sure Sendmail doesn't try to resolve that address with the DNS resolver.

So far, we've set up some variables and classes. If you are unsure of how we will use them, keep on reading. Their purposes and uses will become clear as you see them used in the rules. Now we set up some variables that, in most cases, must be there but are probably the same values in nearly all sendmail.cf files.

8.4. Special Macros

Consider the following lines:

```
# my name
DnMAILER-DAEMON
# UNIX header format
DlFrom $g  $d
# delimiter (operator) characters
Do.:%@!^=/[]
# format of a total name
Dq$?x$x $.<$g>
# Version
DV05AUG93-fma/vix-1.1
# SMTP login message
De$j Sendmail $v ($V) $b
```

Here we set up the name Sendmail will use if it has to send mail back to the
sender, and we define the UNIX envelope From line. The line starting Dl specifies
that the From envelope line (variable 1 — the letter "el") is made up of "From" followed by the value of macro g followed by the value of macro d. The $g is the *mail-
box* of the sender, and the $d is the date the mail was sent. These were explained in
Chapter 7.

Macro o is set to the *delimiters* or punctuation marks in mail addresses. The $q is
the "total name" of a mail address. The line on which $q is defined (Dq) reads:
"Define q to be: The full name of the user ($x) followed by a blank, if and only if $x
is defined, followed by the mail address ($g) within angle brackets. If $x is not
defined, then $q will be the address in brackets." The $?x says "if x is defined."
The $| means "else" (though not present in this rule), and the $. is the "end-if."

So, for example, if $x is defined to be "Paul Vixie" and his mailbox is
"vixie@pa.frobozz.com", then $q will have the value

```
Paul Vixie <vixie@pa.frobozz.com>
```

but if $x is not defined or known, then $q will be

```
<vixie@pa.frobozz.com>
```

When a process connects to our Sendmail socket it will be sent the greeting indicated by the last line in the example. Our host name ($j) will be filled in. The ver-
sion of the running Sendmail ($v) and the version of the Sendmail configuration
(defined by variable V are also filled in, as is the date in ARPAnet format ($b). The
value of the variable V is useful for debugging, but not if we don't remember to

change it when we make a change to this file. For example, it might expand to the following (we've split the line so it will fit on the page):

```
volition.pa.frobozz.com Sendmail 5.6 (05AUG93-fma/vix-1.1) \
            Sun, 29 Aug 93, 19:17:34 -0700
```

8.5. Configuration Options

All of the possible options to Sendmail are listed in Appendix B. They can be given to Sendmail on the command line or in the configuration file. All options lines start with the letter O. Most of these are clear enough that we won't spend much time on them. Using these option lines, we can set locations of files (options A and H, for example) and other defaults.

```
# wait 5 minutes for newaliases to complete
Oa
# location of alias file
OA/etc/aliases
# default delivery mode (deliver in background)
Odbackground
# temporary file mode
OF0600
# default UID
Ou1
# default GID
Og1
# location of help file
OH/usr/lib/sendmail.hf
# log level
OL9
# include sender if she's on an alias to which she's sending
Om
# queue directory
OQ/var/spool/mqueue
```

We see our default delivery mode is with a `background` process. When temporary files are created they are created with reading and writing enabled for owner and no one else (`OF0600`). Further, our default user and group id is 1 (that is user `daemon`). The line that is `OL9` shows us setting the `syslog` log level to 9 (see the `syslog` man pages for more details). This controls how much information gets logged to our `syslog` system logging server. The m option (*m* for "me too") controls what happens when a local user sends mail to an alias in a Sendmail alias list and she is listed in the alias. The options are to include the user or not include her.

```
# read timeout -- violates protocols
Or1h
# status file
OS/etc/sendmail.st
# queue up everything before starting transmission
Os
# use separate envelope/header rewriting rulesets (IDA)
O/
# default timeout interval
OT3d
# load average for forcing "Odq" behaviour
Ox20
# load average for refusing connections
OX12
```

Astute readers will note that the value shown for Ox is larger than the value shown for OX, and that this is opposite from the configuration files you may have seen elsewhere. Setting them as shown here gives Sendmail a range of load average in which it is capable of delivering messages from its queue but incapable of receiving new messages. This is intentional. If you set Ox to be less than OX, Sendmail has instead a range of load averages in which it can receive new mail (thus adding to the queue) but cannot deliver any queued mail. We believe that mail queues should become smaller or stay the same size when the load average is high. After watching our large mail gateway computers melt down many times over the years, we have learned that it is better to let other hosts' mail stay where it was — on other hosts — when our load average is high, than to accept it even though we don't plan to do anything with it until our load average becomes low again. Symptoms of Ox being less than OX are messages like /usr/spool: out of inodes on your system console, and mail messages sent to your local postmaster address asking why mail sometimes takes several days to get through your gateway.[1]

You will read in nearly every sendmail.cf the comment "read timeout — violates protocols." And everyone goes ahead and violates them anyway. As of RFC 1123, this is no longer a protocol violation, since everyone chose to ignore this protocol rule and run the risk of cutting off a slow connection in the interest of saving our host's CPUs from developing psychological problems. This line says "after a hour, if there's no action on the connection — even if you are still "reading" — break the connection."

---

[1] Jeff Mogul deserves the credit for suggesting to us the proper relationship of Ox and OX, and let the record show that Jeff's mail was often unfairly trapped in our queue until we learned this lesson.

In this section, we turn on Boolean option s. Notice that there is no value associated with some options. They are either set or not set. We also include here an option switch in IDA Sendmail and derivatives that allows the use of separate rules for envelope and header fields. The line-setting option T says if a message has been undeliverable for three days (the value of macro T is 3d), return it to the sender. The system manager may set this value to whatever time interval she thinks fits the mail system's and network's needs. The value 3d is "three days," as 12h is "twelve hours," and 65m is "sixty-five minutes." The value 3d is common, 5d is the new recommendation in RFC 1123.

Options x and X are interesting. (You *are* remembering that these are *options* and not *variables*?). In this example, if the load average of this host ever got up to 20, all mail would be put in the mail spool directory and left there until things quieted down. Sendmail would not attempt to deliver the mail until the load average was lower than 20. Further, if the load average got over 12, the running Sendmail would refuse any SMTP connections.

8.6. Precedence, Trust, and Headers

The P instruction in `sendmail.cf` assigns numeric values to character strings that may be used in e-mail messages.

```
Pfirst-class=0
Pspecial-delivery=100
Pjunk=-100
```

These values are used as previously described. There is nothing special about these words or numbers except that `special-delivery` is given a higher mailing priority than the default and anything labeled `junk` has a negative precedence, which means "do not tell me if any mail failed to get delivered." Numbers may always be put in mail headers in place of these descriptive names, but the names are conventions, and these conventions may vary from site to site; some sites may be using `special-delivery=1000` and `junk=-1000`. Each relay that queues your mail will look at the precedence header, and since you do not know what numbers the relay is using, it is better to use names and let each relay translate the name to a number.

```
Troot daemon uucp news avolio vixie
```

This line defines the "Trusted Users" as we described in Chapter 6. It tells Sendmail that any of these users are allowed to use the -f flag of Sendmail, which sets the envelope sender address. This is reasonable for all of these users (we can include the system mail administrators here as well).

```
H?P?Return-Path: <$g>
HReceived: by $j; id $i; $b
H?D?Resent-Date: $a
H?D?Date: $a
H?F?Resent-From: $q
H?F?From: $q
H?x?Full-Name: $x
HSubject:
H?M?Resent-Message-Id: <$t.$i@$j>
H?M?Message-Id: <$t.$i@$j>
```

These are the header definition lines. The first reads, "If the P flag is set on the mailer, the Return-path:, should it be there, is the sender's mailbox in angle brackets." The Received: line is put on no matter what (no check for mailer flag). Values are filled in for $j, and so on. The $i is the queue identifier, and the $b is the date in ARPAnet format. We discussed both of these previously.

We see here, also, how the Message-Id is built. If the M flag is set by the mailer, a Message-Id is added. It is made up of a character representation of the time ($t is in the numeric form *YYMMDDHHMM*, where *YY* is the last two digits of the year, *MM* is the month, and so on) followed by the queue identification and the host's FQDN. For example, consider

```
Message-Id: <9207110505.AA21896@shaman.zk.frobozz.com>
```

8.7. Rulesets 1 and 2

A ruleset starts with the upper-case letter S followed by a number. A ruleset ends when any line other than a rule, comment, blank line, or continuation line is found. So, in our example Ruleset 1 actually goes from the line where S1 is up to but not including the line where S2 is.

```
S1
# empty

S2
# empty
```

Rulesets 1 and 2 are easy to understand because they are short. In fact, they are empty. We are conservative about what we put in them because S1 and S2 are *always* used, one or the other, in rewriting mail headers. Since header rewriting is such a serious business (would *you* like a mail handler in a post office opening up your letters and changing information at the top of your mail inside your envelope?), most header rewriting should be done only in mailer specific rewriting rules. For that reason, we do nothing here.

8.8. Ruleset 3: Focuser

Now we are about to get into the meat of things. If earlier you ignored the suggestion for a double espresso, you might want to reconsider it while you still have your wits about you. It's still not too late.

As we stated, Ruleset 3's job is to focus on the most important piece of information in an address, which is usually the domain part. As it does this it puts the address in *internal* or *canonical* form, which is

local-part<@domain-part>anything-else

For example,

```
vixie@nsl.frobozz.com
```

gets internally turned into

```
vixie<@nsl.frobozz.com>
```

while address

```
decuac!gildor!avolio
```

becomes

```
gildor!avolio<@decuac.UUCP>
```

in our configuration file. Notice that the *local-part* does not have to be a simple user name. It is merely that part of the address that is of no interest to the current host but should be of interest to the next host on the way to delivery.

This latter example shows another of Ruleset 3's jobs: It tags things internally to indicate the form of the original address. Similarily DECnet addressing such as

```
guru::kathryn
```

gets transformed into

```
kathryn<@guru.ENET>
```

by our Ruleset 3. Later we will see how this is used and how to undo it.

We designed Ruleset 3 to be logical in its "execution," and so it considers simple cases and moves on to more complex ones. For example, we first look at the case of an empty address, then at addresses already in canonical form. As we will see, we might call other rulesets that in turn call Ruleset 3, so the address may already be processed. Another "easy" case we look at initially is a mail address in the form

<@dom1, @dom2, . . . @domN:user@domain>

which is using a mechanism called "source routing." While the use of source routing is discouraged by RFC 1123 and by us (as the RFC says, "The choice of transmission route should be left to the mail transport service"), we support its use in this configuration file and consider the parsing of such an address "easy" because the host information in which Sendmail is interested is presented at the front of the address. So

```
<@uk-relay.nyu.edu:graveyard@ic.ac.uk>
```

internally becomes

```
<@uk-relay.nyu.edu>:graveyard@ic.ac.uk
```

which, aside from being discouraged as stated, is a way to circumvent bugs in the DNS or faulty routes.

With all that in mind, we are ready to look at Ruleset 3.

8.9. General Cases

Ruleset 3 begins with some easy rules that take care of a few corner cases.

```
S3
# handle "from:<>" special case
R<>             $@@                    turn into magic token

# simplest case, after an empty address, is a single token
R$-             $@$1

# route-addr's look canonical but aren't
R<@$+:$+>$*      @$1:$2                 unfocus <route-addr>

# already canonical?
R$*<@$+>$*       $@$>7$1<@$2>$3         idempotency is good

# basic textual canonicalization
R$*<$+>$*        $2                     basic RFC822 parsing
```

S3 starts the ruleset. The first rule looks for an empty address. The LHS is <>, which says "match an *open angle bracket* followed immediately by a *closed angle bracket*" with no other characters in the address. If we have processed the address down to nothing, there is something wrong. In this case we transform the address into a single @. On the RHS a leading $@ says "do this transformation and then exit from this ruleset." It is, as the comment says, a "magic token" only because we treat it specially later. So this line says, "If I have an empty address, indicate this by returning a single @ as the address and quit parsing the address."

The second rule in this ruleset is there for expediency. If we have a single token, we must have a local address. We need not look further for a *domain-part*. We take a quick exit out of Ruleset 3.

The next rule (`route-addr`) handles a source route (mentioned earlier) in the form

<@dom1 : other-stuff>

This *looks* like we've focused on a domain part, (because we have an @ followed by other characters immediately inside an open angle bracket), but in fact it is not in canonical form. We strip off the angle brackets in this first case so that we can further process the address. Otherwise, this source route address will be picked up by the line immediately following.

The "`idempotency`" line says "if we already have a string in the form *zero or more tokens*, with *"@" followed by one or more tokens* in angle brackets, followed by *zero or more tokens* then send it all to Ruleset 7 and exit this ruleset with the result." We will see it later, but Ruleset 7 does some cleanup work, making sure all of our domains and pseudodomains are fully qualified.

The last line takes an RFC 822 address such as any of

```
Paul Vixie <vixie@pa.frobozz.com>
Frederick <avolio@dco.frobozz.com> Avolio
<postmaster@frobozz.com> The Postmaster
```

and focuses on the address (really, it temporarily discards the comment information).

```
# make sure <@a,@b,@c:user@d> syntax easy to parse.
# undone later
R@$+,$+        @$1:$2            change all "," to ":"
R@$+:$+        $@$>7<@$1>:$2     handle <route-addr>

# more miscellaneous cleanup
R$+:$*;$*      $@$1:$2;$3        list syntax
R$+@$+         $:$1<@$2>         focus on domain      (A)
R$+<$+@$+>     $1$2<@$3>         move gaze right      (B)
R$+@$+<@$+>    $1%$2<@$3>        a@b@c@d ->a%b%c@d    (C)
```

The first two rules handle source routes. If we are there with

```
@decwrl.dec.com,@uk-relay.nyu.edu:graveyard@ac.ic.uk
```

which is proper source routing notation, we know that we want to focus on `@decwrl.dec.com`. But remember that the Focuser is not very smart. What if this process is already *on* node `decwrl.dec.com`? The address will be taking another trip through this ruleset later on with the first domain stripped off. So, in anticipation of that eventuality, in this rule we change all commas to colons.

All commas? Remember that a rule is applied as long as the results of the RHS transformation match the LHS unless otherwise specified through a control command, either `$:` or `$@`. So this rule will work on all commas in the address, turning something like

@dom1 , *@dom2* , . . . *@domN* : *user@domain*

into

@dom1 : *@dom2* : . . . *@domN* : *user@domain*

and when we're done we will undo this and change all but the last colon back to commas.

After we've done this, we focus on the leading domain name (on the next rule) and go into Ruleset 7, which, as we stated, is what we usually do when leaving Ruleset 3. Note, that in the previous example with address

```
@uk-relay.nyu.edu:graveyard@ac.ic.uk
```

and $1 being `uk-relay.nyu.edu` and $2 being `graveyard@ac.ic.uk`, we would go into Ruleset 7 with

```
<@uk-relay.nyu.edu>:graveyard@ac.ic.uk
```

The line with the "`list syntax`" comment deals with list notation, which is allowed by RFC 822. We could be looking at an address such as

```
Hackers: Paul <vixie@pa.frobozz.com>, Marcus <mjr@dco.frobozz.com>,
         Win <treese@crl.frobozz.com>;, Fred <avolio>
```

In this example, `Paul`, `Marcus`, and `Win` are grouped together as `Hackers`. This is a great idea, but Sendmail does not handle list notation properly. The above example will work, but only because Sendmail will end up looking only at the addresses inside angle brackets, treating the rest as comments. Because of this, we punt this form of address and bail out of the ruleset.

The next three lines should be fairly straightforward. If we have something in @ notation, we focus on the domain part. Notice the $: on the RHS of the rule. If we started with the address

```
reid@ns1.frobozz.com
```

we have

```
reid<@ns1.frobozz.com>
```

after the first pass through this rule. But the LHS of

```
$+@$+
```

says "one or more tokens followed by an @ followed by one or more tokens," and as we've pointed out, "one or more tokens" implies "one or more tokens plus the operators (or punctuation) that glues them together." So, after the first time through, the transformed address can still be processed by this rule (with $+ matching "`reid<`" and the second $+ matching "`ns1.frobozz.com>`"). Therefore, we need the $:, which says that if the LHS of the rule matches the address, "do this only once."

On the second-to-the-last rule in this section, we look for the case of an address with something already within angle brackets, with at least one token between the open angle bracket and the @. In this case we move the open angle bracket over. The last line handles the case of more than one @. We treat the rightmost @ as dominant (the *real* one, if you will) and change any others to percent signs (%).

Now, let's walk a complex address through those last few lines (labeled in the comment area (A), (B), and (C)). We will use the example address

```
maddog@shaman@xirtlu.net@gateway.doghouse.com
```

and the lines specified. Please note that this is an ugly and evil address, which in the real world would never be generated by any but the most mixed-up mail systems. We would rather remove and eat our own livers with rusty spoons than let an address like this get out through one of our mail gateways.

Line	Address after Transformation
(A)	`maddog<@shaman@xirtlu.net@gateway.doghouse.com>`
(B)	`maddog@shaman@xirtlu.net<@gateway.doghouse.com>`
(C)	`maddog%shaman@xirtlu.net<@gateway.doghouse.com>`
(C)	`maddog%shaman%xirtlu.net<@gateway.doghouse.com>`

8.10. Special Mailers: DECnet

If we lived in an RFC 822-only world, our Ruleset 3 could end here. But there are other address forms we need to handle, and we are going to handle DECnet Phase IV addresses as well as UUCP. This is an important discussion even if you don't have any DECnet or UUCP connections, because it shows how to handle other mail address formats and will allow you to add support for other mail formats in the future.

We want to convert all DECnet addresses into :: form and then into @ form with one of our pseudodomains tacked on as a label. We defined this earlier in the file as ENET.

A Phase IV DECnet address is in one of a few forms. The following are all possible for Sendmail to see:

```
decuac::fma
fma@decuac.enet
36.51::fma
fma@36.51.enet
36915::fma
fma@36915.enet
```

UUCP addresses, of course, use "bang" notation, such as

```
research!uunet!grebyn!sluggo
```

where the path the mail must take is explicitly given.[2]

```
# (phase IV)
R$+<@$+.$E>         $@$>7$1<@$2.$E>      already encapsulated IV
R$+<@$-.$-.$=J>     $:$2.$3::$1          u@aa.nnn.DNET
R$+<@$-.$=J>        $:$2::$1             u@node.DNET
```

These rules handle Phase IV DECnet addresses. We have set up this particular configuration file so that any DECnet (any non-SMTP mail for that matter) is sent via a relay host. The first rule says if we are looking at an address in which the part we've focused on is in the form @ followed by anything with a .ENET at the end (remember, that is what $E is), then we are done, and we go into Ruleset 7 for our final touches before leaving the ruleset.

The next two rules are checking for addresses in the form where we have an ending tag that implies DECnet mail (in our case either an ENET or DNET) with two leading tokens (a DECnet address made up of an area number and a host number) or with a single leading token (a node name), or perhaps

```
vixie<@jove.enet>
vixie<@10.853.dnet>
```

We don't just pass them off as is, as we did in the first line. There we had an address that ended in our "official" pseudodomain for Phase IV addresses (ENET). In these lines, we have something that might end in DNET that comes from Phase IV addresses. We switch this around to the "double colon" notation and decide to handle it in a few lines when we handle all such addressing. In this way we don't duplicate rules and effort.

```
# things that are still in @-form are ready to eat
R$+<@$+>            $@$>7$1<@$2>             now canonical
```

By the time we get to the last rule above, anything still in

```
$+<@$+>
```

format is as focused as we're going to get (remembering that that is the only job we have), so we go off to Ruleset 7 and then exit this ruleset.

---

[2] In the "olden days," this was the case. Nowadays, you can't tell from looking at a UUCP address whether all hosts in the path are in fact spelled out. One of the hosts might be a "smart UUCP host" that knows how to route through UUCP or other networks to get to the "next" host in the path.

```
# (phase IV conversions)
R$-.$-::$+        $@$>7$3<@$1.$2.$E>        numeric decnet addr
R$-::$+           $@$>7$2<@$1.$E>           h::u -> u@h.pseudodom
```

By now, we're entering the home stretch. If we have an address such as any of

```
10.853::vixie
jove::vixie
36.31::36.241::avolio
decuac::gildor::avolio
```

we put it into canonical form. Notice that we check for "one single token followed by a dot followed by one single token followed by a double colon followed by one or more tokens" in the first rule and "one single token followed by a double colon followed by one or more tokens" in the second. We know then, that by definition, the node to focus on is the first one, and we do so, tagging this as we put it in canonical form with .$E, which is .ENET. Again we exit from the ruleset by going to Ruleset 7 and then leaving.

8.11. UUCP and Other Special Cases

Since UUCP addresses use a totally different syntax than our canonical form, we detect and convert such addresses here.

```
# UUCP conversions
R$-.$+!$+         $@$>7$3<@$1.$2>          host.domain!user
R$-!$+            $@$>7$2<@$1.UUCP>        resolve uucp names

# convert rightmost % to @ (S7 has rest of magic for this)
R$+%$+            $@$>7$1<@$2>             user%host
```

We handle UUCP addresses here, assuming that anything in the form "one token followed by a dot followed by one or more tokens followed by a bang (!) followed by one or more tokens" is something that can be rendered as an RFC 822 address. We assume this because (1) something to the left of a ! must be a host name and (2) a host name that has an embedded period (or more than one) must be an FQDN, by definition. We transform it into canonical form and send it to Ruleset 7 before ending.

The second rule handles the simple case of basic UUCP bang notation and takes anything in the form

host!*user*

and transforms it into

user@<*host*.UUCP>

Finally, after we have checked for empty addresses, RFC 822 addresses, DECnet addresses in many forms, and UUCP addresses, we check for the case of a % instead of an @ in an address. At this point we've checked for all possible @ addresses. But it is possible, as we shall see, that an address such as

user%other-domain@our-host-name

got handed to us as

user%other-domain

This last rule changes this % to an @, focuses on the domain part, and sends it all to Ruleset 7 before exiting.

That's the end of Ruleset 3, the most complex ruleset we will look at.

8.12. Ruleset 7: Exit Path from Ruleset 3

Ruleset 7 is used to take any specially tagged addresses received from Ruleset 3 and make them legal addresses where appropriate. It also does some address clean up.

```
S7
R$*<@$+%$+>$*        $1%$2<@$3>$4        move @ right after %
R$*<@$+.$E>$*        $@$1<@$2.$E.$P>$3   hide .$E under $P
R$*<@$->$*           $@$1<@$2.$N>$3      qualify hostnames
```

While Ruleset 3 found the rightmost @ in the address, the first rule here checks to make sure there isn't a % to the right of the @. If there is, Ruleset 3 moves the focus — the open angle bracket (<) — over, changes the left @ to a %, and changes the % on the right to a @. So

```
vixie<@cognition%ns1.frobozz.com>
```

becomes

```
vixie%cognition<@ns1.frobozz.com>
```

Next, we take any address in which the focused-on domain part contains a trailing tag indicating DECnet and tacks on our parent domain. For example,

```
vixie<@jove.ENET>
```

becomes

```
vixie<@jove.enet.frobozz.com>
```

The last rule in Ruleset 7 takes the case where the domain focused on is a simple (unqualified) name, and it adds our host's parent domain to the address (which is the only thing we can do with it.)

8.13. Ruleset 4: The Final Cleanup

Ruleset 4 is simple. Remember what Ruleset 4's job is: to postprocess an address to put it back in external form. All it does is undo what Ruleset 3 has done.

```
S4

R@                  $@              handle <> error addr     (A)
R$*<$+>$*           $1$2$3          defocus                  (B)
R@$+:$+:$+          @$1,$2:$3       <route-addr> canonical   (C)
R@$+:$+             $@<@$1:$2>      route-addr needs <>      (D)
```

The first thing we checked for in Ruleset 3 was an empty address. When we found one, we returned from Ruleset 3 with the "magic token." Here we look for it and bail out of this ruleset, leaving it "as is." We will see later where we handle it. The second rule looks for something on which we've focused and removes the "focusing marks" — the angle brackets. Again, continuing with "undoing what Ruleset 3 has done," we match something with an @ followed by one or more tokens followed by a colon (`:`), and if we find it we replace all colons except the final one with commas. We explained why we put it in this form earlier. We are now putting it back in proper "source route" format.

```
@decwrl.dec.com,@uk-relay.nyu.edu:graveyard@ac.ic.uk
```

was put into internal form as

```
<@decwrl.dec.com>:@uk-relay.nyu.edu:graveyard@ac.ic.uk
```

which now gets changed back in Ruleset 4. In our example, when we get into that address into Ruleset 4, the following takes place:

Line	Address After Transformation
(A)	`<@decwrl.dec.com>:@uk-relay.nyu.edu:graveyard@ac.ic.uk`
(B)	`@decwrl.dec.com:@uk-relay.nyu.edu:graveyard@ac.ic.uk`
(C)	`@decwrl.dec.com,@uk-relay.nyu.edu:graveyard@ac.ic.uk`
(D)	`<@decwrl.dec.com,@uk-relay.nyu.edu:graveyard@ac.ic.uk>`

At this point, some `sendmail.cf` files will convert addresses we put in the form

user@domain.TAG

back into their original form. We choose not to do that at this point because the addresses' final form will depend on the *mailer* to be used. For example, if the address at this point is

```
favolio@gramps.ENET
```

and this will be sent via the MAIL11 mailer, the address will have to be finally written as

```
gramps::favolio
```

But if the final mail is the UUCP mailer, the final address will be

our-host`!gramps.enet!favolio`

Therefore, this work is left to the mailer-specific rewriting rules.

8.14. IDA Rulesets 5 and 6

We pointed out earlier that Rulesets 1 and 2 are always applied to the sender and receiver fields, one or the other. Rulesets 1 and 2 are applied to both the envelope and header addresses in many Sendmails. In IDA sendmail, and its derivatives, Rulesets 1 and 2 are applied to the envelope addresses only and Rulesets 5 and 6 are applied to the header addresses.

```
S5
R$+                     $@$>1$1                 same as envelope

S6
R$+                     $@$>2$1                 same as envelope
```

As you can see, we do not make use of these special IDA rulesets. In Ruleset 5, we just call Ruleset 1 on any address we get. We call Ruleset 2 from Ruleset 6. This has the effect of allowing this `sendmail.cf` to work the same across IDA and non-IDA Sendmail configurations.

8.15. Ruleset 8: Stripping off Local Host Names

Ruleset 8 is used primarily to strip the local host and domain information. If it discovers that that host name on which we have focused is the name or the pseudonym of the local host, the Router needs to send the address back to the Focuser with the local host name removed. This action is accomplished by Ruleset 8, which also checks for an empty host name, also considered useless information to the Router.

```
S8

R$+                     $:$>3$1                 needed for recursions
```

```
R$*<@$j>$*              $:$1<@>$2              @my FQDN
R$*<@$=w>$*             $:$1<@>$3              @my alias
R$*<@$=w.$N>$*          $:$1<@>$3              @my alias
```

The first rule has us calling Ruleset 3 with whatever address we have, to make sure it is canonical. The first time through we have a canonical address, since Ruleset 8 is initially called from Ruleset 0 (as we shall see), but later on we can be sure that the address will need to be made canonical again. For example, if we are on node `decuac.frobozz.com` and we start with the address

`vixie%jove.ENET@decuac.frobozz.com`

which becomes

`vixie%jove.ENET<@decuac.frobozz.com>`

it will become

`vixie%jove.ENET`

We can see that we will want that transformed into

`vixie@jove.ENET`

and finally

`vixie<@jove.ENET>`

so a further trip through Ruleset 3, which will accomplish this, is needed.

In the next three rules, we peek into the host name part on which we have focused and if it is *our* host name or one of our pseudonyms, we strip it off and mark it to go back through this ruleset (which again, as we'll see in a few more rules, starts by sending us to Ruleset 3). Here we look for our fully qualified host name ($j), one of our pseudonyms, or one of our pseudonyms with our domain tacked on. In this example, `sendmail.cf` file, class w is not defined and so treated as empty. If our host name is found inside the angle brackets, it is taken away and the @ is left. It will soon be cleaned up.

Why do we leave an @ within the brackets (<@>)? We have to handle the cases of an address in the form *user@domain* as well as source route addresses. If we have a normal address, we want to strip off everything inside the angle brackets plus the angle brackets themselves. But if we have a source route address, we want to strip off everything inside the angle brackets plus the angle brackets *plus* the colon immediately to the right of the closing angle bracket.

Recall that an address in the form

```
@decwrl.dec.com,urc.dco.frobozz.com:avolio@talos.enet.frobozz.com
```

will be canonicalized as

```
<@decwrl.dec.com>:urc.dco.frobozz.com:avolio@talos.enet.frobozz.com
```

and if we are processing this *on* host decwrl.dec.com, we want to strip off
"<@decwrl.dec.com>:" from the address and try again. Notice that each of these
lines is executed only once.

```
R$*<@$N>$*          $:$1<@>$2         @mydomain
R$*<@$=d.$P>$*       $:$1<@>$3         @codomain
```

These next two rules basically do the same as the others. These lines are used
because this host is part of a mail cluster (with shared user names and aliases). So,
just as for the local host name and host pseudonyms, they check for and strip off the
host name part if it is equal to our domain ($N) or one of the other domains that we
equate to "us" ($=d.$P).

```
R$*<@$y.$E.$P>$*     $:$1<@>$2         myname:: (IV)
R$*<@$U.UUCP>$*      $:$1<@>$2         myuucpname!
```

Finally, we do the same for our DECnet name in a Phase IV address. Our DECnet
name is stored in $y; $E is our designator for an original Phase IV address. We also
check for our UUCP name. We aren't actually a UUCP site, but since we want to
include the logic to handle UUCP addresses, this line is included. If defined, $U is
our UUCP name.

```
# here's where we recurse if a change was made
R<@>:$*             $@$>8$1           localhost/route-addr
R$*<@>$*            $@$>8$1$2         localhost
```

We exit this ruleset after one of these rules. These two rules strip off the empty
address if found (the two flavors we just discussed) and send things recursively into
Ruleset 8 again.

8.16. Ruleset 9: SMTP Address Adjustment

Ruleset 9 is called from the Sender rewriting rulesets for SMTP mail in this send-
mail.cf. Its four lines make sure that the host name focused on is a complete host
name.

```
S9
R$*<@$->$*           $:$1<@$2.$N>$3          qualify
R$*<@$+.$=T>$*        $@$1<@$2.$3>$4          trash pseudodom, lv alone
R$*<@$+.$=T.$P>$*     $@$1<@$2.$3.$P>$4       qualified trash, lv alone
```

The first rule's LHS is matched if the host name is unqualified (that is, no domain is attached). In the case of an unqualified host name, we must add our local domain name. This is the only possible handling for an unqualified host name.

In the second rule we look for a host name that is qualified with one of our pseudodomain names. We never want these to appear as top level domains. In our example, we mean something that has a domain part that ends in USENET, ENET, or UUCP. We want to treat these domains as special. They have special meaning, and serve dual purposes. They are recognized as subdomains, under our top level domain, but they indicate special gateways or processes.

This table shows you some transformations that take place in this ruleset (assuming Class T and Macro P are defined as in this `sendmail.cf`).

Address	Becomes
vixie<@gildor>	vixie<@gildor.dco.frobozz.com>
reid<@jove.ENET>	reid<@jove.ENET.FROBOZZ.COM>

Your `sendmail.cf` may or may not have a Ruleset 9. We chose that number at random when we needed a utility ruleset.

8.17. Ruleset 0: Router and Transporter

Ruleset 0 is a special ruleset, as stated earlier. Its job is to end up with three things: a mailer to use as the transport, the next host to which to route the mail, and the address to pass to this host. Ruleset 0 looks at the address — more accurately, it looks at what Ruleset 3 has determined is the most important part of the address — and, based on what is within the angle brackets, it makes its determinations.

Once Ruleset 0 decides on a mailer, host, and address triplet, it exits. It does not continue processing through the rest of the ruleset, nor will we see any explicit "exit from ruleset" commands ($@) on the RHS of a rule.

For example, if we have the address `goldrush@frobozz.com`, it might resolve to something like

Mailer	Host	Address
smtp	frobozz.com	goldrush<@frobozz.com>

Ruleset 4 will take care of the angle brackets (< and >) later.

The RHS of a rule that can accomplish this is

```
$#smtp $@$2 $:goldrush@frobozz.com
```

The string `$#` specifies the mailer to use, `$@` the host name to send to, and `$:` the address to give that host.

Ruleset 0 handles things in the following order:

(1)   Empty address error condition (@)
(2)   Numeric IP address
(3)   The part focused on is not the local host
(4)   Phase IV DECnet address
(5)   UUCP address
(6)   POP special-case address
(7)   Any address in our local domain
(8)   Any address in our parent domain
(9)   Any other complex (with an @) address
(10) Local mail

8.17.1. Special Cases

As with Ruleset 3, Ruleset 0 begins with a few easy rules to catch some corner cases.

```
S0

# special cases
#
R@                 $#local $:$n                        handle <> form
R$*<@[$+]>$*        $#smtp $@[$2] $:$1<@[$2]>$3    numeric IP

# localize if possible (rip off @DOMAINs for which we are authority)
#
R$*<@$+>$*               $:$>8$1<@$2>$3
```

The first rule handles the case of an empty address. In Ruleset 3, if we found ourselves staring at an empty address (open and closed angle brackets with nothing inside), we replaced it with a single @ and returned. This was done in Ruleset 3 because we are without hope at this point and must punt, sending the mail to a human to read and decide what to do with it. The first line says "if there is no address, send it to user `$n` via the `local` mailer." Recall that `$n` was set to be `Mailer-Daemon`, which should be aliased to the local mail or system manager.

Next is the case where the domain part is a numeric IP address. An address such as `fma@[192.5.214.1]` is legal and would be delivered to that address by our example `sendmail.cf`. You could make an argument to change this to go to your Internet relay machine instead, as we do in later examples with other address forms.

The last rule says "for anything that has an @ followed by at least one token, both within angle brackets, make sure we are not focused on our own host name" and it does this by sending the address to Ruleset 8. By the time the address returns from Ruleset 8, it has been cleared of local host information and has been made canonical again.

8.17.2. DECnet Mail

DECnet is not very useful as a networking protocol, but it is quite useful as an example in ruleset perversity. Read on; it isn't as bad as it looks.

We should point out here that one reason we have included examples of what we do with DECnet mail is to show you what you must do when adding a new mailer to your `sendmail.cf` file. The double @ is used so that we can pull out the host name for DECnet and stick it on the front of the address (to make parsing easier later) without changing the rest of the address in any way. The @@ is used to separate these pieces of information. We will first look for something in our basic DECnet Phase IV encapsulated format. If we find it, we will leave it as is except to make a copy of the host name part and stick it on the lefthand side.

If something was in that form and is now in the new form and we have a Phase IV relay defined, we change the address to add the relay's host name as the "focused-on" host name. If there is no Phase IV relay defined (if we are a DECnet machine), we leave the address alone. If the mail has *our* host name tacked onto its righthand side, it was placed there at some other point within this configuration file (an option when building this file). If it is not our host name but that of our DECnet Phase IV relay ($J), the mail is sent via SMTP (the `smtp1` mailer definition).

```
# (phase IV)
R$+<@$+.$E.$P>       $:$2@@$1<@$2.$E.$P>       dup nodename; add @@
R$+@@$+<@$+>         $:$?J$1@@$2%$3<@$J>$|$1@@$2<@$3>$.
R$+@@$+%$+<@$j>      $#mail11 $@$1 $:$1::$2   them is us; use mail11
R$+@@$+%$+<@$J>      $#smtp1 $@$J $:$2<@$3>   undo damage; send
R$+@@$+%$+<@$+>      $:$2<@$3>               undo $?J damage
R$+@@$+<@$+>         $:$2<@$3>               undo !$?J damage
```

You can see that we are looking to match our encapsulated Phase IV address, something like

```
roj<@chef.ENET.FROBOZZ.COM>
```

The transformation — carried out only once — is fairly straightforward and is as we just described. This last example address becomes

```
chef@@roj<@chef.ENET.FROBOZZ.COM>
```

to preserve the address as it was for now but to bring out the host name in which we are interested. The second rule looks quite a bit more complicated, but is not bad once you know how to read it. The RHS reads "if we have a DECnet relay (J) defined, generate the address with $J focused on. If $J is *not* defined, leave it as you found it." So, again as with the example address, since we have a DECnet relay defined (`decnet-relay.dco.frobozz.com`), we get

```
chef@@roj%chef.enet<@decnet-relay.dco.frobozz.com>
```

If, when we get to the third rule, our own host name is the object of our focus, we know this means we want this host to send the mail via the `mail11` mailer (which we will see defined later). If our DECnet relay is the host on which we are focused (next rule), we send the original encapsulated address to it (notice we've dropped the leading $1 and @@). Finally, we undo the strangeness and put the address back the way we found it. So, using our example address, we resolve to

Mailer	Host	Address
smtp	decnet-relay.dco.frobozz.com	roj<@chef.enet>

Why did we go through all of this? The reason is found on the third rule (comment "them is us; use mail11"). If we were going to send the mail ourselves directly via DECnet mail, this would give us the opportunity to strip out the host name to send to without modifying the address any further (and a way to easily undo what we had done).

8.17.3. Final Resolutions

We are rapidly approaching the end of Ruleset 0, and the going gets easier now.

```
R$+.USENET          $:$1.USENET<@usenet.$N>          groupname.USENET

R$*<@$-.UUCP>       $#smtp $@uucp-relay.$N $:$2!$1<@uucp-relay.$N>

# Fake hosts in my domain
#
R$+<@POP>           $#pop $@$j $:$1                  username@POP
```

An address in the form indicated on the LHS of this first rule allows users to use mail to post something to a Usenet news group. For example, a user could address e-mail to address

```
comp.unix.ultrix.usenet
```

to post to the newsgroup `comp.unix.ultrix`. What our Sendmail configuration does is send mail like this to a host that knows what to do with it (such as having a mail alias for each newsgroup) in this example, `usenet.dco.frobozz.com`.

In the next rules we check for UUCP and POP mail indicated by the label showing what kind of mail it is (in these cases, UUCP or POP.)

We've checked for an empty address, numeric IP addresses, the *local* host name, and DECnet addresses, and we just looked for addresses to Usenet newsgroups or UUCP or POP addresses. The only kinds of addresses left are TCP/IP addresses and local addresses.

```
# Real hosts in my domain - our domain; no gateway
R$*<@$*$N>$*          $#smtp1 $@$2$N $:$1<@$2$N>$3

# Parent domain - our domain; no gateway
R$*<@$*$P>$*          $#smtp $@$2$P $:$1<@$2$P>$3

# Nonlocal mail - use gateway
R$*<@$+>$*            $#smtp $@relay.$N $:$1<@$2>$3
```

We choose to handle IP mail in three ways. For e-mail to an address in our local domain ($N), we will send the mail directly via SMTP and have the return address show the host it came from, fully qualified. For hosts in our parent domain ($P), we will also send the mail directly (i.e., without using a relay host), but we will make the return address show only our domain (`avolio@dco.frobozz.com` versus `avolio@gildor.dco.frobozz.com`). Mail will look the same for the third case, external IP mail, but we send mail for external hosts via our relay host(s).

As we see, any domain part we are focused on that ends in our local domain will cause Sendmail to transport the mail by the `smtp1` mailer to that host ($*$N or, on the RHS, 2N). The next rule is similar except that it is for addresses ending in our *parent* domain. Remember that once Ruleset 0 decides what to do with the mail based on the recipient address it is processing, it quits. So if our local domain ($N) is DCO.FROBOZZ.COM and our parent domain is FROBOZZ.COM and we have the address

`ricardo@burfle.dco.frobozz.com`

which at this point is in canonical form

`ricardo<@burfle.dco.frobozz.com>`

the LHS of the first rule matches the address. The $* matches `ricardo`; the <@ matches the literal <@ in the pattern, $* matches `burfle.` (notice, it matches `burfle` followed by the dot); the $N matches FROBOZZ.COM; and the > matches the literal > in pattern. Even though the address given also matches the LHS of the rule under "Parent domain," that mailer and route won't be taken because we never get there, stopping with the first rule ("our domain").

Once we pass these rules, if we still have an address in the form

something<@something-else>

we know we must have an external IP address. We have tested for everything else, that is, we have tested for everything else that we know and can handle. Thus, anything else in that form is for an IP address not in our local or parent domain. In this example, we send it via the smtp mailer to our relay host (relay.$N) with the address we are processing. In our environment, the relay is usually not a host at all, but has associated MX records so that the mail in this case might actually be handled by any one of a number of hosts defined by our name server.

We have now handled all mail addressed to an address containing a host name. Anything else is local mail. We could at this point hand all mail off to the local mailer, but we might support some special forms of local mail (mail other than for a simple user name):

```
R$+.POP          $#pop $@$j $:$1              username.POP

R$+              $#local $:$1                 must be local
```

The "special form" is for users who receive their mail through the Post Office Protocol (POP). A user's .forward file or mail alias indicates that mail for that user (let's use vixie as an example) should go to local address vixie.pop. If this happens, mail is sent to user vixie via the pop mailer.

Now, anything else we have *must* be a local address and so is given to the local mailer. Notice that with the local mailer there is no host name to which to route.

This brings us to the end of Ruleset 0.

8.18. Local Mailer Definitions and Rewriting Rules

Mailer definitions and related rewriting rulesets start next. We group the mailer definitions with their respective rules for ease of reading (as we will see):

```
Mlocal,    P=/bin/mail,        F=rlsDFMmn,  S=10, R=20, A=mail -d $u
Mprog,     P=/bin/sh,          F=lsDFM,     S=10, R=20, A=sh -c $u
Mpop,      P=/usr/lib/mh/spop, F=nsmFDM,    S=10, R=20, A=pop $u
```

These are the mailer definitions for the local, prog, and pop mailers. The local mailer is for all mail Ruleset 0 decides is for delivery to a mailbox on the local host, as we've discussed. The pop mailer is for anyone who gets mail delivered by the Post Office Protocol. We haven't mentioned the prog mailer directly, and it was not mentioned in Ruleset 0, but we have mentioned mailing to programs. Use of the prog mailer is programmed into the Sendmail executable and does not have to be handled in Ruleset 0. If the first character of an address is " | ", the prog mailer is used on the mail.

We see the names of the mailers, the associated programs, the flags for the mailer (described in Appendix C), and the sender and recipient rewriting rules. Also, the command line to execute is included (A=). In mailer definitions, $h is the host to send to (set via $@ when exiting Ruleset 0), and $u is the user name to mail to (set by $: when exiting Ruleset 0).

The local mailer needs arguments: "-r *from*" (r); Final delivery will be performed (1); Quotes are to be stripped from the address before the mailer is called (s); Date:, From:, and Message-ID: headers are wanted (DFM); The mailer can send to multiple mailboxes in one transaction (m); And, it does not want a UNIX-style From envelope line added at the top of the message (n).

As described in the previous chapter, there is a set series of rulesets through which each address passes. One of the series of rulesets is variable, depending on the mailer invoked. These three mailers all use Ruleset 10 for all sender lines and Ruleset 20 for all recipient lines.

```
S10
R@          $n                          errors to mailer-daemon
S20
```

Rulesets 10 and 20 don't do much because we usually don't want or need to rewrite local addresses. The one thing we do handle is the "magic token" we've seen in Rulesets 3 and 0. We have converted an empty address to one consisting of a single @. This special address will go through Ruleset 0 and be matched by the very last line, which will designate it for the local mailer. Here in Ruleset 10 we check for that. If we find it, we rewrite the address, replacing the @ with $n, which was defined near the beginning of the file to be "our name," MAILER-DAEMON. This is the final action to make sure mail with nonsense addresses will be delivered to someone — the mail administrator — for resolution.

Ruleset 20 is empty. We do no special rewriting of any recipient addresses.

8.19. SMTP to Hosts Inside the Local Domain

Here is the mailer definition for "local SMTP mail" smtp1:

```
Msmtp1,      P=[IPC], F=mDFMuX, S=11, R=21, A=IPC $h, E=\r\n
```

As described earlier, we will use this mailer when delivering mail to hosts in our local domain or to any hosts we want to treat this way. We could treat *all* SMTP delivery this way. The smtp1 mailer causes all mail originating at our host to have our host and local domain tacked on to the local addresses if we are not in a mail cluster. If we are part of a mail cluster, mail is sent from this mailer without the local host name attached (as we shall see).

The program used (P=) is not an external program but the internal IPC mechanism. Sendmail does its own SMTP mail transfer. We won't go through the mailer flags with this mailer or subsequent ones, as they are listed in Appendix C, as mentioned.

The Eol (end-of-line) string for this mailer is "carriage return, new line" (\r\n). Ruleset 11 is the sender rewrite ruleset and 21 is for recipients.

```
S11
R$*<@$j>$*              $>3$1$2                 strip local host name
R$*<@$+>$*              $:$>9$1<@$2>$3          canonicalize domain
# (include if aliases shared across localdom)
R$=N                    $@$1<@$j>               qualify nonhidden users

S21
R$+                     $@$>11$1                nothing special here
```

First notice that Ruleset 21 contains one line. It matches anything and goes into Ruleset 11. Therefore, we only have to understand Ruleset 11 to understand how both recipient and sender fields are handled for the smtp1 mailer.

The first rule in S11 matches if our fully qualified host name is the object of focus (<@$j>). If it does match, the angle brackets and their contents are tossed and everything else is sent back for canonicalization to Ruleset 3. When it returns, things continue. Next, we take anything with a "focused-on" domain part and send it, as is, to Ruleset 9, which, as we saw earlier, makes sure that the host name focused on is a complete host name. Notice that since this presumably still returns something in a form that matches the LHS, this rule is only executed once.

If we are part of a Mail Cluster and share *aliases* files, we don't want to put our own host name back on, *except* for certain user names that are generic and so must be addressed in terms of the system name. For example, we want to know which host an error from daemon came from, as it tells us useful information, but in a Mail Cluster, user reid is the same user across all systems. The rule that, as it says, is only present if aliases are shared, checks for a single token matching one of the set of [root, news, uucp, mailer-daemon, and so on], which is the value of class N. If it matches, our fully qualified host name is tacked onto the address with a @.

8.20. SMTP to Hosts Outside the Local Domain

The smtp mailer is used in our case for mail going to any address outside the local domain. Mail through this mailer will have addresses in proper RFC 822 format passed through; local names with no host name will get our external name attached (in our case our local domain) with the exception of the names in class N.

Address	Becomes
avolio	avolio<@DCO.FROBOZZ.COM>
root	root<@gildor.DCO.FROBOZZ.COM>

```
Msmtp,      P=[IPC], F=mDFMuXL, S=12, R=22, A=IPC $h, E=\r\n
```

In this mailer definition, flag L is added to the flags on the smtpl mailer, which says that line lengths should be limited as per RFC 821.

```
S12
R<@$+>$*               $@<@$1>$2               <route-addr> syntax
R$*<@[$+]>$*           $@$1<@[$2]>$3           numeric, leave alone
R$*<@$+>$*             $@$>9$1<@$2>$3          canonicalize domain
R$=N                   $@$1<@$j>               Add $j to local
R$+                    $@$1<@$W>               fix up return address

S22
R$+                    $@$>12$1                nothing special here
```

Once again, the recipient ruleset punts to the sender ruleset. Why not just use the same ruleset? Why not have this line contain the fields

```
S=12,   R=12
```

instead of using 12 and 22? By having them as two separate rulesets, it makes it easier for you to make them do different things later if necessary. For now, one just calls the other so the effect is as though you had one ruleset used in both R= and S=.

The first two rules find source route addresses and numeric IP addresses and leave them alone, exiting from the ruleset ($@). Anything else in @ format gets sent to Ruleset 9, as before, and the address returned is returned from this ruleset.

If we enter Ruleset 12 with the address

```
mjr@hussar
```

it will be changed by Ruleset 9 to

```
mjr@hussar.DCO.FROBOZZ.COM
```

which will then be returned by Ruleset 12. The next rule is similar to the line we looked at in Ruleset 11, and our fully qualified host name gets tacked on for the same reasons. But for every other address, our external name, defined to be $W, gets appended to the address.

8.21. SMTP to the Relay Host

The smtpr mailer is similar to the smtpl mailer.

```
Msmtpr,      P=[IPC], F=mDFMuX, S=13, R=23, A=IPC $h, E=\r\n
S13
R$*<@$j>$*           $>3$1$2              strip local host name
R$*<@$+>$*           $:$>9$1<@$2>$3       canonicalize domain
R$=N                 $@$1<@$j>            qualify nonhidden users
S23
R$+                  $@$>13$1             nothing special here
```

In this particular case, the two happen to be identical. There are two mailers offered for the environment without a Mail Cluster, where sometimes, the host name needs to be left off. For example, if you know mail will be crossing different mail domains, such as from SMTP to DECnet, you might want to hide some of the topology information from the recipients. You could send mail to a relay machine that has an alias for your mailbox (making you look like a local user on that relay machine). Using this mailer allows you to avoid addresses like this on the recipient end:

```
urcdco::"avolio@gildor.dco.frobozz.com"
```

replacing it with the simpler

```
urcdco::avolio
```

which not only is easier and neater to read but provides some safety against misreading or miswriting of that address.

8.22. Final Thoughts on Configuration

(1)   *"Not all things worth doing are worth doing well."*[3] In other words, you want your Sendmail configuration to handle all of the common mail it will see and all of the common addressing formats. It doesn't have to handle every possible address. If you try to handle an address such as

```
banana!orange!apple!other::thing@something.else%altogether
```

you will waste a lot of time and energy, and the way you handle it will no doubt be different from the sender's intention.

---

[3] Tom Peters, in *A Passion For Excellence*.

(2) Understand every line in your `sendmail.cf`. If you don't, even after a long time of staring at a line, take it out and see what happens. Seriously. We have done this many times over the years. A line will have been inherited into your `sendmail.cf`, and you won't be sure that it was ever really needed. If it was needed, you won't know whether it is still needed. So you take it out and see what happens. We do this by taking a line such as

```
R$*<$*<$*<$+>$*>$*>$*         $4        handle nesting
```

and commenting it out like

```
#FMA31OCT92R$*<$*<$*<$+>$*>$*>$*   $4        handle nesting
```

and if things run smoothly for a while — we do try to keep watch on such things — we forget about it. Months later, when making any other change, if we notice it and the date on the comment seems long enough ago to be *safe*, we remove the line.

(3) *"Do not get involved with Sendmail. She is an exotic lover, whispering delicious promises in your ear, flashing her dark eyes at you. But she is insane, and will draw you down in to her madness."*[4]

---

[4] Andrew Molitor, from his `.plan` file.

9

Maintenance and Administration

In this chapter we explain the various duties and methods of mail administration. We will discuss how to analyze `syslog` information and what to look for, common problems, and different ways to fix the things that normally go wrong on a busy mail hub. We'll start with a tour of the "mechanics" behind Sendmail, and later, give you a brief smattering of hints, kinks, and secret handshakes.

9.1. The Files and Directories

Sendmail uses several files to help it do its work. We present and explain them here. Note that different systems keep their Sendmail-related files in different directories. If you don't find Sendmail's configuration files in `/etc`, look for them in `/usr/lib`. If you don't find the `sendmail` binary itself in `/usr/lib`, look for it in `/usr/sbin` and `/usr/etc`. If you don't find the mail queue in `/usr/spool/mqueue`, look in `/var/spool/mqueue` or even `/var/sendmail` or `/var/spool/sendmail`. Vendors love to move this kind of stuff around.

Happy hunting.

`sendmail`

> The Sendmail executable program. Sendmail is usually executed at system start-up time out of one of the system start-up files (often `/etc/rc.local`). On older Berkeley-based systems (ULTRIX, for example) this is in `/usr/lib`, on OSF/1 systems it is in `/usr/sbin`, on BSD 4.3-Reno and later it is in `/usr/libexec`. You'll need to check your system management guide for your system's convention.

`sendmail.cf`

> The Sendmail configuration file. On some systems this is in `/usr/lib`. On others it is in `/etc`. (ULTRIX puts it in `/etc` with a symbolic link from `/usr/lib`.) On OSF/1 it is in the `/var/adm/sendmail` directory.

sendmail.fc

The "frozen" version of the sendmail.cf file. It allows for "quick start-up" of Sendmail. This file is a processed version of the sendmail.cf and it is located in the same directory as sendmail.cf. Invoking Sendmail with the -bz option tells it to write out an image of its data space into this file. Each time Sendmail starts up it reads the configuration file. If sendmail.fc exists, it is read when Sendmail starts up, instead of Sendmail interpreting the sendmail.cf file. This is a performance win only if your disks are faster than your CPU for the amount of processing needed for your particular .cf file. Try it both ways before you decide to freeze. Note that R8 and other modern Sendmails don't offer freeze files at all.

sendmail.hf

The Sendmail help file. Its contents are printed when someone issues the command help to the running Sendmail SMTP port. As almost no human actually sits and types directly to a running Sendmail process, the wisdom of this might seem questionable. However, one day, when you are debugging mail, you will be glad it's there. The location of this file is set from the sendmail.cf file. It is usually put in /etc (ULTRIX) or /usr/lib and is in /var/adm/sendmail on OSF/1. Note that your vendor-supplied .hf file may contain an incorrect address for the maintainer of Sendmail; if so, editing it to point to your local Postmaster address is a reasonable way to fix it.

sendmail.st

Mail statistics are stored here. The auxiliary program mailstats uses it (see below). The location of this file is set from the sendmail.cf file. It is usually in the same place as the other Sendmail files.

sendmail.pid

Contains the process identifier (PID) of the last Sendmail that was started with the -bd option. It is useful if you need to kill Sendmail and restart it with a new .cf or .fc file. Only the modern versions of Sendmail create this file. If it exists, it will probably be in /etc or /var/run.

mailq

A "hard link" to the Sendmail program and prints a report to standard output showing the contents of the Sendmail mail queue.

syslog

Collects log information from Sendmail and other programs that issue syslog calls. Usually it is in /etc or /usr/sbin. This is also the name of the log file, usually, in the mail queue directory (see mqueue, below).

syslog.conf

The syslog configuration file. Usually it is in /etc.

syslog.pid

Contains the process identification number (PID) of the currently running syslog process. It is usually found in /etc or /var/run.

`aliases, aliases.pag, aliases.dir, aliases.db`
> The system-wide mail *aliases* and distribution list database. The `aliases` file is the flat ASCII file. The other files are built from it for use by the Sendmail program. Usually all the "aliases" files are in `/etc` or `/usr/lib`. files.

`newaliases`
> A "hard link" to the Sendmail program. It rebuilds the *aliases* database files after the `aliases` text file is modified. Normally in `/usr/ucb` or `/usr/bin`, it should be in the system manager's execution path. It was put in `/usr/ucb` on Berkeley's early systems to allow any user to edit the `aliases` file — which was left world-writable — and to rebuild it. This, of course, is madness.

`mailstats`
> A program that formats Sendmail statistics found in `sendmail.st`. Your vendor may or may not have included it in your system; most do not.

`mqueue`
> The system mail queue, this directory is where mail messages are processed and queued up. It us the mail room or the central post office of the system, and also where the `syslog` log files are often kept. The full path is usually `/var/spool/mqueue` or `/usr/spool/mqueue`.

`resolv.conf`
> Always found in `/etc`, this file shows your default local domain name (which is unfortunately not used by Sendmail or available to `.cf` programmers) and a list of default name servers for the host. We mention this file only so that we have a chance to recommend that a busy Sendmail host's name servers should be *close* and *fast*. Running a "caching-only" name server on a host just because of a busy Sendmail is common and recommended.

`svc.conf, nsswitch.conf`
> Vendors, those loveable guys, have by and large decided that their name service client configurations are not complex enough. You may find that your system will only use DNS (or NIS, or whatever you are hoping for it to use) if you edit some file down in `/etc`. Often, the command "`man gethostent`" will give you clues.

9.2. The Mail Queue

When Sendmail places mail in the mail queue it stores different pieces of information for each mail message in different files. The names of these files include a prefix followed by a queue identifier. All files related to the same message have similar names with different prefixes. The body of a file name whose prefix is `qf` is the queue identifier. The body of the other files related to a given message is usually also a queue identifier except in rare cases.

The queue identifier is made from two letters followed by the PID of the process responsible for putting the message in the queue. In the example we use AA as the two letters starting the queue id because this is most common. When making a queue id, Sendmail starts with AA, tacks on the PID, and checks to make sure that there is no other message with that identifier in the queue. If it finds one (rare but possible) it tries AB and then AC and so on up to AZ and BA, BB, and so forth.

dfAA*nnnnn*
> The data file, that is, the body of the letter.

lfAA*nnnnn*
> (Pre-5.65 only) The lock file. The job is currently being processed, another Sendmail will not try to process it. This keeps multiple instances of Sendmail from "working on" the same piece of mail. Sendmail versions 5.65 and later do not use lock files, but instead use flock(2) on the qf file.

qfAA*nnnnn*
> The queue control file. Mail envelope information, status information, creation time information, and the headers are here. A complete list of what is contained in a qf file is given below.

tfAA*nnnnn*
> A temporary file. All other queue files begin as a tf file, which is renamed to its true name after it has been created.

xfAA*nnnnn*
> A transcript file. This shows everything that happens during the mail transfer. When mail is delivered (or when Sendmail gives up for a time) this file goes away.

nfAA*nnnnn*
> A file is created when Sendmail has decided on a file id and is making sure that another Sendmail process has not decided on that exact same id. These files exist only for a few milliseconds. The only places *you* will probably ever see mention of these are here, in the documentation, and in the source code.

The df files are straightforward — they contain the body of the mail message. Everything except the envelope information *and the header information* is contained in the df file. This is different from p-mail, in which the header information is at the top of the letter inside of the envelope.

The qf files contain most of the data in which we are interested (unless you're into reading other people's mail). Figure 9-1 is an example of a qf file. We leave it to you to determine its name. The leading character indicates the type of each line.

P   is the current message priority. This number is initially based on the priority header — if any — given in the mail headers (see Chapter 4) and the size of the message, and it is modified based on the time it sits in the queue. The longer it sits, the higher the priority.

Sendmail uses the priorities to decide the order in which to process mail in a queue. The software takes into account factors such as the number of recipients, the size of the mail message, and the time it has been in the queue (unable to be delivered).

When a mail message is passed to Sendmail and dropped into the queue, it is given a priority derived by using a formula similar to the following:

```
size + CreationTime - (Class * ClassFactor)
    + (#Recipients * RecipientFactor)
```

`Class` is something set up in your `sendmail.cf` (for example, `Junk=-100`) and added by a UA to the header of a mail message. Since most e-mail does not have this header, it is sent with the default class of 0. (Of course, now that you know about this...) `ClassFactor` and `RecipientFactor` are variables in the Sendmail source code and are used to give higher magnitudes to `Class` and number of recipients (which in the source code we have are 1800 and 1000 respectively).

```
P695447232
T695159735
K695401658
N69
I18487
DdfAA02849
MDeferred
S<avolio@gildor.dco.frobozz.com>
R<person@yourtown.us>
R<vixie@al.org>
E<xmen-request@dco.frobozz.com>
H?P?return-path: <avolio@gildor.dco.frobozz.com>
Hdate: Sat, 11 Jan 92 14:55:34 -0500
Hfrom: avolio@gildor.dco.frobozz.com (Frederick M. Avolio)
Hmessage-id: <9201111955.AA13478@gildor.dco.frobozz.com>
Hto: xmen@dco.frobozz.com
Herrors-to: xmen-request@dco.frobozz.com
Hsubject: xcd
```

Figure 9-1. Example Queue File

The bigger this number is, the lower the priority it is given. So, in general with regular mail (Class = 0), the larger it is and the more recipients it has, the lower its priority (the higher the number). Sendmail gives preference to small, single-connection messages.

Each time Sendmail processes a message that is in the queue (because it hasn't been able to send it) a TimeFactor is applied to the message, so that the longer it sits in the queue the higher the number and the lower the priority still. The TimeFactor in our source code was 9000.

Think about this scheme a bit. It's a good one. If *most* e-mail messages get through a queue the first time Sendmail attempts to send them, but one or two (or ten) large mail messages can't be sent immediately (let's say a network connection is down), we don't want the other mail messages waiting behind them in the queue each time it is run.

T   is the time (a long integer) showing the time (in seconds since 1970) that the message was first put into the mail queue.

K   (*KJS only*) is the time (in seconds since 1970) of the last delivery attempt.

N   (*KJS only*) is the number of times Sendmail has attempted to deliver this mail message (and failed, of course, since it is still in the queue).

I   (*KJS only*) is the data file's (df*) inode number, which can be used to rebuild your mail queue directory in the event that your system crashes in a dirty way, corrupting the mqueue directory. A dirty crash can result in all of your mail queue files being moved into the file system lost+found directory, with names like #01234 (for the file whose inode number is 1234). If the qf file has only the *name* of the df file, you can't put Humpty-Dumpty back together again. Therefore, *KJS* also puts the df file's inode number into the corresponding qf file.

D   is the name of the data file (the df file).

M   is status information (saying why it is still in the queue), put here to be printed by the mailq command.

S   sender's e-mail address. This is *envelope* information.

R   (there may be multiple R lines) contains the e-mail address of one of the recipients of the mail message. While not all of the addresses on the R lines may be on the same computer, they are all reached via the same next hop. The *route* they take goes through the same next stop. This is a way that e-mail is bundled, as we discussed earlier. This, too, is *envelope* information.

E   if there is a separate Errors-to: header, E holds the address of the person to whom mail errors should go. This is often used by people who maintain a mail distribution list.

H   H lines are header lines as they appear in the original mail or as they have been added by Sendmail or other mail processors along the way. We discuss the format of H lines further and header lines in general in Chapter 8.

The xf, lf, and tf files are less interesting. The xf files contain the comments between the local Sendmail and the last remote transport to which it tried to hand off the message. These files are generally very short-lived. The lf files are empty and act as lock files. If lfAA18487 exists, it means that Sendmail is currently working on the mail message in dfAA18487 with header file qfAA18487. If the system crashes or Sendmail crashes and burns ("No way, Ted!" "Yes way, Bill!"), these lock files are left behind. Usually these files are deleted at system start-up. A good thing to remember if you are restarting a crashed Sendmail process is that none of the mail with lock files left around after a crash will be sent. You must remove these files first. The nf files are downright boring.

9.3. Adding a New Mailer

The steps in adding a new mailer are fairly straightforward. The header translations, mailer definitions, and testing are what take a lot of thought.

(1)   Determine the address formats. You need to understand what addresses will look like from this new mail environment and what you have to do, if you care to, to transform them for any other mail arena you support. If you were adding UUCP you'd be looking for addresses in bang notation.

(2)   Write the rules in Ruleset 3 to recognize mail from this mailer and tag it. This means determining how to recognize it and defining the tag to use and writing the lines to do that. Again, with the UUCP mail example, this means deciding to change addresses like

```
decwrl!decuac!avolio
```

into

```
decuac!avolio<@decwrl.UUCP>
```

for later handling. Rules we might add to Ruleset 3 are

```
# UUCP conversions
R$-.$+!$+          $@$>7$3<@$1.$2>      host.domain!user
R$-!$+             $@$>7$2<@$1.UUCP>    resolve uucp names
```

(3)   Add lines in Ruleset 0 to recognize it and dispatch it. We need to recognize
        the form we decided on in the additional lines to Ruleset 3 (in this case
        $+<@$+.UUCP>) and decide what we will do with them.

```
# UUCP
#
R$*<@$-.UUCP>    $#uucp $@$2 $:$2!$1    use our own uucp
```

(4)   Write the mailer definition. This is separate, of course, from writing the
        mailer itself (which is beyond our scope). At this point, the numbers for the
        rewriting rules are picked.

(5)   Write the S= and R= rewriting rules to rewrite from canonical form to the
        form needed by the mailer.

```
#####          UUCP mailers
Muucp, P=/usr/bin/uux, F=sDFhuU, S=15, R=25, M=100000,
       A=uux - -r $h!rmail ($u)

S15
R$*<@$+>$*      $@$1<@$2>$3        domain form is ok
R$+            $:$>25$1           do unto sender as to recipient
R$U!$+         $@$U!$1            already has our node name
R$+            $@$U!$1            tack on our hostname.

S25
R$*<@$+>$*      $@$1<@$2>$3        domain form is ok
R$-!$+         $@$1!$2            !-form is ok; done
R$+!$+         $@$>3$2<@$1>       looks like domain; chg to u@dom
```

(6)   Test the dickens out of it with Sendmail in test mode. Test all the sender and
        receiver possibilities with all possible mail address formats.

9.4. Testing Configurations

The rules and rulesets of sendmail.cf constitute a programming language, which
means that a sendmail.cf file can be considered a program. Programs — even
programs in use and generally considered to "work" — often have bugs. Bugs tend
to creep in whenever a program is changed in some way; in particular, fixing one bug
often has the side effect of creating others. The sendmail.cf file makes it very
easy to add bugs, since almost every complex thing a programmer wants to do has to
be done indirectly and using clever side effects.

Sendmail includes a limited debugging environment for `sendmail.cf` files. By "limited" we mean that there is no way to change the value of macros or classes while inside the debugger; to do this, you must exit the debugger, edit the `sendmail.cf` file, and restart the debugger. Likewise, while tracing the execution of the `sendmail.cf` file, you can't change the level of granularity of the trace output without exiting the debugger and restarting it with a different command line option. There are no breakpoints. There is no way to examine the value of a macro or class. Even with these limitations, the debugging environment available for `sendmail.cf` files is useful, and once you get the hang of it you will be able find bugs, fix them, and test your fixes.

9.4.1. Sendmail `-C`

The `-C` command line option tells Sendmail to use some configuration file other than its usual one (which could be `/etc/sendmail.cf` or `/usr/lib/sendmail.cf` or perhaps `/var/adm/sendmail/sendmail.cf` — every vendor has its own idea of where the default `sendmail.cf` should be kept). The `-C` command line option is magic in the way that Sendmail usually is. If you just say `-C` — that is, you do not specify a file name — then Sendmail will search for a `sendmail.cf` file in your current working directory. If you specify a file (e.g., `-Ctest.cf`), Sendmail will use that file. Note that no space is necessary or allowed between the `-C` and the file name.

You should use the `-C` option to test configuration files before you install them in the default system-level directory; it is better to find bugs in new configuration files by testing them privately than by installing them and having mail bounce while you fine-tune things.

9.4.2. Sendmail `-bt`

The `-bt` command line option causes Sendmail to start up in its debugging environment, which it calls "ADDRESS TEST MODE." In the examples below, we have been forced to "fold" some lines for readability. We indicate this by ending the example line with a back-slash (\).

```
% sendmail -bt
ADDRESS TEST MODE
Enter <ruleset> <address>
>
```

The `>` is a prompt, at which you can enter debugging commands, which are of the form "*rulesets addresses*" where *rulesets* is a comma-separated list of rulesets to be called and *addresses* is a comma-separated list of addresses to be sent to those rule-sets. Some Sendmail configurations automatically call Ruleset 3, without the user specifying it. We'll use a Sendmail that doesn't do this.

The simplest case is where you have one ruleset and one address, as in

```
> 3,0 postmaster
rewrite: ruleset  3    input: "postmaster"
rewrite: ruleset  3 returns: "postmaster"
rewrite: ruleset  0    input: "postmaster"
rewrite: ruleset  0 returns: "^V" "local" "^X" "postmaster"
>
```

or

```
> 3,0 postmaster@al.org
rewrite: ruleset  3    input: "postmaster" "@" "al" "." "org"
rewrite: ruleset  6    input: "postmaster" "<" "@" "al" "." "org" ">"
rewrite: ruleset  6 returns: "postmaster" "<" "@" "al" "." "org" ">"
rewrite: ruleset  3 returns: "postmaster" "<" "@" "al" "." "org" ">"
rewrite: ruleset  0    input: "postmaster" "<" "@" "al" "." "org" ">"
rewrite: ruleset  0 returns: "^V" "tcpr"  \
           "^W" "inet-gw" "." "vix" "." "com"  \
           "^X" "postmaster" "<" "@" "al" "." "org" ">"
>
```

As each ruleset is entered and exited, the address as it exists at that point is displayed along with the ruleset number. When the last ruleset has been called, you are returned to the > prompt. Notice how, in the second example, Ruleset 3 calls Ruleset 6 (implying that the sendmail.cf file has a $>6 operation somewhere in Ruleset 3); this shows up on the trace even though Ruleset 6 is not on the list of rulesets that we asked Sendmail to run on this address.

Sendmail is not helpful if you enter an *address* but forget to enter any *rulesets*; it will silently ignore your command and offer you another > prompt, as in

```
> postmaster@al.org
>
```

We've just seen an example of using -bt to determine the route a message will take. Let's see how we use it to test header rewriting rules.

If we are on node gildor.dco.frobozz.com, and we are sending e-mail to vixie@al.org and fma@urc.dco.frobozz.com, we know that in one case we will send mail via our smtp mailer and in the other via our smtp1 mailer. When we look at these in our configuration file, we see that the S= rule for the smtp mailer is

12 and for the `smtp1` mailer, 11. We want to see, in these examples, what the
`From:` header will look like if user `avolio` is sending the mail.

Let's test both of these addresses:

```
% sendmail -bt
ADDRESS TEST MODE
Enter <ruleset> <address>
> 3,1,12,4 avolio
rewrite: ruleset  3   input: "avolio"
rewrite: ruleset  3 returns: "avolio"
rewrite: ruleset  1   input: "avolio"
rewrite: ruleset  1 returns: "avolio"
rewrite: ruleset 12   input: "avolio"
rewrite: ruleset 12 returns: "avolio" \
          "<" "@" "DCO" "." "FROBOZZ" "." "COM" ">"
rewrite: ruleset  4   input: "avolio" \
          "<" "@" "DCO" "." "FROBOZZ" "." "COM" ">"
rewrite: ruleset  4 returns: "avolio" \
          "@" "DCO" "." "FROBOZZ" "." "COM"
>
```

We see, and it is no surprise, that our *domain* rather than our fully qualified host
name is attached to the local name `avolio`. That is how it will appear in mail to
`vixie@al.org`.

```
> 3,1,11,4 avolio
rewrite: ruleset  3   input: "avolio"
rewrite: ruleset  3 returns: "avolio"
rewrite: ruleset  1   input: "avolio"
rewrite: ruleset  1 returns: "avolio"
rewrite: ruleset 11   input: "avolio"
rewrite: ruleset 11 returns: "avolio"
rewrite: ruleset  4   input: "avolio"
rewrite: ruleset  4 returns: "avolio"
>
```

Observe that, since we are set up as a Mail Cluster any outgoing mail to users in
our domain (part of the Mail Cluster) will see the unqualified name `avolio` as the
sender.

Finally, let's see what happens if we send this out of the `root` account, which is
one that is always host-qualified, even in a Mail Cluster.

```
> 3,1,11,4 root
rewrite: ruleset  3    input: "root"
rewrite: ruleset  3 returns: "root"
rewrite: ruleset  1    input: "root"
rewrite: ruleset  1 returns: "root"
rewrite: ruleset 11    input: "root"
rewrite: ruleset 11 returns: "root" \
         "<" "@" "gildor" "." "DCO" "." "FROBOZZ" "." "COM" ">"
rewrite: ruleset  4    input: "root" \
         "<" "@" "gildor" "." "DCO" "." "FROBOZZ" "." "COM" ">"
rewrite: ruleset  4 returns: "root" \
         "@" "gildor" "." "DCO" "." "FROBOZZ" "." "COM"
>
```

9.4.2.1. IDA Notes on -bt

A non-IDA Sendmail will always call Ruleset 3 before calling any other rulesets, even when running in -bt mode. IDA wisely avoids calling ruleset 3 during testing. It is sometimes necessary while debugging a new rule or ruleset to send input to a rule without having it first pass through Ruleset 3. Thus, in our examples you'll see that we had to specify a leading "3" on our list of rulesets to be called. In a non-IDA Sendmail this is a bad thing to do, since before Sendmail calls the first ruleset given on the -bt command line, it calls Ruleset 3 — Therefore, if you specify a leading "3" you will cause Ruleset 3 to be called *twice*. This can be a bad thing if your Ruleset 3 is not idempotent, and this IDAism is one of the leading reasons why Ruleset 3 *should be* idempotent. Let's see what IDA Sendmail will do if we don't give it the leading "3,":

```
> 0 postmaster
rewrite: ruleset  0    input: postmaster
rewrite: ruleset  0 returns: $# local $: postmaster
>
```

and

```
> 0 postmaster@al.org
rewrite: ruleset  0    input: postmaster @ al . org
rewrite: ruleset  0 returns: $# local $: postmaster @ al . org
>
```

Obviously, the second example didn't work — postmaster@al.org is not a local address. This demonstrates why Sendmail always calls Ruleset 3 to canonicalize addresses: With no <brackets> around the @*domain*, Ruleset 0 honestly believes that there is nothing special about this address and that it must belong to the `local` mailer. Let's try it again, this time calling Ruleset 3 first:

```
> 3,0 postmaster@al.org
rewrite: ruleset  3    input: postmaster @ al . org
rewrite: ruleset  6    input: postmaster < @ al . org >
rewrite: ruleset  6 returns: postmaster < @ al . org >
rewrite: ruleset  3 returns: postmaster < @ al . org >
rewrite: ruleset  0    input: postmaster < @ al . org >
rewrite: ruleset  0 returns: $# tcpr $@ inet-gw . vix . com \
         $: postmaster < @ al . org >
>
```

Running Ruleset 3 first was obviously the missing magic. You could also specify the focus manually, as in

```
> 0 postmaster<@al.org>
rewrite: ruleset  0    input: postmaster < @ al . org >
rewrite: ruleset  3    input: postmaster @ al . org
rewrite: ruleset  6    input: postmaster < @ al . org >
rewrite: ruleset  6 returns: postmaster < @ al . org >
rewrite: ruleset  3 returns: postmaster < @ al . org >
rewrite: ruleset  0 returns: $# local $: postmaster . al
>
```

Here we see Ruleset 0 stripping off the focus and calling Ruleset 3. This demonstrates the fact that like a 150-kg gorilla, Sendmail does whatever it wants to do. It's fun to watch, though.

The other thing IDA Sendmail does differently from non-IDA Sendmail when running in address test mode is to format the output in a less arcane way. Since no useful purpose is served by printing quotes (") around tokens in the tracing output, IDA leaves them out. And while the (*mailer, host, user*) tuple is in fact represented as a token stream with control characters delimiting the parts, there is no need for most `sendmail.cf` programmers to see those control characters in their raw form. Therefore, where standard Sendmail prints

```
rewrite: ruleset  0 returns: "^V" "tcpr" \
         "^W" "inet-gw" "." "vix" "." "com" \
         "^X" "postmaster" "<" "@" "al" "." "org" ">"
```

IDA Sendmail prints

```
rewrite: ruleset  0 returns: $# tcpr $@ inet-gw . vix . com \
    $: postmaster < @ al . org >
```

where each character represents the same return from Ruleset 0:

```
$#tcpr $@inet-gw.vix.com $:postmaster<@al.org>
```

9.4.3. Sendmail -o

The -o command line option can be used to specify an option that would normally be set with a "O" line in the sendmail.cf file, or to override some option that actually *is* specified with an "O" line in whatever configuration file you are using. All of the options described for the "O" line in configuration files are available with the -o command line option. The most common use of the option during debugging is to specify a queue directory other than the standard one (e.g., -oQ/usr/spool/testq) so that your test messages don't pollute the main mail queue. You might also set the delivery option to "queued" (-odq) to force Sendmail to drop the message in your alternate queue and abandon it there so you can examine it at your leisure.

9.4.4. Sendmail -d

The -d command line option turns on debugging options internal to Sendmail. These options are of the form "*class1[-class2].level*", where *class1* and *class2* are numbers representing groups of similar debugging information and *level* is a number representing the level of detail you want to see for those classes. Higher numbers indicate greater detail. The debugging goes to standard output. The -d command line option takes a comma-separated list of these *class1[-class2].level* specifications, as in the following:

-d0.4,21.3

> Says that for debugging class 0 we want to see any debugging messages that are at levels 4 and below; also, for class 21 we want levels 3 and below.

-d0-40.4

> Says that for debugging classes 0 through 40, we want to see any debugging messages that are at levels 4 and below.

The degenerate case is "-d" with no argument following it; this is the same as saying "-d0-99.1" — that is, select level-1 debugging detail for every debugging class. This is almost never going to be what you want.

Debugging classes and levels vary somewhat from vendor to vendor, since individual vendors would have had their own special porting problems getting Sendmail to run on their computer, and they likely added debugging output that focused on those special problems. Some vendors are less generous; they provide Sendmail binaries with no internal debugging at all — for these systems, the -d command line option is a no-op. If you discover that your Sendmail has the wrong internal debugging configuration built into it, or worse, that it has no internal debugging at all, you should complain to your vendor and plan to build your own Sendmail from sources.

The most common debugging classes and levels are described in Appendix G. No doubt these will be out of date by the time this book is published. For an up-to-date list, get the sources and read them. In the table in Appendix G, descriptions in (parenthesis) are actions — actual changes in Sendmail's behavior caused by this debugging *class* and *level*. All other descriptions shown in the table are of debugging output.

9.4.4.1. Sendmail -d21.3 Example

Debug class 21, level 3, is the same output that the -bt command line option shows, except that where -bt shows you a trace of a specific address run through a specific list of rulesets, -d21.3 can be used in an actual delivery, thus showing you all of the rewriting that occurs. Since there will always be times when you can't quite figure out which ruleset is being called for some address that isn't being rewritten the way you like, you should try out -d21.3 so that when you need it, you'll know how it works.

Here is the /bin/sh script we used to generate the trace output used in the following discussion:

```
sendmail -v -d21.3 root <<EOF
From: HdrFrom
To: HdrTo
Cc: HdrCC

body
EOF
```

Given the input shown (and the -v flag on the command line, which is the "verbose" flag), Sendmail prints an amazing amount of output that shows each of the various rewrite rulesets as they are entered and exited. The trace output is usually rather hard to read because there is no visual cue that clearly shows you when one address rewrite has been completed and another has begun. The trick is to look for lines that say "ruleset 4 returns" — these tell you that a rewrite is complete, since ruleset 4 is always the last one called.

Let's have a look:

```
rewrite: ruleset  3    input: vixie
rewrite: ruleset  3 returns: vixie
rewrite: ruleset  0    input: vixie
rewrite: ruleset  0 returns: $# local $: vixie
rewrite: ruleset  2    input: vixie
rewrite: ruleset  2 returns: vixie
rewrite: ruleset 20    input: vixie
rewrite: ruleset 20 returns: vixie
rewrite: ruleset  4    input: vixie
rewrite: ruleset  4 returns: vixie
```

Here we see the envelope sender ("vixie," since that is the login name of the user who ran Sendmail to generate this example) being rewritten through rulesets 3, 0, 2, 20, and 4. One can reasonably ask at this point: "Why is the sender being rewritten through ruleset 0, since ruleset 0 handles the recipients?" Sendmail is just doing its job. The address has to be parsed and resolved through ruleset 0 so that Sendmail can guess which mailer this message logically "came from." One of the per-mailer "flags" ("c") binds to the "come-from" mailer rather than to the usual "goes-to" mailer. In case you haven't memorized all of the predefined ruleset numbers by now, here is an explanation of why these particular rulesets were called:

3   canonicalizes the address, which basically means adding angle brackets around the @*domain* (if there is one) to "focus" on it. There is nothing to focus on in this address, so Ruleset 3 did nothing — the address came out looking the same way it looked going in.

0   examines the address. Based on the domain, pseudodomain, or addressing syntax, it chooses the outgoing mailer that would be used to reach this address if this address were a recipient — which it clearly is not, but see the discussion above.

2   recipient preprocessing. This ruleset is run on all recipients, header and envelope alike (except in IDA where you can split them up if you want to). It's called *pre*processing because it's run before the mailer-specific recipient rewrite ruleset, which for mailer local in our sendmail.cf is...

20   mailer-specific recipient processing. This is run on all recipients that go through this mailer. The sendmail.cf file evidently has rule R=20 in the Mlocal declaration. Since this address is simple, there's nothing to do.

4   final postprocessing and cleanup. This undoes any special thing done by Ruleset 3 (or any other ruleset for that matter, though by convention only Ruleset 3 speaks in this way to Ruleset 4 — you can think of them as "like parentheses" in that they match and that one begins and the other ends. Once again, since this address is simple, there is nothing to do.

The trace continues:

```
rewrite: ruleset  3    input: vixie
rewrite: ruleset  3 returns: vixie
rewrite: ruleset  1    input: vixie
rewrite: ruleset  1 returns: vixie
rewrite: ruleset  4    input: vixie
rewrite: ruleset  4 returns: vixie
```

There's nothing unusual here. Rulesets 3 and 4 are called because they are always called; Ruleset 1 is the sender preprocessing ruleset (still called the *preprocessing* ruleset even here where there is no mailer-specific ruleset to be called after it). This is the normal sequence of rulesets that are called for *envelope* senders.

The trace continues:

```
rewrite: ruleset  3    input: root
rewrite: ruleset  3 returns: root
rewrite: ruleset  0    input: root
rewrite: ruleset  0 returns: $# local $: root
rewrite: ruleset  2    input: root
rewrite: ruleset  2 returns: root
rewrite: ruleset 20    input: root
rewrite: ruleset 20 returns: root
rewrite: ruleset  4    input: root
rewrite: ruleset  4 returns: root
```

We know that `root` is the envelope recipient, since that was the recipient named on the `sendmail` command line in the test script. This is the normal sequence of things that happen to an envelope recipient, and the discussion above applies fully.

Next, we see our old friend back again:

```
rewrite: ruleset  3    input: vixie
rewrite: ruleset  3 returns: vixie
rewrite: ruleset  1    input: vixie
rewrite: ruleset  1 returns: vixie
rewrite: ruleset 10    input: vixie
rewrite: ruleset 10 returns: vixie
rewrite: ruleset  4    input: vixie
rewrite: ruleset  4 returns: vixie
root... Connecting to  (local)...
```

You could reasonably ask: "Why are we doing this again, and why are we calling Ruleset 10 this time?" The answer is that Sendmail is not always efficient. The first rewrite of the envelope sender was done for one of Sendmail's internal purposes; this one is being done for a different internal purpose. Note that this second rewrite calls the mailer-specific sender ruleset (number 10) because for `Mlocal` in our send-mail.cf, S=10, and that this was not possible in the first rewrite since the outgoing mailer was not yet known. The "`Connecting to`" shows that Sendmail is sending the mail to a local user via the `local` mailer.

The trace continues:

```
rewrite: ruleset  3    input: HdrFrom
rewrite: ruleset  3 returns: HdrFrom
rewrite: ruleset  1    input: HdrFrom
rewrite: ruleset  1 returns: HdrFrom
rewrite: ruleset 10    input: HdrFrom
rewrite: ruleset 10 returns: HdrFrom
rewrite: ruleset  4    input: HdrFrom
rewrite: ruleset  4 returns: HdrFrom
```

Are you getting the hang of this yet? The header "from" address was passed through Rulesets 3, 1, 10, and 4. These were all explained above. The only thing of interest is that in IDA, Ruleset 5 is called instead of Ruleset 1 if "O/" is set. In fact, our Sendmail system uses this IDA feature, and we end up calling Ruleset 1 from Ruleset 5 after we get done doing the things to the header addresses that we don't also want to do to the envelope addresses.

The trace continues:

```
rewrite: ruleset  3    input: HdrTo
rewrite: ruleset  3 returns: HdrTo
rewrite: ruleset  2    input: HdrTo
rewrite: ruleset  2 returns: HdrTo
rewrite: ruleset 20    input: HdrTo
rewrite: ruleset 20 returns: HdrTo
rewrite: ruleset  4    input: HdrTo
rewrite: ruleset  4 returns: HdrTo
rewrite: ruleset  3    input: HdrCC
rewrite: ruleset  3 returns: HdrCC
rewrite: ruleset  2    input: HdrCC
rewrite: ruleset  2 returns: HdrCC
rewrite: ruleset 20    input: HdrCC
rewrite: ruleset 20 returns: HdrCC
rewrite: ruleset  4    input: HdrCC
rewrite: ruleset  4 returns: HdrCC
```

Both the header "to" and header "cc" addresses are rewritten in the same way. As before, IDA would have done this differently, since header recipients are sent through Ruleset 6 rather than Ruleset 2; our Sendmail configuration calls Ruleset 2 after doing its header-specific rewrites.

Last but not least, a sight for sore eyes:

```
root... Sent
```

Just to be complete about it, here's the mail as it was received by `root`:

```
From vixie Sun Nov  1 01:20:20 1992
Received: by cognition.pa.frobozz.com; id AA06747; \
          Sun, 1 Nov 92 01:20:19 -0800
Date: Sun, 1 Nov 92 01:20:19 -0800
Message-Id: <9211010920.AA06747@cognition.pa.frobozz.com>
From: HdrFrom
To: HdrTo
Cc: HdrCC

body
```

There should be no real surprises here to you, except perhaps that the mail was received by `root` and `root` is not one of the recipients shown in the headers. This is because header recipients don't affect where the mail is sent; in fact, both the recipient headers used in our example contain nonexistent, unreachable addresses. Sendmail does not care whether these addresses are reachable; all it cares about is the envelope. The header is only important because it has to be rewritten to be valid in whatever other domains or networks Sendmail may send it to. The distinction between header and envelope addresses is absolutely crucial to understanding how Sendmail works and how to make it do what you want it to do.

9.5. Running Sendmail from InetD

Given Sendmail's apparent memory requirements, it is occasionally tempting to run it "on demand" from the InetD rather than running it all the time as a listener ("`sendmail -bd -q30m`"). This is accomplished by adding an entry such as

```
smtp stream tcp nowait root /usr/lib/sendmail sendmail -bs
```

in your `/etc/inetd.conf` file. We recommend against this practice for the following reasons:

(1)   A real Sendmail listener will watch the system load average and stop accepting incoming mail when the load average gets too high. You will miss this feature if you don't have it, and InetD doesn't have it.

(2)   Since the "periodic queue run" function is usually performed by the listener, if you don't run a listener you will need to "run the queue" periodically from your Cron Daemon with something like

```
23 * * * * root /usr/lib/sendmail -q
```

While not difficult, this *does* add another place where something can go wrong. Sendmail, however monolithic, has the advantage of either working completely or not — it can't fail to run the queue without also failing to do a lot of other very noticeable things.

(3)   The overhead of exec'ing a new SMTP server is higher than that of just fork'ing a process from the listener. This additional overhead can degrade the performance of your system.

(4)   Finally, the apparent memory requirements of a Sendmail listener are not as bad as they look. All UNIX-like systems are capable of "swapping out" a process if it is not doing anything. Thus, a Sendmail listener not receiving incoming mail or running the queue is eligible to have all of its memory given to more active processes. When incoming mail does arrive, the listener will have to be swapped or paged in from secondary storage. At this time it will use perhaps a small amount more memory than InetD does but only for a very brief time, since once an SMTP connection has been accepted, it will be handled by a subprocess of the listener — which is the same size as that of the "sendmail -bs" process run by InetD.

In summary, it's fun to run Sendmail from InetD, but it's not especially useful. Try it if you want to get a better sense of what "sendmail -bd -q30m" does, but we think you'll end up going back to using a normal listener just to avoid the extra work involved in doing it by hand with other tools.

9.6. Analyzing syslog

As Sendmail runs, it writes transaction records using the syslog facility. The syslog facility can be configured to mix Sendmail's log records in with everything else it receives, or it can be set up to write a separate log file just for Sendmail. Sendmail's syslog volume will probably dwarf all the rest of your syslog traffic combined; this follows from the fact that syslog was written to be part of Sendmail originally. It makes sense that Sendmail will always be syslog's best customer.

You might find your Sendmail logs in any of the following places:

```
/var/spool/mqueue/syslog
/var/log/syslog
/var/log/maillog
/var/log/sendmail
```

It all depends on what you've got in your syslog configuration file. The file will probably be named /etc/syslog.conf, but you know how vendors love to move stuff around, so if you don't find it at first, keep looking.

The format of Sendmail's syslog records varies according to the whim of your vendor or whichever clever person you got your Sendmail from. Even Berkeley Sendmail's syslog record format has evolved a little over time, so be prepared for variation among the different kinds of hosts you maintain. It is especially important to keep format variations in mind when you write Perl or AWK scripts that postprocess the syslog files. The examples we'll show here came from King James Sendmail, aka DECWRL-IDA Sendmail. Note that Sendmail can log a lot of data per mail message, or it can log very little. See Appendix F for details of log level settings. In our examples we will break long lines with backslash (\) characters; in a real syslog file these lines are just very long.

In Figure 9-2 we see the simplest kind of syslog transaction. A mail message came in and was quickly delivered. Let's tear this example apart and see just what we've got. Everything happened on Aug 22; the mail came in at 02:02:40 and left at 02:02:41, a total of one second (delay=00:00:01, to be exact), which is reasonable for short, local messages. The host where all of this took place was named gw, though in fact the actual name was longer — syslog elides the domain name when it logs a host name, since there are often hundreds of thousands of log entries in a day's syslog file and putting the fully qualified host name on every entry would make a large file into a huge file. The application that logged these records was, as we suspected, called sendmail. The PID of the Sendmail that received the message was 8622; the PID of the Sendmail that delivered it was 8624.

The message ID was 9308220902.AA08622@frobozz.com, and the queue ID was AA08622. (Remember, the queue ID will be reused, but the message ID is meant to be unique in the period between Big Bangs.) The mail came from root and was 30192 bytes long. The class=0 is essentially boilerplate. The message was received from local, as opposed to having been received over the network. (Note that mail from uucp always says received from local, since Sendmail knows only that it came from a local program, and it has no concept of a local program that is actually a network agent.) The status of this delivery was Sent, and the delivery method was (local /usr/libexec/mail.local), which means that the local mailer was used ("$#local") and that the program used to deliver the mail was /usr/libexec/mail.local.

```
Aug 22 02:02:40 gw sendmail[8622]: AA08622: \
        message-id=<9308220902.AA08622@frobozz.com>
Aug 22 02:02:40 gw sendmail[8622]: AA08622: \
        from=root, size=30192, class=0, received from local
Aug 22 02:02:41 gw sendmail[8624]: AA08622: \
        to=vixie, delay=00:00:01, stat=Sent \
        (local /usr/libexec/mail.local)
```

Figure 9-2. Syslog Example #1

Well, that was easy. Ready for a harder one? Have a look at Figure 9-3. This one is almost the same as Figure 9-2, except that the mail originated from another host. This fact can be seen from the message ID, which has another host's name in it, and from the notation received from risc-ns.ing.uniroma1.it (151.100.4.2).

Given that the message is from the MAILER-DAEMON address on the same host that it was received from, this is probably a "bounced mail notification." Note that the two-second delay (delay=00:00:02) is the delay within the current system, not the delay from the moment that the mail was originally entered into the mail system over on risc-ns.ing.uniroma1.it or wherever it might have originated (the sender's location).

It's important to note that while there is only one message-id= log record per transaction, and only one from= log record per transaction, there can be multiple to= log records per transaction — one per recipient. In fact, there can even be many per recipient, since if the mail is initially undeliverable, that undeliverability will be logged, and later, when the queue is emptied, those attempts will also be logged. Until the recipient is logged with the notation "stat=Sent", you'll know that the message is still kicking around in your mail queue.

Note that the log records for a given transaction might not be near each other in the syslog file, or even be in the same syslog file, since the mail might be undeliverable for several days and the usual syslog file only contains one day's worth of traffic. Programs that analyze syslog files and produce mail volume reports generally need to be given all of the aged log files so that they can see the source of messages which have been in the queue since before the current day. But if it were easy, *everybody* would be doing it.

```
Aug 22 02:58:30 gw sendmail[9730]: AA09730: \
        message-id=<9308221658.AA25146@risc-ns.ing.uniroma1.it>
Aug 22 02:58:30 gw sendmail[9730]: AA09730: \
        from=<MAILER-DAEMON@risc-ns.ing.uniroma1.it>, \
        size=1985, class=0, received from \
        risc-ns.ing.uniroma1.it (151.100.4.2)
Aug 22 02:58:30 gw sendmail[9732]: AA09730: \
        to=vixie, delay=00:00:02, stat=Sent \
        (local /usr/libexec/mail.local)
```

Figure 9-3. Syslog Example #2

9.7. Resolving Common Problems

If the mail to `postmaster` or `mailer-daemon` eventually ends up in a mailbox with your name on it, you'll need to learn to recognize and resolve certain problems. We will present some of the more common problems you will run up against and give suggestions for resolving them. Some problems you encounter won't be covered here, but by their nature they will be few and fleeting. These types of problems will cause you to think hard and spend hours testing configurations if the problems are clearly a fault of *your* mail gateway. But that's one reason God gave you a brain bigger than a monkey's (although monkeys usually get the proper amount of sleep and you won't).

9.7.1. Undeliverable Mail

The most common group of errors you will see, if you are the `postmaster`, is undeliverable mail. For one reason or another an error in transmission has occurred and the mail, which is usually returned to the sender on an error, can't be returned. This allows us to engage in one of the more interesting of pastimes for Postmasters: reading other people's mail with impunity! No, not really. What we must do, though, is read the headers of the message and glean what we can from them.

(1) Who sent the error message? It is, in all probability, from a MAILER-DAEMON, but which one? It may also be from a user who has received mail bounced by a MAILER-DAEMON. We want to know what system generated the error message.

(2) What is the error? Almost every MTA generates human-readable error messages. Read the subject line and text added on by the MAILER-DAEMON, and try to determine what the problem was.

(3) Whose error is it? What agent on what system?

If the problem is with another system, mail a copy of the pertinent header lines to the `postmaster` account on that other host with a brief note of explanation.

Sometimes that error was caused by user error — someone mistyping an address, for example. Again, this sort of error usually gets back to the sender. If it doesn't, there is almost always a problem with a mail configuration somewhere in addition to the original user error, anyway.

In this case, send a copy of the mail, with a brief note to the intended recipient, if possible, and "carbon copy" the original sender. If there is a mail configuration problem, suggest that the sender send a note to the `postmaster` responsible, or do it yourself.

If you can't tell how to get to the intended recipient, send a copy to the sender with a note. If you can't figure out either the sender or recipient's proper address, and you have already looked up their names in the corporate phone book and tried everything else, read the mail. Read it to see if either party's full name is mentioned or if there is anything else that might help you get it delivered.

Finally, if all else fails, put it in the dead letter box. That is, you delete it.

9.7.2. Queued Mail

Messages often sit around in your mail queue. Maybe they are hanging around because they are temporarily undeliverable, or perhaps you have specified Odq in your sendmail.cf such that new mail is queued immediately with no attempt at an initial delivery. If you get into the habit of scanning your mail queue periodically, you'll get a feel for how it should look, how many messages in the queue are "normal," and so forth. You might also be contacted by a user who has had mail returned because of being unable to send for a certain number of days. This is usually a message that *was* in your queue, perhaps, but was returned to the sender after being in the queue after the queue timeout was reached.

If the problem stems from a system being unreachable, there are various ways to test its reachability. First, you test to see if the system is reachable at all.

(1)   How does mail get to the "unreachable" system? Using Sendmail in test mode (sendmail -bt), test with the address on Ruleset 0 to see how the message is sent to the particular address.

(2)   If the message goes directly to the host via SMTP, query the name server (for example, with nslookup) to see if there are any MX records for the host. The host may be reachable, but if there are MX records for the host, you must check the reachability of the host(s) specified by the MX record(s).

(3)   If the system (either the intended host or its MX hosts) is reachable, and it is reachable via IP for SMTP mail, connect to its Sendmail server to see if *it* is reachable. On most systems, you can do this with the command

telnet *host-name* smtp

which will usually put you in communication with the other host's Sendmail process. If you get an invitation, you know that it is reachable. The quit command will disconnect you. If you end up connected to a service with which you cannot communicate (you don't know the commands), remember that you are connected via telnet. A control-] (ASCII 035) will get you to the telnet prompt and you can quit out of it that way.

(4)   Try running the queue in verbose mode (`sendmail -q -v`) to see what happens when Sendmail attempts to send the mail. In this way you'll see what the Sendmail processes on both machines are saying to each other as they try to exchange the message.

(5)   If you see a way clear to push the mail through to the intended recipient, perhaps via another system, you can edit the q file in the spool directory, changing the envelope recipient line to a correct one. This is quite reasonable and proper to do. The postal service does it all the time when an address on an envelope is incorrect, and it is sometimes the only way to get the mail through.

Sometimes, in going through the above exercises, you'll notice that a host's Sendmail process is confused about its host name. When you (through `telnet`) or Sendmail connect to another host's Sendmail process, the foreign host's Sendmail announces its system name and some configuration information in what is called the "Sendmail login message." You can often tell from this line whether the foreign host's host-name is set correctly.

If Sendmail is configured or run with an erroneous host name, the infamous "I refuse to talk to myself" error is generated. This is because the foreign Sendmail gets an address that should be local but doesn't match its view of its own name. The alternative is an infinitely long mail loop, so this obscure error message is to be preferred.

9.7.3. Tracing Mail Bounces

On a machine under our management at TIS (we'll call it `important.gov`), we received an example of falsified or spoofed mail that someone had made to look as if it had come from an important person on that machine.[1] This mail didn't constitute a threat and probably wasn't meant to be taken seriously by the recipients. We include this as a real-life example of a mail message that was received and that needed to be traced. Analysis was done for demonstration purposes only, to show how to figure out how and why mail bounced, and to try to trace electronic mail. We don't recommend this type of analysis on all forged e-mail of a non-threatening nature, since the time spent does not justify the benefits gleaned (none).

---

[1] Mail spoofing is easy. Just as it is easy to fake p-mail, it is easy to fake e-mail to look like it came from someone else. The only solution is digital signatures, available with such things as Privacy Enhanced Mail.

We received this mail by accident. The sender intended to mail it to a group of addresses on a mailing list, but an error condition caused it to be routed to us, unbeknownst to the sender. We have changed the names and the message text to protect the foolish. Everything else is unchanged.

Here is spoofed message as originally sent (but with host names changed):

```
Received: from IMPORTAN.GOV (aaaaaa.bbbbb.cccc.dddd.eee) by
    fffff.ggg.dddd.eee with SMTP id AA00559
    (5.65c/IDA-1.4.4 for distrib1@fffff.ggg.dddd.eee);
    Thu, 10 Jun 1993 17:02:17 -0400
Date: Thu, 10 Jun 1993 17:02:17 -0400
From: vip@important.gov
Message-Id: <199306102102.AA00559@fffff.ggg.dddd.eee>
Apparently-To: distrib1@fffff.ggg.dddd.eee

This is an important message .....

Yrs truly,
important person
```

Please notice the first line. A machine, `fffff.ggg.dddd.eee`, received this from another host. The other host claimed to be IMPORTAN.GOV. Notice the misspelling. Someone — probably on `fffff.ggg.dddd.eee` — decided to play a joke. That someone was probably logged on `aaaaaa.bbbbb.cccc.dddd.eee` (see the host name in parentheses).

This person probably did the following:

(1) Connected to the network mail socket on `fffff.ggg.dddd.eee` via telnet.

(2) Specified the host name of his or her host to `fffff` as IMPORTAN.GOV. The mail software took that and then showed — in parentheses — what *it* thought the host name was: `aaaaaa.bbbbb.cccc.dddd.eee`. It told the mail server that it had mail for mailing list `distrib1` on that host and that it was from `vip@important.gov`. The person then typed in the text of the message, but didn't do a great job, since he or she didn't remember to include the (normal but not required) `Subject:` line or a `To:` header line (the Sendmail MTA adds an `Apparently-to:` line when no `To:` line exists, as we've mentioned).

Once the message was sent, the following events occurred:

(1) The mailer on `fffff.ggg.dddd.eee` encountered an error condition. The error message "`Options MUST PRECEDE persons`," is unknown to us, and of no real interest, except that it caused the message to bounce.

```
    . . .
From: Mail Delivery Subsystem <MAILER-DAEMON@fffff.ggg.dddd.eee>
Message-Id: <199306102102.AA00609@fffff.ggg.dddd.eee>
To: vip
Cc: Postmaster@fffff.ggg.dddd.eee
Subject: Returned mail: unknown mailer error 5

    ----- Transcript of session follows -----
mail: Options MUST PRECEDE persons
554 distribl@fffff.ggg.dddd.eee... unknown mailer error 5

    ----- Unsent message follows -----
    . . .
```

When a message is "bounced" as the result of an error it is returned to the sender with information about the problem. As far as the mailer could determine in this circumstance, the sender was vip@important.gov. So, the returned message was sent from the MAILER-DAEMON to Important.Gov for user vip.

(2)   There was no user named vip on the host Important.Gov, so the bounced message was bounced back to the sender, who is in this case, MAILER-DAEMON@fffff.ggg.dddd.eee.

```
    . . .
From: MAILER-DAEMON@important.gov (Mail Delivery Subsystem)
Subject: Returned mail: User unknown
Message-Id: <9306102105.AA01806@important.gov>
To: MAILER-DAEMON@fffff.ggg.dddd.eee

    ----- Transcript of session follows -----
550 <vip@important.gov>... User unknown

    ----- Recipients of this delivery -----
Bounced, cannot deliver:
    <vip@important.gov>

    ----- Unsent message follows -----
    . . .
```

(3)   Finally, the same strange error on the original machine caused mail from our MAILER-DAEMON to their MAILER-DAEMON to bounce back to us and so it got to the system manager on the Important.Gov machine (which is how we got it).

The entire message as received here is shown in Figure 9-4 and Figure 9-5.

```
From MAILER-DAEMON@fffff.ggg.dddd.eee Thu Jun 10 17:06:51 1993
Received: by important.gov (5.65/fma/mjr-120691);
     id AA01824; Thu, 10 Jun 93 17:06:49 -0400
Received: from fffff.ggg.dddd.eee/131.158.51.20 via smap
Received: by fffff.ggg.dddd.eee id AA00630
     (5.65c/IDA-1.4.4 for <MAILER-DAEMON@important.gov>);
     Thu, 10 Jun 1993 17:05:09 -0400
Date: Thu, 10 Jun 1993 17:05:09 -0400
From: Mail Delivery Subsystem <MAILER-DAEMON@fffff.ggg.dddd.eee>
Message-Id: <199306102105.AA00630@fffff.ggg.dddd.eee>
To: MAILER-DAEMON
Cc: Postmaster@fffff.ggg.dddd.eee
Subject: Returned mail: unknown mailer error 5
Status: R

     ----- Transcript of session follows -----
mail: Options MUST PRECEDE persons
554 root... unknown mailer error 5

     ----- Unsent message follows -----
Received: from important.gov by fffff.ggg.dddd.eee
     with SMTP id AA00628
     (5.65c/IDA-1.4.4 for <MAILER-DAEMON@fffff.ggg.dddd.eee>);
     Thu, 10 Jun 1993 17:05:09 -0400
Received: by important.gov (5.65/fma/mjr-120691);
        id AA01806; Thu, 10 Jun 93 17:05:49 -0400
Date: Thu, 10 Jun 93 17:05:49 -0400
From: MAILER-DAEMON@important.gov (Mail Delivery Subsystem)
Subject: Returned mail: User unknown
Message-Id: <9306102105.AA01806@important.gov>
To: MAILER-DAEMON@fffff.ggg.dddd.eee

     ----- Transcript of session follows -----
550 <vip@important.gov>... User unknown

     ----- Recipients of this delivery -----
Bounced, cannot deliver:
   <vip@important.gov>

     ----- Unsent message follows -----
Received: by important.gov (5.65/fma/mjr-120691);
        id AA01804; Thu, 10 Jun 93 17:05:49 -0400
```

Figure 9-4. Bounce, Part 1

```
Received: from fffff.ggg.dddd.eee/131.158.51.20 via smap
Received: from IMPORTAN.GOV (aaaaaa.bbbbb.cccc.dddd.eee)
     by fffff.ggg.dddd.eee id AA00609
     5.65c/IDA-1.4.4 for <vip@important.gov>);
     Thu, 10 Jun 1993 17:02:17 -0400
Date: Thu, 10 Jun 1993 17:02:17 -0400
From: Mail Delivery Subsystem <MAILER-
DAEMON@fffff.ggg.dddd.eee>
Message-Id: <199306102102.AA00609@fffff.ggg.dddd.eee>
To: vip
Cc: Postmaster@fffff.ggg.dddd.eee
Subject: Returned mail: unknown mailer error 5

     ----- Transcript of session follows -----
mail: Options MUST PRECEDE persons
554 distrib1@fffff.ggg.dddd.eee... unknown mailer error 5

     ----- Unsent message follows -----
Received: from IMPORTAN.GOV (aaaaaa.bbbbb.cccc.dddd.eee)
     by fffff.ggg.dddd.eee with SMTP id AA00559
     (5.65c/IDA-1.4.4 for distrib1@fffff.ggg.dddd.eee);
     Thu, 10 Jun 1993 17:02:17 -0400
Date: Thu, 10 Jun 1993 17:02:17 -0400
From: vip@important.gov
Message-Id: <199306102102.AA00559@fffff.ggg.dddd.eee>
Apparently-To: distrib1@fffff.ggg.dddd.eee

This is an important message .....

Yrs truly,
important person
```

Figure 9-5. Bounce, Part 2

9.8. Delivery Options and Queue Management

The configuration file option "d" selects a delivery strategy to be used after a message is received by Sendmail. Note that the delivery decision is made only after a message has been completely received — there is no "cut-through retransmission" involved. When Sendmail has completely received a message, that message is stored in several files in the *queue*, and until Sendmail releases them these files are *locked* against possible processing by a *queue run* (à la "sendmail -q").

There are three delivery options available to Sendmail once it has received an entire message. It can simply exit ("Odq"), in which case the *queue* files will be automatically *unlocked* and the message will be eligible for processing during the next *queue run*. Sendmail can also start an immediate delivery attempt ("Odi"), in which case the process that received the message makes a *routing decision* and enters the *delivery* phase. Finally, Sendmail can create a subprocess (via fork) to attempt a delivery in the *background* ("Odb"). *Background* and *queued* deliveries are useful because the original Sendmail process exits immediately after receiving the message, allowing the process that originally called Sendmail also to exit or otherwise proceed with its business.

On systems that process a large amount of mail, it is important to get the queueing strategy right or your performance will be abysmal. Depending on your kernel, getting the queuing strategy wrong might even crash your machine if you dump enough mail into it all at once.

9.8.1. An Example: UUCP Delivery

When mail comes in via UUCP, it is queued inside the local UUCP subsystem until a periodic daemon called uuxqt runs. The job of uuxqt is to locate all the UUCP jobs for which all the necessary files have arrived and "execute" them, which means to run whatever program the job has stapled to its underwear. For mail jobs, that program is usually rmail, which simply rewrites a few headers and addresses and then runs a sendmail process to actually accept the mail. Now, some instances of UUCP have a way to run multiple uuxqt daemons in parallel, which can be good if your Sendmail is configured with "Odi" ("Ooption delivery immediate"), since it will allow several Sendmails to work on the incoming UUCP traffic simultaneously.

However, many older UUCP implementations do not permit multiple uuxqt processes to run in parallel; and on such systems setting "Odi" is a disaster, because it can take hours for a stack of incoming UUCP mail to be processed. If this is your situation, it is very important to make sure that UUCP's incoming mail is processed with something other than "Odi." However, we recommend against "Odb" ("background"), since this has the effect of starting as many concurrent Sendmail processes as there are incoming UUCP mail messages, and for large numbers of processes this will quickly run your machine out of virtual memory and other vital resources. What's left, then, is "Odi" ("immediate"), which will cause each incoming message to be put into the queue and left there for the next *queue run*, which processes things serially and will therefore not start up *N* processes to handle *N* messages; it will run at most one subprocess at a time. Beware even of "Odq," though, since it essentially turns rmail into a "reformat and copy" operation, and it can end up running you out of disk space if you have more traffic in your UUCP queue than you have free space in your Sendmail queue.

9.8.2. Multiple Strategies

What you will discover if you begin to experiment with various delivery strategies is that no single strategy is right for all of your incoming mail. Consider the case of incoming SMTP mail, which tends *not* to arrive in large blocks as UUCP mail; for SMTP mail it is almost always better to use "Odb," since this lets the sender's SMTP client off the line as soon as possible (thus freeing up system and network resources) and then gives each message a chance to be immediately delivered or forwarded. Since success is hopefully your average case, this means that you get the message out of your queue as soon as possible and the recipient actually receives it as soon as possible. However, because we've determined that UUCP has different queuing requirements, what we need is the ability to use different strategies for different kinds of incoming mail. Can we really do that?

Yes. If you start your SMTP listener from /etc/rc.local with a delivery option different from the one specified in sendmail.cf, then the command line's specification will override the configuration file's. Thus, you could put "Odq" or "Odi" in your sendmail.cf and yet start your listener with the "-odb" option. Mail coming in via SMTP is handled by subprocesses of the listener, so they inherit the delivery strategy from the listener and thus do the right thing. Astute readers will note that the *queue run* is also performed by a subprocess of the listener, and for such subprocesses *background* delivery may not be what you want. Don't worry, be happy, and look at "OY" to see how Sendmail solves this problem.

Mail coming in via UUCP will start a new Sendmail process for each message, and this Sendmail will look at the sendmail.cf file to find its delivery strategy. Thus, UUCP appears poised to do the right thing. However, whatever you specify in the sendmail.cf will also affect original mail messages crossing the boundary from local *user agents* into Sendmail in its capacity as *transport agent*. It is possible, even likely, that your users will complain that because you use "Odi" in your sendmail.cf, they have to wait an irritatingly long time after pressing their Send keys before they are released to do other work. Or, users being the capricious folks they are, they might complain that because you specified "Odq" in your sendmail.cf, they never get to see immediate error messages when they send to a bungled address. Or they might also complain that your "Odq" is enforcing a minimum (average) delay on every message they send. You can't win. Or can you?

Yes, and the solution is not necessarily to reeducate your users. What you can do is get the source to the rmail program and edit, recompile, and reinstall it with explicit code inside to set the delivery option on the command line rmail uses to start its Sendmail subprocess. This allows you to specify the delivery strategy that works best for whatever UUCP you have, without affecting any other kind of incoming (or originating!) mail. Getting the source to rmail is not hard; there are several free versions available and most Sendmail source kits you can get via Anonymous FTP will include at least one and possibly several different rmail sources. We believe it should be possible to specify this without editing source code, but we have no faith that any[2] vendor is going to provide so detailed a management interface.

9.8.3. Other Transport Agents

At least one *user agent* uses SMTP for the submission of original messages to its transport agent. This approach is gaining popularity, as it allows user agents to be programmed without regard to the specific transport agent in use. For example, there are other SMTP listeners available besides Sendmail, and they mostly don't come with a sendmail command for use by user agents, but they will all accept incoming SMTP transactions. There is also at least one *transport agent* known to us that, after it receives a DECnet mail message, uses SMTP to submit the message to the local transport. The catch is that it uses SMTP over *pipes*, by starting up a Sendmail sub-process with the "-bs" option. Such agents, if you can get their source code, can be modified exactly as we recommend doing for rmail, which will let you get your delivery strategy set up correctly for each kind of mail your system receives.

---

[2] Note that BSD/OS from BSDi provides /etc/uucp/uuxqt_hook, so we could be wrong.

10

Miscellaneous Factoids

No book on Sendmail would be complete without a chapter full of odds and ends. There are many facts about Sendmail that are important to some people but not to others; this chapter contains the briefest smattering of these facts.

It often happens that there are tens or hundreds of hosts running Sendmail, all of which are maintained by the same small, overworked, underpaid group of system administrators. You can strike terror into one of these poor souls by asking her how many different `sendmail.cf` files are running around on the network, and, if she found a bug in the original `sendmail.cf` file from which most of these were cloned, how long it would take her to propagate the fix outward to all hosts. If you ask her this question and she begins her answer with a smug smile, you are probably about to hear about m4 or Ease.

10.1. m4

m4 is a macro processor available on most UNIX systems. One of its main uses is to make an application's input or configuration files more readable or more tunable. Besides being able to define macros that are expanded in a file, m4 supports conditional expansion, arithmetic, file manipulation, and some specialized string processing. m4 is the mother of all macro preprocessors, at least by today's standards, and though it has at least its quota of warts, it is shipped with most UNIX-like operating systems. Sometimes being there is all it takes to win.

Many of the so-called "`sendmail.cf` construction kits" in the world use m4 as their engine. With m4, you can create a template file, or set of files, which is processed into a working `sendmail.cf` for each host or kind of host on your network. If you want to fix some bug or change some behaviour in all of your machines, you make a change to the template file and recreate all your host-specific `sendmail.cf` files with one happy little `make` command in the master source directory.

m4 has a leg up on its competitors for this job principally because it has no relevant competitors, but also because it had this job when Sendmail was first written and continues to be the `sendmail.cf` construction tool for the latest Berkeley Sendmail as of this writing. Some folks have been known to use cpp, the C preprocessor, but to do this you must go to extraordinary lengths to convert your working `sendmail.cf` files into the beginning cpp template. For example, Sendmail's comment character for `sendmail.cf` is a pound sign (#) and cpp uses this same character to introduce its commands (`#define`, `#ifdef`, et al.)

We will not present any specific examples of using m4 for a configuration system, since there are so many such examples in the world and they are each highly complex, very subtle, and well documented in their accompanying README files. Generally you will find a few template files that are "included" by a per-host or per-host-type *driver* file; the driver file defines certain high level *macros* that control the expansion of the template files into the kind of `sendmail.cf` file that you want.

It is rare that Sendmail's ability to discover the name of the host it runs on, or the name of that host's parent domain, is good enough to allow you to run the same `sendmail.cf` file on more than one host. Sendmail's abilities in this area depend upon, among other things, whether you are running the same version of Sendmail on all your hosts. Since every vendor has its own idea of how to initialize $w and maybe $=w or $D, the chances of running a given `sendmail.cf` on more than one kind of host are at best dim — unless you build your own Sendmail from source, as we do. The best you can do is try to make your `sendmail.cf` as insensitive as possible to variables such as its host's name, and often this is possible if you qualify your addresses with some shared, generic domain name rather than letting each individual host "tack on" and later remove its own name.

Assuming that you have the same Sendmail version running everywhere (which means either that you built it yourself or that all your hosts run the same brand and version of operating system), or that you can write `sendmail.cf` files which are not sensitive to particulars such as local host names, then you can try to build one `sendmail.cf` for all of your workstations and another for all of your spoolers and another for all of your relays. But be prepared for Sendmail and your vendor to gang up on you and club you senseless with their mutual misunderstanding of the fairly reasonable thing that you want to do.

Be prepared, also, for m4 to be less than entirely cooperative. m4 is a purist's macro processor, and it is extremely literal about doing exactly what you've asked of it, no matter how silly. For example, while many macro processors "eat" the *newlines* that terminate its commands, m4 doesn't do this because *newlines* are not the terminators. Have a look at this:

```
define(MyDomain,al.org)
```

Intuitively, a line like this one should define the macro MyDomain to have the value al.org with no side effects. Au contraire. It does define that macro to that value, but it also inserts a newline into your output file at the point after this define. Why? Because you put one there. There *is* a newline after the ")", right? If you want m4 to elide that newline, you need to tell it explicitly, as in

```
define(MyDomain,al.org)dnl
```

m4 predefines the dnl macro to be a command that *D*eletes up to the following *N*ew-*L*ine. Here, there is nothing following the dnl except a newline; however, you could introduce an m4 level "comment" in this way, as in

```
define(MyDomain,al.org)dnl     my domain name
```

This kind of comment will not appear in the generated sendmail.cf file, which can be useful if the comment is relevant to m4's work but will be irrelevant and confusing in the resulting sendmail.cf file.

Generally, you should read all available documentation for m4. You should run some examples in a terminal window so that you have a basic idea of what a macro processor is and what it does, and then you should proceed very, very carefully with whatever m4-based "sendmail.cf construction kit" you wish to try. It's a good idea to read the generated sendmail.cf files at first to make sure you're getting what you expect.

10.2. Ease

When Ease was last published on the Usenet newsgroup comp.sources.unix, the moderator of that newsgroup added the following introductory comments:

> If you would like to write:
> ```
> if ( exactly_one ! one_or_more )      /* uucphost!user */
>         return (RULESET_6 ($2<@$1."uucp">));
> ```
> ...instead of:
> ```
> R$-!$+              $@$>6$2<@$1.uucp>            uucphost!user
> ```
> ...then you want this package. If you don't understand the above, you may want to unpack this and look at it, since it provides an excellent high-level way of looking at the otherwise inscrutable sendmail.cf philosophy.

We agree completely with these comments.[1] Ease is to sendmail.cf as a compiler is to an assembler. (And come to think of it, don't you agree that sendmail.cf's format and philosophy closely resemble assembly language?)

---

[1] which makes sense if you know who the comp.sources.unix moderator was. (-:

Ease's advantage over editing raw `sendmail.cf` files is that the syntax is expansive and easy on the eyes. Compare

```
R$*<@[$+]>$*    $:$1<@$[[$2]$]>$3    lookup addr
```

against

```
/* lookup addr */
if ( zero_or_more <@[ one_or_more ]> zero_or_more )
        next ($1<@ canon ([$2])>$3);
```

and you might agree. Since you can translate your existing `sendmail.cf` files into Ease and then translate them back and `diff` them just to make sure nothing was changed or lost, it's pretty easy to get started with Ease.

Ease's advantage over m4 is that it has all the same macro and "file include" capabilities but none of the "purisms" that make m4 so darned hard to use.

The reason that Ease is not a big player in the mainstream Sendmail community is that there are many, many variants of Sendmail and each one has been extended by some well meaning (we're sure) vendor or hacker, with the result that there are a lot of `sendmail.cf` syntax extensions loose in the world of which Ease is ignorant. Keeping Ease up to date with all of them would be pretty hard to do, though any reader of this book could help out by using Ease, adding to it whatever syntax extensions his or her local Sendmail has, and mailing source patches back to the current maintainer of Ease.[2]

Try Archie (see Appendix K) for information on getting a copy of Ease.

10.3. `rdist`

Generating all your `sendmail.cf` files from a single source pool, using a tool like m4 or Ease is a good thing to do if you can get over the hump of getting it going for the first time. However, you will still need some way to get the generated `sendmail.cf` files out to the hosts where they need to run. To be sure, you can (and many people do) install them by hand, but this is prohibitively difficult when you have hundreds or thousands of hosts to maintain. Generally, the more hosts you have, the less experienced and less technically adept the average user seems to be. Therefore you can't appeal to your user community to help you out with this one; what you need is some technology.

---

[2] Ease is currently maintained by Bruce G. Barnett, and was originally written by James S. Schoner and Arnold D. Robbins.

Chances are good that you already have some kind of administrative file update mechanism to keep your distributed /etc/hosts, /etc/passwd, and other files synchronized on various sets of your hosts. If you don't, you should consider doing so, since once you have the basic mechanism set up it is trivial to add another file (or a whole directory) to any update mechanism you use. It is particularly easy to do this if you use rdist, but we recognize that some vendors recommend the use of NFS, at least on diskless workstations, to point individual hosts' configuration files directly at master copies of them. Use NFS at your own discretion; we believe in autonomy of users and workstations, and we believe that both should continue to get work done even when one of your major file servers takes a power hit.

rdist isn't hard to get running. Once you have it running well manually, you'll set up a Cron entry to run the rdist for you periodically, or you'll have your config-uration source directory's Makefile do it for you whenever a new sendmail.cf file is made. Let's take a look at a simple Distfile, which is the configuration file for rdist, in Figure 10-1. This example makes some simplifying assumptions: that your vendor's Sendmail (or the one you installed) works together with your gener-ated sendmail.cf files so that you can share a configuration file among many hosts of the same type; that your Sendmail uses frozen configuration files; that your rdist will chdir you to the path shown in the install line, and that your hosts are named as shown. Your mileage *will* (not "may") vary.

If the Distfile shown in Figure 10-1 is run in a source directory containing a "sendmail.cf construction kit" that generates files workstation.cf, server.cf, and gateway.cf, the effect should be that these files will be copied to

---

```
WORKSTATIONS = ( torrey gnomea pablo )
SERVERS = ( jove acetes saturn )
GATEWAYS = ( hydra wombat cerberus )

SENDMAIL_CF = ( workstation.cf server.cf gateway.cf )
FILES = ( ${SENDMAIL_CF} )

${FILES} -> ${HOSTS}
  install /etc;
special workstation.cf "cp workstation.cf sendmail.cf; sendmail -bz";
special server.cf      "cp server.cf sendmail.cf; sendmail -bz";
special gateway.cf     "cp workstation.cf sendmail.cf; sendmail -bz";
```

Figure 10-1. Sample Distfile

---

the hosts shown in the sample `Distfile` and copied to the `sendmail.cf` name; the frozen configuration file will then be recreated based on this new file. Note that for completeness, the running Sendmail listener ("`-bd  -q30m`") should be restarted. However, most Sendmails don't create a `sendmail.pid` file, and it is therefore very difficult to find them reliably. It is usually sufficient to refreeze the configuration file — every host reboots sooner or later. Depending on the level of your ambition and your Sendmail's capabilities, you could arrange for a restart. This technique will not be shown here, since mistakes can often lead to killing process 0, which on a UNIX host is a very bad thing. Our lawyers insist that you learn this technique without our help.

As always, you should read the `rdist` man page to learn more about it. If your computer doesn't have `rdist`, don't dispair — like most of the useful software on your average UNIX host, `rdist`'s source code is freely redistributable. Look in Appendix K to find out where to get it.

10.4. Mailer Flag C

As long as we're on the subject of miscellaneous items that don't really belong any-where else, let's consider the implications of the `C` mailer flag. Assume the following mail message:

```
From: foo@bar
To: blat@zowie
Cc: fnarg

splut
```

If this message is sent using a `sendmail.cf` file that specifies no "`C`" flag on any mailer definition, through a command such as

```
sendmail -froot@zippo vixie < /tmp/msg
```

(assuming that `vixie` is the user that should receive the test message and that `/tmp/msg` is the file you stored the test message in), then the message will be delivered with no surprises:

```
Return-Path: root@zippo
Date: Wed, 28 Oct 92 08:22:54 -0800
Message-Id: <9210281622.AA04721@cognition.al.org>
From: foo@bar
To: blat@zowie
Cc: fnarg

splut
```

If, on the other hand, the definition in sendmail.cf of the mailer that will be used to reach the envelope sender (which we set to root@zippo using the -f command line option), contains the "c" mailer flag in its "Flags=" clause, then the message will be delivered with a twist:

```
Return-Path: root@zippo
Date: Wed, 28 Oct 92 08:36:32 -0800
Message-Id: <9210281636.AA04887@cognition.al.org>
From: foo@bar
To: blat@zowie
Cc: fnarg@zippo

splut
```

Note that the Cc: header has an @zippo on it, even though none was present in the input. The "c" mailer flag is designed to let your Sendmail make up for deficiencies in other hosts' Sendmails, the assumption being that a Sendmail should not send out mail with unqualified header recipients unless the envelope sender is likewise unqualified.

The "c" mailer flag is dangerous and you shouldn't use it — ever. There are two reasons for this: First, if there is a bug in someone else's Sendmail, that Sendmail should be fixed, not yours. Fixing a bug in one place is always better than fixing it in 1,000,000 places. Second, the assumption made by the "c" option is incorrect: In mail sent inside a mail cluster, headers *will not* be qualified but envelopes *will* be. As with many other well intentioned fix-ups, the "c" mailer flag solves a problem that should be solved elsewhere and differently, while simultaneously causing a new problem that can't be solved at all.

Appendix A

Command Line Arguments

Arguments may be passed to sendmail on the command line. A list of arguments follows.

-b*mode*

> Set the sendmail operation mode. Possible modes are

Mode	Meaning
a	ARPAnet mode
d	Run in the background as a daemon
i	Write out the `aliases` database (same as `newaliases`)
m	Default mode (deliver)
p	Show information about the mail queue
s	Run server SMTP
t	Run in test mode
v	Run in address verification mode (doesn't do mail delivery)
z	Create the frozen configuration file `sendmail.fc`

-C[*filename*]

> Tells sendmail to use a different configuration file from the real one. This is usually used with -bt when testing a new configuration file. Some versions of Sendmail interpret a lone -C (with no file name) as -Csendmail.cf (send-mail.cf in the current working directory.)

-c ·

> The same as the argument -oc, which turns on the c option (see Appendix B).

-d*level*

> Sets the debugging level as explained in the chapter on maintenance and testing.

-e*mode*

> The same as the argument -oe*mode*, which turns on the e option with the given *mode* (see Appendix B).

-F*name*

> Sets the full name of the sender of the mail to *name*. The default is to use the GCOS field from the sender's `passwd` file entry.

> `sendmail -fvixie@pa.frobozz.com -F`

> sets the sender's address to `vixie@pa.frobozz.com`, as above, and the full name of the sender to "`Paul Vixie`".

-f*address*

> Sets the sender address to *address*. Only a "trusted user" may use this option unless the *address* is the user's. This is most often used when a message is being delivered via a mailer running as a special user, such as `daemon` or `uucp`. The reason only "trusted users" may use this option is that it is otherwise too easy to forge mail (that is, send mail that appears to come from someone else — a popular sport at the growing number of K12 schools on the Internet).

> `sendmail -fvixie@pa.frobozz.com` *user@domain*

> sets the sender to `vixie@pa.frobozz.com`. If -f*address* is not given, Sendmail extracts this information from the header or, if that fails, by getting the user's name from the operating system's login records.

> Note that the presence of this option and the "trusted user" restrictions do not prevent forgeries, which are still trivially possible via `telnet`.

-h*number*

> Sets the "hop count" to *number*. The hop count is the number of systems the message has passed through, determined by the number of `Received` headers added to the message. If the hop count reaches *number*, the message is returned to the sender with an error indicating "`too many hops`". Sendmail is compiled with a default hop count to use when the h flag is not specified.

-I

> Initialize the `aliases` database upon startup. This is equivilent to -bi except that with -I, Sendmail continues to execute and process its other arguments after initializing the database.

-i

> The same as the argument -oi, which turns on the i option (see Appendix B).

-m

> The same as the argument -om, which turns on the m option (see Appendix B).

-n

> Turns off Sendmail's aliasing mechanisms (`/etc/aliases` and `.forward` files).

-o*Xvalue*

> Sets option *X* to value *value*. The full set of options is described in Appendix

B. This command line argument provides a way to override option values as specified in `sendmail.cf`.

-q*time*

Runs the mail queue, trying to send mail. If the optional time is given, when Sendmail has gone through the queue, it will wait until that time interval and run the queue again. If no time is given, Sendmail only runs through it once.

```
sendmail -q1h
```

says "Try to run through the mail queue every hour." Other examples are

Time	Meaning
30m	30 minutes
5d	5 days
2h	2 hours
1h15m	1 hour, 15 minutes (75 minutes)

-s

The same as the argument -os, which turns on the s option (see Appendix B).

-T*value*

The same as the argument -oT*value*, which sets the T option to the given *value* (see Appendix B).

-t

Reads header lines from the message (for To:, Cc:, and Bcc: lines) and uses that data as the envelope information for the message delivery. Any addresses on the command line are treated as addresses to skip.

-v

Turns on verbose mode. See the comments on option v in Appendix B.

Appendix B

Configuration Options

Configuration options, as we have seen, may be set from the command line using the -o argument flag or in the sendmail.cf file. Usually, a Sendmail option cannot be set by anyone but a trusted user.

A*file*

Uses *file* as the aliases database.

a*min*

Waits up to *min* minutes for the aliases database to be rebuilt, and if it hasn't been rebuilt by then, rebuilds it. This is to allow for editing and rebuilding of an aliases database on a running system.

B*char*

Unquoted spaces in addresses are replaced by the character *char* if set.

c

If a mailer is marked as being expensive (in its mailer definition in the Sendmail configuration file), don't connect immediately. Instead, wait until the mail is picked up for delivery in a normal run of the mail queue.

C*number*

Sets the checkpoint value. For a message with multiple addressees, after *number* connections have been made, Sendmail updates the information in the qf file as to which addresses have not been tried and which addresses have been queued. Suppose a message has an addressee list of 100 addresses and the message has been sent to 90 of the addresses when the system crashes. If the checkpoint value is zero (the default), or if the value is 90 or greater, the message will be resent to all 100 addressees. A small value for the checkpoint is sensible even though for very long address lists it could add a slight delay to the overall processing time.

dmode

Sets the delivery mode, one of

Mode	Meaning
i	Interactive
b	Background
q	Queue the message for later delivery

D

Tells Sendmail to rebuild the `aliases` database if necessary. It checks the creation dates of the ASCII `aliases` file and the database version of the file. If the ASCII file (for example, `/etc/aliases`) is newer than the database files (`/etc/aliases.dir` and `/etc/aliases.pag`), and if this option is set, Sendmail will rebuild the database.

emode

Sets the error disposal mode. The possibilities are

Mode	Meaning
p	Print the error messages (default) on standard output.
q	Return status on exit but don't print error messages.
m	Mail back errors to the sender (even if the sender is logged in).
w	Write back errors to the sender (mail if user not logged in).
e	Mail back errors and always return 0 as if no error occured.

f

Retains (or generates) the UNIX-style `From` envelope lines.

Fmode

The file mode to use when creating temporary files.

gid

Sets the default group id for mailers to run as.

Hfile

Specifies the Sendmail help file for SMTP sessions.

i

If set, Sendmail ignores dots in incoming messages.

Llevel

Sets the default log level for `syslog` logging.

m

Sends to the sender also, even if the sender is in an alias expansion.

Mxvalue

Sets the value of a macro; in a configuration file, the line `OMUblat` is identical in function to the line `DUblat` with the dubious exception that the "D" line will process formatted control characters such as `\r` (carriage return, ASCII

0x0D), \n (line feed, ASCII 0x0A), \f (form feed, ASCII 0x0C), and \b (back space, ASCII 0x08), and that processing of "D" lines stops when the first comma not surrounded by quotes is found; none of this magic happens for OM lines. M is intended for command line use only.

n*value*

Checks addresses for form and validity on the RHS during a rebuild of an aliases database.

o

If set, the logic to parse old format addresses is included, with space between addresses instead of commas.

P*address*

Whenever mail is bounced by the local Sendmail, a copy of the bounced message is sent to the Postmaster at the *address* given.

q*factor*

If set, Sendmail uses *factor* in conjunction with the *lav* value from the x option, to determine the priority of a message in the queue. Messages of low priority will remain in the queue if the load average of the system is equal to or greater than the value of *lav* while messages of higher priority may be sent if the load average has not yet reached the upper critical bound as specified by the *lav* value from option x. The default value of *factor* is 10000.

Q*dir*

Sets the mail queue directory.

r*time*

If set, network reads will be terminated after this time interval. For example, if *time* is 1h, the timeout interval is one hour.

s

Forces Sendmail to copy each message to the queue directory prior to processing. The messages are not removed from the queue until delivery has been made. If this option is not set, Sendmail reads messages directly into volatile memory where they are lost if a system crash occurs during processing.

S*file*

The location of the Sendmail statistics file (for example, /etc/sendmail.st.

T*time*

Sets the queue timeout. For example, if *time* is 3d, mail left in the queue longer than three days will be returned to the Sender.

u*id*

Option u sets the default userid for mailers.

v

Run in verbose mode. Not as verbose as debug mode, but Sendmail will let you see what is going on and watch the interaction with other MTAs with which it connects. It should only be run from the command line.

x*lav*

> When the system load average is greater than *lav*, messages get queued instead of sent. Sendmail will not try to send them until the load average is below this value.

x*lav*

> When the load average exceeds *this* load average, the running Sendmail daemon refuses any attempts to connect to it.

y*fact*

> In the formula

```
size + CreationTime - (Class * ClassFactor)
    + (#Recipients * RecipientFactor)
```

> *fact* is plugged in for the `RecipientFactor`. The more recipients, the higher the penalty.

Y

> If set, Sendmail will deliver each job run from the queue in a separate process. The Y option is used to help systems with low memory cope with the large amounts of memory Sendmail uses when running the queue. This is normally not a problem on modern computers.

z*fact*

> In the above formula, *fact* is plugged in for `ClassFactor`. Messages with a higher precedence get better treatment.

z*fact*

> Added to the priority of a message every time Sendmail attempts to send the message and fails. This effectively decreases the priority of the message.

Appendix C

Mailer Flags

The following flags may be set in the mailer description. They tell Sendmail what is expected by the individual mailers.

B

> For use with BSMTP (Batched SMTP) in IDA Sendmail and derivatives. B tells Sendmail not to read replies to SMTP commands but to assume that they all work. This is used when creating a BSMTP envelope around a message.

C

> Tells Sendmail that the envelope sender's domain, if any, should be added to any header recipient that doesn't already have one.

D

> The mailer wants a Date: header line.

E

> Any lines in the body of the message that begin with the string From will have a > added to the beginning of the line. The > is not automatically stripped off. Its purpose is to prevent a mail UA from reading a line beginning with From as the beginning of a new mail message.

e

> The mailer is expensive to connect to. Always queue the mail rather than sending it immediately. The e flag is used in conjunction with option c (see Appendix B).

F

> The mailer wants a From: header line.

f

> The mailer needs an "-f*sender*" argument passed so it will know who sent the mail.

h

> The mailer cares about upper case in host names. Sendmail shouldn't change the case.

I

> The mailer will be speaking SMTP to another Sendmail process. The I flag is used for efficiency, but is not needed, and it requires knowledge of the remote host.

L

> Line-length limiting is expected for this mailer (RFC 821). High-order bits are stripped as well.

l

> Tells Sendmail that this mailer is going to make final local delivery. This has some implications. It is in the local mailer that Return-receipt-to: headers and owner-aliases will work. If it is a local mailer and Sendmail sees a Return-receipt-to: header, a delivery receipt is returned to the address on that header line.

M

> The mailer wants a Message-Id: header line.

m

> Tells Sendmail that the mailer can send to multiple users on the same host with one transaction. This flag is used during the grouping or bundling of mail that Sendmail goes through as it readies mail for transfer. If this flag is set, it means that if there is a message for multiple addressees on a remote host, only one copy of the message need be sent, with the whole list of intended addressees on that host attached.

n

> If set, tells Sendmail not to insert a UNIX-style From line on the top of the message. This option is needed for UUCP, local, file, or program mailers, but not for SMTP or MAIL11.

P

> The mailer wants a Return-Path: line.

p

> If set, Sendmail will use the return-path in the SMTP MAIL From: command when transferring the message.

r

> Similar to the f flag, except Sendmail puts "-*rremoteuser*" on the argument list.

S

> Don't reset the userid before calling the mailer. Normally, Sendmail resets the userid of the running process to the user who initiated mail (in the case of locally generated mail). This flag is used for special cases or special mailers where the mail administrator really needs to override this feature.

s

> If set, Sendmail strips quotes off of the address before calling the mailer.

U

The mailer wants UNIX-style `From` lines with "`Remote from`" information. (required by some UUCP implementations).

u

The mailer cares about upper case in user names. Sendmail shouldn't change the case.

X

The mailer uses the hidden dot algorithm[1] as specified in RFC 821.

x

The mailer wants a `Full-Name:` header line.

---

[1]A line beginning with a dot will have an extra dot prepended. Since a period on a line by itself terminates the message, this algorithm makes sure that the message will not be prematurely ended. The extra dot is stripped off at the other end.

Appendix D

Sample Sendmail.cf

This is the sendmail.cf file used in our walkthrough. All comments are attached. This is *not* a model configuration file that you should run on your computer, unless your computer and its network are exactly the same as the ones we use.

```
############################################################
############################################################
###
###                SENDMAIL CONFIGURATION FILE
###
### WRL internal version -- works on servers or workstations
###
### Paul Vixie, forked off on 9-December-90
### Paul Vixie, major MAIL11/MR work on 17-July-1991
### Paul Vixie, Todd Kaehler and Fred Avolio: parameterized, Aug92
###
### $Header: /usr/src/kjs-930504a/RCS/book.cf,v1.11 1993/08/05 21:53:43
###
############################################################
############################################################

## predefined
#   $y decnet node name (if known) (if running a recent binary)
#   $w fully-qualified hostname
#   $j same as $w (except IDA, which is all-lower-case,
#                  strip-at-first-dot)
##

############################################################
###        local info
############################################################

# parent domain
DPFROBOZZ.COM
```

```
# my domain
DNDCO.$P

# name exported on external internet mail
DW$N

# my official hostname
Dj$w.$N

#   $=J[.$P] is gatewayed through $J or sent via DECNET/MAIL11
#   if $J ($K) is undefined; will just use MX records (i.e. $#smtp)
#   if set to $j will cause mail to be sent via mail11 from this host
#
# Easynet/Mail11
#
# (DNET is hardcoded here because DEC's mail11d generates it; $=J should not
#   include $E or $F since these are likely to be multi-token which only IDA
#   can handle in class matches. UTK Mail11D generates .DNET or .ENET (dependi
#   on your compile-time configuration).   $=J must include whatever your Mail
#   is generating which in the case of UTK with .ENET would make you want to
#   set your ENET to ENET.)
#
CJDNET ENET
DJdecnet-relay.$N
DEENET
#
# UUCP
#DUMy-UUCP-Name
#
#CwMy Nicknames
# aliases at the $P level -- we think we are authoritative for these
#
Cd

#
# usernames which will be @host qualified on outbound localdom mail
#
CNroot news uucp mailer-daemon rdist nobody daemon

#
# trash top level domains -- don't use $[...$] on names ending with these
#
CTUUCP USENET ENET

############################################################
#
#   General configuration information
#
############################################################

##########################
###    Special macros    ###
```

```
##########################

# my name
DnMAILER-DAEMON
# UNIX header format
DlFrom $g  $d
# delimiter (operator) characters
Do.:%@!^=/[]
# format of a total name
Dq$?x$x $.<$g>
#Dq$g$?x ($x)$.
DV05AUG93-fma/vix-1.1
# SMTP login message
De$j Sendmail $v ($V) $b


##################
###   Options   ###
##################

# wait 5 minutes for newaliases to complete
Oa
# location of alias file
OA/etc/aliases
# default delivery mode (deliver in background)
Odbackground
# temporary file mode
OF0600
# default UID
Ou1
# default GID
Og1
# location of help file
OH/usr/lib/sendmail.hf
# log level
OL9
# include sender if she's on an alias to which she's sending
Om
# queue directory
OQ/var/spool/mqueue
# read timeout -- violates protocols
Or1h
# status file
OS/etc/sendmail.st
# queue up everything before starting transmission
Os
# use separate envelope/header rewriting rulesets (IDA)
O/
# default timeout interval
OT3d
# load average for forcing "Odq" behaviour
Ox20
# load average for refusing connections
```

```
OX12

###############################
###    Message precedences    ###
###############################

Pfirst-class=0
Pspecial-delivery=100
Pjunk=-100

#########################
###    Trusted users    ###
#########################

Troot daemon uucp news avolio

############################
###    Format of headers    ###
############################

H?P?Return-Path: <$g>
HReceived: by $j; id $i; $b
H?D?Resent-Date: $a
H?D?Date: $a
H?F?Resent-From: $q
H?F?From: $q
H?x?Full-Name: $x
HSubject:
H?M?Resent-Message-Id: <$t.$i@$j>
H?M?Message-Id: <$t.$i@$j>

##########################
###    Rewriting rules    ###
##########################


###############################
#   Sender Field Pre-rewriting   #
###############################
S1
# empty

#################################
#   Recipient Field Pre-rewriting   #
#################################
S2
# empty

#########################
#   Name Canonicalization   #
#########################
S3
```

```
# handle "from:<>" special case
R<>             $@@                     turn into magic token

# simplest case, after an empty address, is a single token
R$-             $@$1

# route-addr's look canonical but aren't
R<@$+:$+>$*      @$1:$2                 unfocus <route-addr>

# already canonical?
R$*<@$+>$*       $@$>7$1<@$2>$3    idempotency is good

# basic textual canonicalization -- note lack of RFC733 heuristic here
R$*<$+>$*        $2                     basic RFC822 parsing

# make sure <@a,@b,@c:user@d> syntax is easy to parse -- undone later
R@$+,$+          @$1:$2                 change all "," to ":"
R@$+:$+          $@$>7<@$1>:$2          handle <route-addr>

# more miscellaneous cleanup
R$+:$*;$*        $@$1:$2;$3             list syntax
R$+@$+           $:$1<@$2>              focus on domain
R$+<$+@$+>       $1$2<@$3>              move gaze right
R$+@$+<@$+>      $1%$2<@$3>             a@b@c@d ->a%b%c@d

#
# DECNet.  First turn all these addresses into :: form then back to @-form
# with a .pseudodomain approporiate to the protocol (phaseIV/phaseV/MR)
#

# (phase IV)
R$+<@$+.$E>      $@$>7$1<@$2.$E>           already encapsulated IV
R$+<@$-.$-.$=J>  $:$2.$3::$1               u@aa.nnn.DNET
R$+<@$-.$=J>     $:$2::$1                  u@node.DNET

# (all decnet addresses
#   are now in ::-format,
#   including the ones
#   that came in that way;
#   and the .DNET is gone.)

# things that are still in @-form are ready to eat
R$+<@$+>         $@$>7$1<@$2>             now canonical

# (phase IV conversions)
R$-.$-::$+       $@$>7$3<@$1.$2.$E>       numeric decnet addr
R$-::$+          $@$>7$2<@$1.$E>          h::u -> u@h.pseudodom

# UUCP conversions
R$-.$+!$+        $@$>7$3<@$1.$2>          host.domain!user
R$-!$+           $@$>7$2<@$1.UUCP>        resolve uucp names
```

```
# convert rightmost % to @ (ruleset 7 has the rest of the magic for this)
R$+%$+              $@$>7$1<@$2>              user%host

# (ruleset 3 ends here.  we don't exit through
#   $>7 here as with the other exits from ruleset 3
#   since we only exit through S7 when we make a
#   change.)

##### special local conversions (exit path from S3)
S7
R$*<@$+%$+>$*      $1%$2<@$3>$4              move @ right after %
R$*<@$+.$E>$*      $@$1<@$2.$E.$P>$3         hide .$E under $P
R$*<@$->$*         $@$1<@$2.$N>$3            qualify hostnames


################################
#  Final Output Post-rewriting  #
################################
S4

R@                 $@                       handle <> error addr
R$*<$+>$*          $1$2$3                   defocus
R@$+:$+:$+         @$1,$2:$3                <route-addr> canonical
R@$+:$+            $@<@$1:$2>               route-addr needs <>


################################
#  (IDA) header senders        #
################################
S5
R$+                $@$>1$1                  same as envelope


################################
#  (IDA) header recipients     #
################################
S6
R$+                $@$>2$1                  same as envelope


################################
#  Utility: strip local domain  #
################################

# this is necessarily tricky.  S0 needs to strip off the local host(s) and
# it may take several passes to do that (consider $-%$j%$j%$j or $U!$-@$j).
# this requires iterate-until-no-change, which is a semantic not directly
# provided by sendmail.  sendmail does permit recursion, though, which we
# use.  S0 calls S8, which calls itself whenever it makes a change, else falls
# out the bottom when it has nothing left to strip.
#
# S8 starts by calling S3 since on the subsequent recursive calls, a change
# will have been made and the canonicalization will have been lost.  we would
# like to use $>8$>3 but that doesn't work the way you'd expect.  the cost
# here is that S3 gets called once at the top even though S3 was called before
# S0 so there's nothing for it to do.  this is why S3 must be idempotent and
```

```
# also why S3's "no change needed" condition is so close to its top.

S8

R$+                     $:$>3$1                 needed for recursions

R$*<@$j>$*              $:$1<@>$2               @myfqdm
R$*<@$=w>$*             $:$1<@>$3               @my alias
R$*<@$=w.$N>$*          $:$1<@>$3               @my alias

# next two lines only used if have aliases for all
R$*<@$N>$*              $:$1<@>$2               @mydomain
R$*<@$=d.$P>$*          $:$1<@>$3               @codomain
R$*<@$y.$E.$P>$*        $:$1<@>$2               myname:: (IV)
R$*<@$U.UUCP>$*         $:$1<@>$2               myuucpname!
# here's where we recurse if a change was made
R<@>:$*                 $@$>8$1                 localhost/route-addr
R$*<@>$*                $@$>8$1$2               localhost
#######################################
#  Utility: canonicalize local domain  #
#######################################
S9

R$*<@$->$*              $:$1<@$2.$N>$3          qualify
R$*<@$+.$=T>$*          $@$1<@$2.$3>$4          trash pseudodom, leave alone
R$*<@$+.$=T.$P>$*       $@$1<@$2.$3.$P>$4       qualified trash, leave alone

###########################################################
###########################################################
#####
#####                    RULESET 0
#####
###########################################################
###########################################################

S0

# special cases
#
R@                      $#local $:$n                    handle <> form
R$*<@[$+]>$*            $#smtp $@[$2] $:$1<@[$2]>$3     numeric internet spec

# localize if possible (rip off @DOMAINs for which we are authoritative)
#
R$*<@$+>$*              $:$>8$1<@$2>$3

# DECNet/Mail11
#
# (phase IV)
R$*<@$+.$E.$P>          $:$2@@$1<@$2.$E.$P>             dup nodename; add @@
R$+@@$+<@$+>            $:$?J$1@@$2%$3<@$J>$|$1@@$2<@$3>$.      mk @relay or lv alone
R$+@@$+%$+<@$j>         $#mail11 $@$1 $:$1::$2          them is us; use mail11
```

```
R$+@@$+%$+<@$J>        $#smtp1 $@$J $:$2<@$3>              undo damage; send now
R$+@@$+%$+<@$+>        $:$2<@$3>                           undo $?J damage
R$+@@$+<@$+>           $:$2<@$3>                           undo !$?J damage

R$+.USENET            $:$1.USENET<@usenet.$N>  groupname.USENET

R$*<@$-.UUCP>          $#smtp $@uucp-relay.$N $:$2!$1<@uucp-relay.$N>

# Fake hosts in my domain
#
R$+<@POP>             $#pop $@$j $:$1                     username@POP

# Real hosts in my domain
#
R$*<@$*$N>$*           $#smtp1 $@$2$N $:$1<@$2$N>$3    our domain; no gw
#R$*<@$*$N>$*          $#smtp1 $@relay.$N $:$1<@$2$N>$3  our domain w/ gw

# Parent domain
#
R$*<@$*$P>$*           $#smtp $@$2$P $:$1<@$2$P>$3      our top domain; no gw
#R$*<@$*$P>$*          $#smtp $@relay.$P $:$1<@$2$P>$3 our top domain w/ gw

# Nonlocal mail
#
R$*<@$+>$*             $#smtp $@relay.$N $:$1<@$2>$3    use gateway
#R$*<@$+>$*            $#smtp $@$2 $:$1<@$2>$3          go direct

# Local mail
#

R$+.POP              $#pop $@$j $:$1                     username.POP

R$+                  $#local $:$1                        must be local

############################################################
############################################################
#####
#####              Local, POP and Program mailers
#####
############################################################
############################################################

Mlocal,    P=/bin/mail, F=rlsDFMmn, S=10, R=20, A=mail -d $u
Mprog,     P=/bin/sh,   F=lsDFM,    S=10, R=20, A=sh -c $u
Mpop,      P=/usr/lib/mh/spop, F=nsmFDM, S=10, R=20, A=pop $u

S10
R@         $n                                errors to mailer-daemon

S20
```

```
###########################################################
###########################################################
#####
#####          SMTP to hosts inside the local domain
#####
###########################################################
###########################################################

Msmtpl,      P=[IPC], F=mDFMuX, S=11, R=21, A=IPC $h, E=\r\n

# (we pull off the local hostname in all cases, and then selectively add it
#  back on. we would add it back if the aliases aren't shared across all
#  hosts in this domain, or if the user is root or one of the others that
#  we want to know the hostname for.)
#
S11
R$*<@$j>$*          $>3$1$2                 strip local host name
R$*<@$+>$*          $:$>9$1<@$2>$3          canonicalize domain
# include if aliases are shared across local domain
R$=N                $@$1<@$j>               qualify nonhidden users

# include if aliases are NOT shared across local domain
#R$*<@$+>$*         $@$1<@$2>$3             already has @domain
#R$+               $@$1<@$j>               add our hostname
# (by running S11 on recipients, we get the above behaviour on To: and Cc:
#  headers, as well as for the envelope recipient. this is good since we
#  always call $#smtpl with hostname attached, which means that we won't be
#  down here at all if $j is in the address (that would have been stripped
#  in S0), and we will therefore qualify any domain-less addresses with our
#  own hostname before sending them to other hosts in our domain. this is
#  all ugly but it's what you have to do if your aliases aren't shared. --vix)
#
S21
R$+                 $@$>11$1                nothing special here

###########################################################
###########################################################
#####
#####          SMTP to hosts outside the local domain
#####
###########################################################
###########################################################

Msmtp,      P=[IPC], F=mDFMuXL, S=12, R=22, A=IPC $h, E=\r\n

S12
R<@$+>$*            $@<@$1>$2               <route-addr> syntax
R$*<@[$+]>$*        $@$1<@[$2]>$3           numeric, lv alone
R$*<@$+>$*          $@$>9$1<@$2>$3          canonicalize domain
R$=N                $@$1<@$j>               Add $j to local
R$+                 $@$1<@$W>               fix up return addr
```

```
S22
R$+                  $@$>12$1                          nothing special here

############################################################
############################################################
#####
#####                  SMTP to relay host
#####
############################################################
############################################################

Msmtpr,     P=[IPC], F=mDFMuX, S=13, R=23, A=IPC $h, E=\r\n

# (we pull off the local hostname in all cases, and then selectively add it
#  back on.  we would add it back if the user is root or one of the others
#  for which we want to know the hostname.  Otherwise we want to look like we
#  are a local user on the relay machine.  This is to allow for "cleaner"
#  addresses when crossing mail domains. --FMA)
#
S13
R$*<@$j>$*           $>3$1$2                           strip local host name
R$*<@$+>$*           $:$>9$1<@$2>$3                    canonicalize domain
R$=N                 $@$1<@$j>                         qualify nonhidden users

S23
R$+                  $@$>13$1                          nothing special here

############################################################
############################################################
#####
#####                  DECNET/MAIL11
#####
############################################################
############################################################

# (note that you will need an ultrix or osf1 sendmail binary to use this)
Mmail11, P=, F=mnSXxH, S=14, R=24/29,
           A=mail11 $f $x $h

# (mail11 senders)
S14
# (phase IV)
R$+<@$+.$E.$P>                $@$2::$1              phaseIV back to :: form

# (mail11 recip env)
S24
R$+                          $@$>14$1              nothing special here

# (mail11 recip hdr)
S29
# next line is for CC: headers which most mail11 receivers won't qualify
R$-                          $@$y::$1              tack on our nodename
```

```
R$+                          $@$>14$1          nothing special here

############################################################
############################################################
#####
#####           UUCP Mailer
#####
############################################################
############################################################
Muucp,     P=/usr/bin/uuc, F-sDFhuU,  S=15,  R=25,  M=100000,
           A=uux - $h!rmail ($u)
S15
R$*<@$+>$*                   $@$1<$2>$3        domain form is okay
R$+                          $:$>25$1          do unto sender as recipient
R$U!$+                       $@$U!$1            already has our UUCP name
R$+                          $@$U!$1            tack on our UUCP name

S25
R$*<@$+>$*                   $@$1<@$2>$3        domain form is okay
R$-!$+                       $@$1!$2            !-form is okay; done
R$+!$+                       $@$>3$2<@$1>       more than 1 token before !.
```

Appendix E

Simple `sendmail.cf`

This is a very simple `sendmail.cf` for a client that handles local delivery only. Anything else gets pushed off to the relay host. This file was made originally for a client that also had no local delivery; all mail got sent to the Mail Hub. The mail spool directory was NFS-mounted, so no local delivery was needed.

This is offered to you as an example.

```
# Thanks to Peter Churchyard,              Ox8
# Imperial College, London.                OX12
#                                          Pfirst-class=0
# Your local domain.                       Pspecial-delivery=100
DDdco.frobozz.com                          Pjunk=-100
                                           Troot daemon uucp
# Your full hostname                       H?F?From: $q
Dj$w                                       H?D?Date: $a
#Dj$w.$D                                   H?M?Message-Id: <$p.$t@$j>
DRrelayhost.dco.frobozz.com                HSubject:
DVsimple
Dnmailer-daemon                            S0
DlFrom $g $d remote from $U                R$*@$j  $#local$:$1     optional
Do@.%                                      R$*@$w  $#local$:$1     optional
Dq$?x$x <$g>$|$g$.                         R$-     $#local$:$1     optional
De$j Sendmail $v/$V ready at $b            R$*     $#remote$@$R$:$1
Odbackground                               S1
Om                                         S2
OF0644                                     S3
Og1                                        R$*<$+>$*          $2
OH/etc/sendmail.hf                         S4
OL6                                        Mremote, P=[IPC], F=nsmFDMuXC, \
Oo                                                 S=10, R=10, A=IPC $h
OQ/var/spool/mqueue                        Mlocal, P=/bin/mail, F=lsDFrmn, \
Or1h                                               S=10, R=10, A=mail -r $f -d $u
OS/etc/sendmail.st                         Mprog, P=/bin/echo, F=lsDFMmn, \
OT3d                                               S=10, R=10, A=mail $u
Ou1                                        S10
```

Appendix F

Log Levels

Sendmail's logging facility is tiered such that each log message has a certain *level* and you can specify in sendmail.cf which levels you care about. The vast majority of sendmail.cf files in use have the *log level* set to 9 (i.e., OL9), which means that messages with log level 9 or lower will be generated, and messages with log level 10 or higher will not be generated. Using the table in this appendix, you should be able to make an informed decision about your OL*x* setting, on the basis of the kinds of messages you think you need to see in your logs. It is common to boost the OL*x* value when working on a hard mail problem.

Note that Sendmail's log levels are distinct from syslog's log levels; that is, each message Sendmail sends to syslog has a syslog *priority* attached to it, but these priorities are values like LOG_INFO and LOG_ALERT, which are internal to syslog and have nothing to do with the Sendmail log level. We believe that a more consistent design would have led to a direct mapping between Sendmail log levels and syslog priority levels, since there is no reason why syslog should rank the priorities of messages differently than Sendmail does.

As you will see, log levels 10 and higher are of interest mostly to someone who is debugging Sendmail; they are rarely used by the average Postmaster.

The obvious degenerate case holds: If you set the log level to 0, no messages are logged. No Postmaster has ever done this and lived to tell about it. OL9 really is a reasonable default.

Log Level	Messages	Notes
22	unlink-fail ???	Debugging
21	unlink ???	Debugging
20	open transcript unlock	Debugging

Log Level	Messages	Notes
17	`assigned id`	Debugging
16	`queueup, qf=???, df=???`	Debugging
12	`connected, pid=???`	Debugging
	`finis, pid=???`	Debugging
	`in background, pid=???`	Debugging
	`runqueue ???, pid=???`	Debugging
	`dowork, pid=???`	Debugging
11	`dropenvelope`	Debugging
10	`locked`	Debugging
	`too young`	Debugging (*KJS*)
9	`message-id=???`	Message has entered Sendmail
8	`??? aliases, longest ??? bytes, \`	
	`??? bytes total`	
7	`rebuilding alias database`	
	`alias database out of date`	
6	`alias database rebuilt`	
5	`stat=queued`	(*non-KJS*)
4	`stat=tempfail`	
	`stat=sent`	(*non-KJS*)
3	`stat=queued`	(*KJS*)
	`stat=failure`	
	`stat=sent`	(*KJS*)
2	`header parse error; \`	(*KJS*)
	`dropping message`	
	`from=???, size=???, \`	
	`class=???, received from ???`	
1	`unexpected close on \`	
	`connection from ???`	
	`cannot get connection`	For main listener socket
	`from=??? unparseable, \`	
	`received from ???`	
	`cannot prescan from (???)`	
	`SYSERR ???`	Serious problem
	`savemail HELP!!!!`	Internal error
	`SMTP DEBUG or SHOW \`	Security concern
	`command from ??? (???)`	

Appendix G

Debug Classes

These are the debug classes for running Sendmail in debug mode (-d).

Class	Type	Level	Description
0	General	1	Don't fork as often
		4	Setting of $j, $w, $=w
		15	Dump configuration file
		44	Print argument vector
1	Envelope	1	Envelope sender
2	Exiting	1	Final exit status
5	Timers	4	Alarm tick
		5	Event added; event cleared
		6	Activity in alarm tick
6	Error notifications	1	Each error; returns to sender
		5	dead.letter versus mail back error text
7	Queue file names	1	Created a new queue file name
		2	Used an existing queue file name
		20	Trying a new queue file name
8	DNS	1	MX RR lookups; name canonicalization

Class	Type	Level	Description
9	More DNS	1	maphostname (for $[and $])
		2	(turn on resolver debugging [*KJS* only])
10	Delivery	1	General trace; envelope dump
11	Mailers	1	Mailer open
12	Remotely visible names (*KJS* only)	1	Before and after
		2	Ruleset numbers of a mailer's S= and R=
13	Sending to recipient list	1	General
		3	Checking for errors
		4	errors-to whom? (owner-*xxx*)
14	Headers	2	Headers with comma-separated lists
15	SMTP listener	1	Initialization; load average
		2	Incoming connection
		15	(turns on kernel socket debugging)
16	SMTP client	1	Outbound connection
		14	(turns on kernel socket debugging)
18	More SMTP client	1	Can't open connection; protocol trace
		100	(pause per protocol element)
20	Address resolving, Calling of Rulesets 3 and 0	1	Before and after
21	Rulesets	2	Entry and exit of each ruleset; Miscellaneous (output like -bt)
		3	Rulesets calling rulesets with $>
		4	Rewritten addresses
		10	Rule did not match
		12	Testing and application of each rule
		15	Replacements form RHS
		35	Internal form of each rule

Class	Type	Level	Description
22	Address tokenizing	36	Each token
		45	Before
		101	Each character
25	Sending to recipient lists	1	Recipient lists and "control" address
26	Sending to recipients	1	Each recipient; duplicate suppression
		6	/etc/passwd lookups (per recipient)
27	Aliases	1	Expansion; forwarding; miscellaneous
		3	Database searches
30	Message collection	1	End of header
		2	Parsing From header
		3	Added Apparently-To header
31	Header processing	6	Each header
32	Header collection	1	Collected header
33	Address parsing, stripping of comments	1	Before and after
35	Macros	9	Definitions
		24	Expansions
36	Symbol tables (macros, classes)	5	Each reference
		9	Hash values
37	Configuration file	1	Setting an option
40	Queueing	1	Writing qf* file; dump work queue; processing queue entry
		4	Reading queued qf* file
		5	Get/set "control" address/user
41	Queueing	2	qf* file disappeared — skipping

Class	Type	Level	Description
45	More delivery	1	Setting sender; setting userid to sender
50	More delivery	1	Dropping envelope
51	Queue control	4	(do not remove xf* file)
52	Process control	1	Disconnection from parent and tty
		5	(prevent disconnection from parent)
60	Database	1	Dbm file opens and searches

Appendix H

RFC 1311

RFC 1311 describes a series of RFCs called STDs — "Standards." This RFC introduces them as well as lists, in *its* appendix, all the relevant standards in IP/TCP networking and their associated RFCs.

The RFC begins on the following page.

Network Working Group   Internet Activities Board
Request for Comments: 1311   J. Postel, Editor
                                                                    March 1992

                        Introduction to the STD Notes

Status of this Memo

This RFC describes a new sub-series of RFCs, called STDs (Standards). Distribution
of this memo is unlimited.

1. Introduction

The STDs are a subseries of notes within the RFC series that are the Internet standards. The intent is to identify clearly for the Internet community those RFCs which
document Internet standards.

2. The Assignment of STD Numbers

There is a need to be very clear about which specifications have completed the full
process of standardization in the Internet. To do this an STD number will be assigned
to a specification when it reaches the Standard maturity level. Note that specifications may be either Technical Specifications (TS) or Applicability Statements (AS).

When a specification reaches the final stage of the standardization process and the
IAB has designated it a standard for the Internet, an STD number will be assigned to
that specification.

The existing standards have been assigned STD numbers (see Appendix).

The standard for a particular protocol will always have the same STD number.

> If at some future time a protocol is reworked and a new document is produced as
> the specification of that standard and the new specification is designated by the IAB
> as a standard for the Internet, then the new document will be labeled with the same
> STD number (of course, that new document will have a new RFC number).

Multiple Documents for One Standard:

> A STD number identifies a standard not a document. A document is identified
> by its RFC number. If the specification of a standard is spread over several docu-
> ments they will each carry the same STD number.

> For example, the Domain Name System (DNS) is currently specified by the com-
> bination of RFCs 1034 and 1035. Both of these documents are now labeled
> STD-13.

> To be completely clear the DNS "Concepts and Facilities" document can be referenced as "STD-13/RFC-1034".

In such cases, whenever possible, the set of documents defining a particular standard will cross reference each other.

One Standard or Multiple Standards:

One difficult decision is deciding whether a set of documents describe one standard or multiple standards. In the Appendix, one can see that there are several cases in which one STD applies to multiple RFCs (see STDs 5, 13, and 20). There is one case in which a family of specifications has multiple STD numbers; that is the Telnet Options.

The general rule is that a separate STD number is used when the specification is logically separable. That is, logically separable options are assigned distinct STD numbers while amendments and non-optional extensions use the same STD number as the base specification.

Multiple Versions or Editions of a Standard:

It may occur that the documentation of a standard is updated or replaced with a new document. In such cases, the same STD number will be used to label the standard. No version numbers will be attached to STD numbers. There need be no confusion about having the up-to-date document about STD-9 since each version of the document will have a distinct RFC number (and of course a different date).

The complete identification of a specification and its document is the combination of the STD and the RFC. For example, "STD-13/RFC-1035" completely identifies the current version of the second part of the Domain Name System specification.

> To completely identify all of the DNS standard the citation would be "STD-13/RFC-1034/RFC-1035".

One way to think of this is that an acronym (like TCP) refers to a concept, which is called a protocol. An RFC number (like RFC-793) indicates the specific version of the protocol specification. An STD number (like STD-7) designates the status of the protocol.

2. Why an RFC Subseries ?

There are several reasons why the STDs are part of the larger RFC series of notes.

The foremost reason is that the distribution mechanisms for RFCs are tried and true. Anyone who can get an RFC, can automatically get a STD. More important, anyone who knows of the RFC series can easily find the STDs.

Another reason for making STDs part of the RFC series is that the maintenance mechanisms for RFCs are already in place. It makes sense to maintain similar documents in a similar way.

3. Format Rules

Since the STDs are a part of the RFC series, they must conform to "Request for Comments on Request for Comments: Instructions to RFC Authors" (RFC-1111) with respect to format.

3.1 Status Statement

Each STD RFC must include on its first page the "Status of this Memo" section which contains a paragraph describing the intention of the RFC. This section is meant to convey the status approved by the Internet Activities Board (IAB).

3.2. Distribution Statement

Each STD RFC will also include a "distribution statement". As the purpose of the STD series is to disseminate information, there is no reason for the distribution to be anything other than "unlimited".

Typically, the distribution statement will simply be the sentence "Distribution of this memo is unlimited." appended to the "Status of this Memo" section.

3.3. Security Considerations

All STD RFCs must contain a section that discusses the security considerations of the procedures that are the main topic of the RFC.

3.4. Author's Address

Each STD RFC must have at the very end a section giving the author's address, including the name and postal address, the telephone number, and the Internet email address.

In the case of multiple authors, each of the authors will be listed. In the case of a document produced by a group, the editor of the document will be listed and optionally the chair of the group may be listed.

4. The STD Publication

New documents can only become STD RFCs through an action of the IAB. The publication of STDs will be performed by the RFC Editor.

5. STD Announcements

New STD RFCs are announced to the RFC distribution list maintained by the Network Information Center (NIC). Contact the NIC to be added or deleted from this mailing list by sending an email message to

```
RFC-REQUEST@NIC.DDN.MIL
```

6. Obtaining STDs

STD RFCs may be obtained in the same way as any RFC.

Details on obtaining RFCs via FTP or EMAIL may be obtained by sending an EMAIL message to "rfc-info@ISI.EDU" with the message body "help:ways_to_get_rfcs". For example:

```
To: rfc-info@ISI.EDU
Subject: getting rfcs

help: ways_to_get_rfcs
```

The current standards are listed in the "IAB Official Protocol Standards" (which is STD-1), whose current edition is RFC-1280.

Security Considerations

Security issues are not discussed in this memo.

Author's Address

Jon Postel USC/Information Sciences Institute 4676 Admiralty Way Marina del Rey, CA 90292

Phone: 310-822-1511 Fax: 310-823-6714

Email: Postel@ISI.EDU

Appendix — The Grandfathered STDs

Protocol	Name	Status	RFC	STD
	IAB Official Protocol Standards	Req	1280	1
	Assigned Numbers	Req	1060	2
	Host Requirements	Req	1122,1123	3
	Gateway Requirements	Req	1009	4
IP	Internet Protocol	Req	791	5
	as amended by:			
	IP Subnet Extension	Req	950	5
	IP Broadcast Datagrams	Req	919	5
	IP Broadcast Datagrams with Subnets	Req	922	5
ICMP	Internet Control Message Protocol	Req	792	5
IGMP	Internet Group Multicast Protocol	Rec	1112	5
UDP	User Datagram Protocol	Rec	768	6
TCP	Transmission Control Protocol	Rec	793	7
TELNET	Telnet Protocol	Rec	854,855	8
FTP	File Transfer Protocol	Rec	959	9
SMTP	Simple Mail Transfer Protocol	Rec	821	10
MAIL	Format of Electronic Mail Messages	Rec	822	11
CONTENT	Content Type Header Field	Rec	1049	11
NTP	Network Time Protocol	Rec	1119	12
DOMAIN	Domain Name System	Rec	1034,1035	13
DNS-MX	Mail Routing and the Domain System	Rec	974	14
SNMP	Simple Network Management Protocol	Rec	1157	15
SMI	Structure of Management Information	Rec	1155	16
MIB-II	Management Information Base-II	Rec	1213	17
EGP	Exterior Gateway Protocol	Rec	904	18
NETBIOS	NetBIOS Service Protocols	Ele	1001,1002	19
ECHO	Echo Protocol	Rec	862	20
DISCARD	Discard Protocol	Ele	863	21
CHARGEN	Character Generator Protocol	Ele	864	22
QUOTE	Quote of the Day Protocol	Ele	865	23
USERS	Active Users Protocol	Ele	866	24
DAYTIME	Daytime Protocol	Ele	867	25
TIME	Time Server Protocol	Ele	868	26

Telnet Options		Opt	Sta	RFC	TD
TOPT-BIN	Binary Transmission	0	Rec	856	27
TOPT-ECH	Echo	1	Rec	857	28
TOPT-SUP	Suppress Go Ahead	3	Rec	858	29
TOPT-STA	Status	5	Rec	859	30
TOPT-TIM	Timing Mark	6	Rec	860	31
TOPT-EXT	Extended-Options-List	255	Rec	861	32

Appendix I

RFC 822

RFC 822 describes the standard for ARPA Internet text messages. This appendix contains Appendix A from RFC 822, which presents examples of valid Internet e-mail addresses. This excerpt is from the Preface of RFC 822:

> By 1977, the Arpanet employed several informal standards for the text messages (mail) sent among its host computers. It was felt necessary to codify these practices and provide for those features that seemed imminent. The result of that effort was Request for Comments RFC 733, "Standard for the Format of ARPA Network Text Message," by Crocker, Vittal, Pogran, and Henderson. The specification attempted to avoid major changes in existing software, while permitting several new features.
>
> This document revises the specifications in RFC 733, in order to serve the needs of the larger and more complex ARPA Internet. Some of RFC 733's features failed to gain adequate acceptance. In order to simplify the standard and the software that follows it, these features have been removed. A different addressing scheme is used, to handle the case of inter-network mail; and the concept of re-transmission has been introduced.
>
> This specification is intended for use in the ARPA Internet. However, an attempt has been made to free it of any dependence on that environment, so that it can be applied to other network text message systems.

Standard for ARPA Internet Text Messages   David H. Crocker
Request for Comments: 822   August 13, 1982

A. EXAMPLES

A.1. ADDRESSES

A.1.1. `Alfred Neuman <Neuman@BBN-TENEXA>`

A.1.2. `Neuman@BBN-TENEXA`

These two "Alfred Neuman" examples have identical semantics, as far as the operation of the local host's mail sending (distribution) program (also sometimes called its "mailer") and the remote host's mail protocol server are concerned. In the first example, the "`Alfred Neuman`" is ignored by the mailer, as "`Neuman@BBN-TENEXA`" completely specifies the recipient. The second example contains no superfluous information, and, again, "`Neuman@BBN-TENEXA`" is the intended recipient.

> Note: When the message crosses name-domain boundaries, then these specifications must be changed, so as to indicate the remainder of the hierarchy, starting with the top level.

A.1.3. `"George`

This form might be used to indicate that a single mailbox is shared by several users. The quoted string is ignored by the originating host's mailer, because "`Shared@Group.Arpanet`" completely specifies the destination mailbox.

A.1.4. `Wilt . (the Stilt) Chamberlain@NBA.US`

The "`(the Stilt)`" is a comment, which is *not* included in the destination mailbox address handed to the originating system's mailer. The local-part of the address is the string "`Wilt.Chamberlain`", with *no* space between the first and second words.

A.1.5. Address Lists

```
Gourmets:   Pompous  Person <WhoZiWhatZit@Cordon-Bleu>,
                     Childs@WGBH.Boston, Galloping Gourmet@
                     ANT.Down-Under (Australian National Television),
                     Cheapie@Discount-Liquors;,
Cruisers:   Port@Portugal,  Jones@SEA;,
                     Another@Somewhere.SomeOrg
```

This group list example points out the use of comments and the mixing of
addresses and groups.

A.2. ORIGINATOR ITEMS

A.2.1. Author-sent
George Jones logs into his host as Jones. He sends mail himself.

```
From:   Jones@Group.Org
```

or

```
From:   George Jones <Jones@Group.Org>
```


A.2.2. Secretary-sent
George Jones logs in as Jones on his host. His secretary, who logs in as Secy
sends mail for him. Replies to the mail should go to George.

```
From:      George Jones <Jones@Group>
Sender:    Secy@Other-Group
```


A.2.3. Secretary-sent, for user of shared directory
George Jones' secretary sends mail for George. Replies should go to George.

```
From:      George Jones<Shared@Group.Org>
Sender:    Secy@Other-Group
```

> Note that there need not be a space between "Jones" and the "<", but adding a
> space enhances readability (as is the case in other examples).

A.2.4. Committee activity, with one author

George is a member of a committee. He wishes to have any replies to his message go to all committee members.

```
From:       George Jones <Jones@Host.Net>
Sender:     Jones@Host
Reply-To:   The Committee: Jones@Host.Net,
            Smith@Other.Org,
            Doe@Somewhere-Else;
```

> Note that if George had not included himself in the enumeration of The Committee, he would not have gotten an implicit reply; the presence of the "Reply-to" field *supersedes* the sending of a reply to the person named in the "From" field.

A.2.5. Secretary acting as full agent of author

George Jones asks his secretary (Secy@Host) to send a message for him in his capacity as Group. He wants his secretary to handle all replies.

```
From:       George Jones <Group@Host>
Sender:     Secy@Host
Reply-To:   Secy@Host
```

A.2.6. Agent for user without online mailbox

A friend of George's, Sarah, is visiting. George's secretary sends some mail to a friend of Sarah in computerland. Replies should go to George, whose mailbox is Jones at Registry.

```
From:       Sarah Friendly <Secy@Registry>
Sender:     Secy-Name <Secy@Registry>
Reply-To:   Jones@Registry.
```

A.2.7. Agent for member of a committee

George's secretary sends out a message which was authored jointly by all the members of a committee. Note that the name of the committee cannot be specified, since <group> names are not permitted in the From field.

```
From:    Jones@Host,
         Smith@Other-Host,
         Doe@Somewhere-Else
Sender:  Secy@SHost
```

A.3. COMPLETE HEADERS

A.3.1. Minimum required

```
Date:      26 Aug 76 1429 EDT
From:      Jones@Registry.Org
Bcc:
```

or

```
Date:      26 Aug 76 1429 EDT
From:      Jones@Registry.Org
To:        Smith@Registry.Org
```

Note that the "Bcc" field may be empty, while the "To" field is required to have at least one address.

A.3.2. Using some of the additional fields

```
Date:         26 Aug 76 1430 EDT
From:         George Jones<Group@Host>
Sender:       Secy@SHOST
To:           "Al Neuman"@Mad-Host,
              Sam.Irving@Other-Host
Message-ID:   <some.string@SHOST>
```

A.3.3. About as complex as you're going to get

```
Date        :  27 Aug 76 0932 PDT
From        :  Ken Davis <KDavis@This-Host.This-net>
Subject     :  Re: The Syntax in the RFC
Sender      :  KSecy@Other-Host
Reply-To    :  Sam.Irving@Reg.Organization
To          :  George Jones <Group@Some-Reg.An-Org>,
               Al.Neuman@MAD.Publisher
cc          :  Important folk:
               Tom Softwood <Balsa@Tree.Root>,
               "Sam Irving"@Other-Host;,
               Standard Distribution:
               /main/davis/people/standard@Other-Host,
               "<Jones>standard.dist.3"@Tops-20-Host>;
Comment     :  Sam is away on business. He asked me to handle
               his mail for him.  He'll be able to provide  a
               more accurate explanation when he returns
               next week.
In-Reply-To: <some.string@DBM.Group>, George's message
X-Special-action:  This is a sample of user-defined field-names.
               There could also be a field-name
               "Special-action", but its name might later be
               preempted
Message-ID: <4231.629.XYzi-What@Other-Host>
```

Appendix J

domain-template.txt

NETINFO:DOMAIN-TEMPLATE.TXT   04/93
To establish a domain, the following information must be sent to the InterNIC Domain Registrar (HOSTMASTER@INTERNIC.NET). Questions may be addressed to the Hostmaster by electronic mail at the above address, or by phone at (703) 742-4777 or (800) 444-4345.

NOTE: The key people must have electronic mailboxes and "handles," unique NIC database identifiers. If you have access to WHOIS, please check to see if you are registered and if so, make sure the information is current. Include only your handle and any changes (if any) that need to be made in your entry. If you do not have access to WHOIS, please provide all the information indicated and a handle will be assigned.

(1) The name of the top level domain to join (EDU, COM, MIL, GOV, NET, ORG).
      1. Top level domain:

(2) The name of the domain (up to 12 characters). This is the name that will be used in tables and lists associating the domain with the domain server addresses. [While, from a technical standpoint, domain names can be quite long we recommend the use of shorter, more user-friendly names.]
      2. Complete Domain Name:

(3) The name and address of the organization establishing the domain.
      3a. Organization name:
      3b. Organization address:

(4) The date you expect the domain to be fully operational.
      4. Date operational:

(5) The handle of the administrative head of the organization -- or this person's name, mailing address, phone number, organization, and network mailbox. This is the contact point for administrative and policy questions about the domain. In the case of a research project, this should be the principal investigator.

NOTE: Both the Administrative and the Technical/Zone contact of a domain MUST have a network mailbox, even if the mailbox is to be within the proposed domain.

Administrative Contact

5a. Handle (if known) :
5b. Name (Last, First) :
5c. Organization:
5d. Mail Address:

5e. Phone Number:
5f. Net Mailbox :

(6) The handle of the technical contact for the domain -- or the person's name, mailing address, phone number, organization, and network mailbox. This is the contact point for problems concerning the domain or zone, as well as for updating information about the domain or zone.

Technical and Zone Contact

6a. Handle (if known):
6b. Name (Last, First) :
6c. Organization:
6d. Mail Address:

6e. Phone Number:
6f. Net Mailbox :

(7) Domains must provide at least two independent servers on Government-sponsored networks that provide the domain service for translating names to addresses for hosts in this domain.

* If you are applying for a domain and a network number assignment simultaneously

and a host on your proposed network will be used as a server for the domain, you must wait until you receive your network number assigment and have given the server(s) a netaddress before sending in the domain application. Sending in the domain application without complete information in Sections 7 and 8 of this template will result in the delay of the domain registration.

Also, establishing the servers in physically separate locations and on different PSNs and/or networks is strongly recommended.

NOTE: All new hosts acting as servers will appear in the DNS root servers but will not apppear in the HOSTS.TXT file unless otherwise requested.

Primary Server: HOSTNAME, NETADDRESS, HARDWARE, SOFTWARE

7a. Primary Server Hostname:
7b. Primary Server Netaddress:
7c. Primary Server Hardware:
7d. Primary Server Software:

(8) The Secondary server information.

8a. Secondary Server Hostname:
8b. Secondary Server Netaddress:
8c. Secondary Server Hardware:
8d. Secondary Server Software:

(9) If any currently registered hosts will be renamed into the new domain, please specify old hostname, netaddress, and new hostname.

For example:

```
BAR-FOO2.XYZ.COM (26.8.0.193) -> FOO2.BAR.COM
BAR-FOO3.XYZ.COM (192.7.3.193) -> FOO3.BAR.COM
BAR-FOO4.ARPA (34.6.0.193) -> FOO4.BAR.COM
```

(10) Please describe your organization briefly.

> For example: Our Corporation is a consulting organization of people working with UNIX and the C language in an electronic networking environment. It sponsors two technical conferences annually and distributes a bimonthly newsletter.

For further information contact InterNIC Registration Services:

Via electronic mail:	HOSTMASTER@INTERNIC.NET
Via telephone:	(800) 444-4345 or (703) 742-4777
Via postal mail:	Network Solutions InterNIC Registration Services
	505 Huntmar Park Drive
	Herndon, VA 22070

RECOMMENDED READING

Feinler, E.J.; Jacobsen, O.J.; Stahl, M.K.; Ward, C.A., eds. DDN Protocol Handbook: Menlo Park, CA: SRI International, DDN Network Information Center; 1985 December; NIC 50004 and NIC 50005 and NIC 50006. 2749 p.

Garcia-Luna-Aceves, J.J.; Stahl, M.K.; Ward, C.A., eds. Internet Protocol Handbook: The Domain Name System (DNS) Handbook. Menlo Park, CA: SRI International, Network Information Systems Center; 1989 August; 219 p. AD A214 698.

Postel, J.B.; Reynolds, J.K. Domain Requirements. Marina del Rey, CA: University of Southern California, Information Sciences Inst.; 1984 October; RFC 920. 14 p. (RS.INTERNIC.NET POLICY RFC920.TXT).

Harrenstien, K.; Stahl, M.K.; Feinler, E.J. DoD Internet Host Table Specification. Menlo Park, CA: SRI International, DDN Network Information Center; 1985 October; RFC 952. 6 p. (RS.INTERNIC.NET POLICY RFC952.TXT). Obsoletes: RFC 810

Harrenstien, K.; Stahl, M.K.; Feinler, E.J. Hostname Server. Menlo Park, CA: SRI International, DDN Network Information Center; 1985 October; RFC 953. 5 p. (NIC.DDN.MIL RFC:RFC953.TXT). Obsoletes: RFC 811

Partridge, C. Mail Routing and the Domain System. Cambridge, MA: BBN Labs., Inc.; 1986 January; RFC 974. 7 p. (RS.INTERNIC.NET POLICY RFC974.TXT).

Lazear, W.D. MILNET Name Domain Transition. McLean, VA: MITRE Corp.; 1987 November; RFC 1031. 10 p. (RS.INTERNIC.NET POLICY RFC1031.TXT).

Stahl, M.K. Domain Administrators Guide. Menlo Park, CA: SRI International, DDN Network Information Center; 1987 November; RFC 1032. 14 p. (RS.INTERNIC.NET POLICY RFC1032.TXT).

Lottor, M. Domain Administrators Operations Guide. Menlo Park, CA: SRI International, DDN Network Information Center; 1987 November; RFC 1033. 22 p. (RS.INTERNIC.NET POLICY RFC1033.TXT)

Mockapetris, P. Domain Names - Concepts and Facilities. Marina del Rey, CA: University of Southern California, Information Sciences Inst.; 1987 November; RFC 1034. 55 p. (RS.INTERNIC.NET POLICY RFC1034.TXT). Updated-by: RFC 1101 Obsoletes: RFC 973; RFC 882; RFC 883

Mockapetris, P. Domain names - Implementation and Specification. Marina del Rey, CA: University of Southern California, Information Sciences Inst.; 1987 November; RFC 1035. 55 p. (RS.INTERNIC.NET POLICY RFC1035.TXT). Updated-by: RFC 1101 Obsoletes: RFC 973; RFC 882; RFC 883

Mockapetris, P. DNS Encoding of Network Names and Other Types. Marina del Rey, CA: University of Southern California, Information Sciences Inst.; 1989 April; RFC 1101. 14 p. (RS.INTERNIC.NET POLICY RFC1101.TXT). Updates: RFC 1034; RFC 1035

Appendix K

Other Resources

The Internet contains several resources of interest to Postmasters. These include Usenet newsgroups, Requests For Comments ("RFCs"), Anonymous FTP servers, and resource discovery services. There are also several useful e-mail servers that provide access to Internet resources for users who do not have a direct Internet connection and who therefore cannot use FTP or TELNET. At the end of this appendix you will find our recommended reading list.

K.1. Usenet

Usenet is a loosely defined, worldwide association of hosts that exchange articles on thousands of topics, from cooking to C language programming to cyberpunk to sex to multimedia to computer architecture. Each host on the Usenet has a local group of users who post articles and read articles posted by other users. Participating in Usenet can take anywhere from 15 minutes to 24 hours a day, depending on your interests.

You should read the `comp.mail.sendmail` newsgroup from Usenet. It is also a good idea to read `comp.bugs.4bsd`, which is where patches first appear for each new major bug in Sendmail. Reading this group may convince you to start building your Sendmail from source if you aren't already doing that. Then there are a number of security-related newsgroups, but most of these are theoretical — the only one you should be sure to read is `comp.security.announce`, which is where virtually all new security-related bugs in Sendmail are first announced. Note that security bugs tend to be announced without patches, since it is almost always possible for a Bad Person to guess from a patch what the original security hole was and then exploit this knowledge on any host that has not yet been patched.

Usenet is available via the NNTP protocol over IP/TCP if you have a direct IP connection to the Internet; UUCP nodes can also participate, although at the time of this writing, a complete Usenet feed requires many hours per day with the fastest dial-up modems available. (Historians please note: The news volume was ˜30 MB/day in late 1992 and ˜150 MB/day in early 1994.) Usenet is not resource-intensive if you only subscribe to a limited set of newsgroups. To join Usenet, you need an NNTP or UUCP (or other, more obscure) connection to one or more existing Usenet nodes. To find these nodes, ask your friends.

You will also need some software; we recommend the INN package, written by Rich Salz of the Open Software Foundation with support from UUNET Technologies, Inc. INN can be had via Anonymous FTP as

```
ftp.uu.net:˜ftp/networking/news/nntp/inn/*
```

or

```
gatekeeper.dec.com:˜ftp/pub/news/inn/*
```

If you don't have Internet access, you won't be able to FTP this file. In that case you will have to find someone who will sell you a tape. Try UUNET Technologies, 3110 Fairview Park Drive, Suite 570, Falls Church, VA 22042-4239, USA, +1 (703) 204-8000. You should first inquire via e-mail to make sure they are still selling tapes; try <root@uunet.uu.net>.

INN only supports the inter-host transport of Usenet articles. The user agent software, which your users will need in order to read and post articles through your INN transport, is packaged separately. There are quite a few different, good Usenet user agents, but you should start simply and use rn, which is available as

```
ftp.uu.net:˜ftp/networking/news/rn/*
```

or

```
gatekeeper.dec.com:˜ftp/pub/news/rn/*
```

As before, if you don't have Internet access, you can try buying a tape from UUNET.

Usenet is free. All of the software described above is free. You can buy a supported Usenet feed and supported Usenet software, but the overwhelming majority of Usenet participants provide their own support and use free software.

K.2. Requests for Comments ("RFCs")

Internet RFCs are the publication vehicle for all Internet standards (all Internet standards are RFCs, but not all RFCs are Internet standards). Of the RFCs that exist at the time of this writing, we recommend that you read 821, 822, 974, 1034, 1035, 1123, 1311, and, for extra credit, 976. If you have any interest in history, you will probably enjoy reading *all* of the RFCs, in order — just don't try to read them all in the same month.

Periodically, an RFC will be superseded by a newer RFC. This is one good reason to read each new RFC as it comes out — that way you will know when one of the older ones has been superseded. But there's a deeper problem here. Let's say you want to know which RFCs describe some Internet protocol or convention. Imagine for an instant that you find an RFC that purports to describe the thing you want to know about. How are you to know that this RFC has not been superseded?

The answer has been, for a long time, that you have to locate the latest RFC-index and scan it, looking for all RFCs that appear from their titles to be related to what you are attempting to learn; then you skim the top of each such RFC looking for the declaration of which RFCs have been superseded by this one. This process is tedious and error-prone. To the great relief of many, there is now a better way. See Appendix ? for a complete copy of RFC 1311, which describes the STD Notes.

The easiest way to acquire RFCs is via Anonymous FTP from `ftp.nisc.sri.com:~ftp/rfc/*` or `nic.ddn.mil:~ftp/rfc/*`. If you don't have a direct Internet connection, you can order paper copies from SRI International, 333 Ravenswood Avenue, Menlo Park, CA 94025, USA, +1 (415) 859-6387. SRI International also has a subscription service that will mail you paper copies of all new RFCs. [1]

Additionally, RFCs may be requested through e-mail from SRI's automated mail server at `<mail-server@nisc.sri.com>`. In the body of the message, indicate the RFC to be sent, for example,

```
send rfcNNNN
```

where NNNN is the number of the RFC. For PostScript RFCs, specify the extension, for example,

```
send rfcNNNN.ps
```

Multiple requests can be sent in a single message by specifying each request on a separate line. Request the RFC index by typing `send rfc-index`.[1]

K.3. Anonymous FTP

The Internet File Transfer Protocol (FTP) makes it possible for a host to provide so-called *anonymous* access to an archive of exported files. By anonymous, we mean that you don't need any special account or password to access such an archive. There are literally thousands of FTP servers in existence at the time of this writing; it

---

[1] These paragraphs were taken directly from the comments in `rfc-index`.

would be useless to list them all, since the list changes hourly. There are some well-known servers that are probably going to be around for a long time; `ftp.uu.net`, `gatekeeper.dec.com`, and `wuarchive.wustl.edu` are all examples of long-lived Anonymous FTP server hosts.

Setting up your own Anonymous FTP server is not at all difficult if you have a modern UNIX computer to build it out of. But the thing you will do most with Anonymous FTP is access servers other than your own. As mentioned earlier, there is some very useful free software out there — all you have to do is pull it over, build it, install it, and start using it. When you see a reference like

`ftp.frobozz.com:~ftp/pub/frbz/README`

you should read it as several distinct components:

Reference Component	Meaning
`ftp.frobozz.com:`	FTP server's host name is `ftp.frobozz.com`
`~ftp/`	This file is available via Anonymous FTP
`pub/frbz/README`	This is the file you should ask FTP for

When you connect to an FTP server that has been advertised as having anonymous access, enter `anonymous` as your user name and enter your fully qualified e-mail address as your password. This information is logged by the system administrators of the FTP server host, and it is only polite to give them your address since they are giving you files. (We will discuss how to access FTP files if you only have e-mail service and no FTP shortly.)

K.4. Resource Discovery Services

As the Internet grows, the probability will increase that some datum of interest to you is available out there somewhere, but in the absence of any coherent index or search mechanism, the probability of your *finding* that datum will actually decrease. Several experimental services have been created to solve this problem; while the ideal "coherent index" is not a realistic possibility, real progress has been made through Archie and Gopher.

K.4.1. Archie

Archie is an archive searching system that functions by retrieving a complete directory from every major FTP server on the Internet, storing it in a local database, and permitting anonymous users to log into the Archie server host to search this database. There are a lot of Archie servers, and each of them will give you the complete list of the others when you log into it. If you see this list and have reason to believe that one of the others listed is closer to you than the one you are using, then disconnect and try the closer server. Archie also has its own protocol, and if you are willing to invest the effort in getting an Archie client running, you will probably like it a lot more than you'll like Archive-over-telnet. Archie servers known to exist at the time of this writing follows:

Hostname	IP Address	Location
archie.rutgers.edu	128.6.18.15	Rutgers University
archie.unl.edu	129.93.1.14	University of Nebraska in Lincoln
archie.ans.net	147.225.1.2	Advanced Networks and Services
archie.mcgill.ca	132.206.2.3	Canada (original Archie site)
archie.au	139.130.4.6	Australia
archie.funet.fi	128.214.6.100	Finland
archie.doc.ic.ac.uk	146.169.11.3	UK/England
archie.cs.huji.ac.il	132.65.6.15	Israel
archie.wide.ad.jp	133.4.3.6	Japan
archie.ncu.edu.tw	140.115.19.24	Taiwan

We won't include instructions here on how to use Archie, since there is adequate online help after you telnet in. Figure K-1 contains an example that might motivate you.

You can use Archie through e-mail if you don't have a direct connection to the Internet. The best way to learn how to use it is to ask it for help; it will cheerfully send you a help file if you type something like

```
% echo help | mail -s foo archie@archie.sura.net
```

However, in the interests of providing motivational examples, here is the mail message that duplicates the previous query:

```
To: archie@archie.sura.net
Subject: foo bar

prog kjs.tar.Z
```

We understand that work is already under way on a companion program for Archie, called Jughead, but this may only be a rumour.

K.4.2. The Internet Gopher

The Internet Gopher is a more general resource discovery tool than Archie, which means that it is more difficult for Gopher to do the thing that Archie does well, but that there are a lot more things you can do in Gopher than in Archie. Gopher has keyword searches of its online databases; it has the ability to ftp files for you after it locates them; it can proxy-telnet you to other online information tools (various university and government libraries, for example).

```
% telnet archie.sura.net
Trying...
Connected to nic.sura.net.
Escape character is '^]'.

UNIX (nic.sura.net)

login: archie
Last login: Fri Oct 30 04:45:25 from relay.pipex.net

                Welcome to the ARCHIE server at SURAnet
archie> show search
# 'search' (type string) has the value 'regex'.
archie> set search exact
archie> prog kjs.tar.Z
# matches / % database searched:   2 /100%

Host uxc.cso.uiuc.edu    (128.174.5.50)
Last updated 03:51 20 Oct 1992

    Location: /mail
      FILE        rw-r--r--    886221  Jun  5 10:51   kjs.tar.Z
Host nic.funet.fi   (128.214.6.100)
Last updated 03:04 15 Oct 1992

    Location: /pub/unix/DEC
      FILE        rw-rw-r--    830749  Jan 24  1992   kjs.tar.Z
archie> quit
Connection closed by foreign host.
```

Figure K-1

Gopher really expects you to run its client on your host, so there are very few publicly available gopher accounts and those that exist are called "courtesy" accounts. If you try out one of these "courtesy" accounts and you decide that you like Gopher and expect to use it in the future, you should immediately invest the minimal effort to get a Gopher client running on your local host.

Figure K-2, Figure K-3, and Figure K-4 show an example of Gopher usage, using the courtesy account gopher on the gopher.uiuc.edu host. There is also a courtesy account on the consultant.micro.umn.edu host. We first connected via telnet. What's notable about this example is that it took a total of 19 seconds from the login prompt to the last display shown. Gopher is *very fast.*

In fact, we hit return at that point and were shown, after about 30 seconds' delay, the first page of RFC 1211. The 30-second delay was because Gopher had to retrieve the RFC from ftp.nisc.sri.com, and the connection was slow that day.

```
            Internet Gopher Client v1.03, Courtesy Account

                   Root gopher server: gopher.uiuc.edu

       1.   Welcome to the U of Illinois Gopher.
       2.   Campus Announcements (9/30/92)/
       3.   What's New? (10/16/92).
       4.   Information about Gopher/
       5.   Keyword Search of Gopher Menus <?>
       6.   U of Illinois Campus Information/
       7.   Champaign-Urbana & Regional Information/
  -->  8.   Computer Documentation/
       9.   Libraries/
       10.  Newspapers, Newsletters, and Weather/
       11.  Other Gopher and Information Servers/
       12.  Phone Books (PH)/
       13.  Internet File Server (ftp) Sites/

Press ? for Help, q to Quit, u to go up a menu         Page: 1/1
```

Figure K-2. First screen after logging into Gopher

```
            Internet Gopher Client v1.03, Courtesy Account
                      Computer Documentation
       1.   CCSO Fall 1992 Short Courses-Classes.
       2.   CCSO's Navigator Information/
       3.   CCSO's Quick Reference Guides/
       4.   CCSO's UIUCnet Newsletter/
       5.   CICNet Resource Guide/
       6.   Frequently Asked Questions on the Network/
  -->  7.   Keyword Search of RFCs (Internet Standards) <?>
       8.   Keyword Search of Unix Manuals <?>
       9.   Miscellaneous Technical Documents/
       10.  Software and Manuals for Sale (CCSO)/
       11.  Software: Educational Discounts.
       12.  Unix Manuals/
Index word(s) to search for: HELO
```

Figure K-3. Second screen after logging into Gopher

```
            Internet Gopher Client v1.03, Courtesy Account
           Keyword Search of RFCs (Internet Standards): HELO
  --> 1.  RFCs/1024: HEMS variable definitions : Stanford October'87
      2.  RFCs/1123: Requirements for Internet hosts - application..
      3.  RFCs/1211: Problems with the maintenance of large mailing
      4.  RFCs/821: Simple Mail Transfer Protocol : Simple Mail Tran
      5.  RFCs/937:  Post Office Protocol: Version 2 : ICE PROTOCOL
      6.  RFCs/976: UUCP mail interchange format standard

Press ? for Help, q to Quit, u to go up a menu          Page: 1/1
```

Figure K-4. Third screen after logging into Gopher

K.5. Mail-Based services

We showed above in the discussion of RFCs, you can retrieve RFCs from SRI International by sending a specially coded mail message to a particular nonhuman address on one of SRI's computers. We also showed a mail-based interface to the Archie resource discovery service. Mail-based services are becoming very popular on the Internet, since any two addresses in the world can probably exchange mail through various gateways; e-mail is the one end-to-end protocol that works almost everywhere and for which gateway translation issues have had the most time to mature.

While there are many mail-based servers, the only type of interest to Postmasters that has not already been discussed above is the ftp-by-mail server. There are several of these, all unfortunately called `ftpmail` even though their user interfaces are incompatible. All are descended, in spirit at least, from the old BITFTP server on the BITNET. When the BITFTP server became severely loaded, its administrators decided to restrict its user population to BITNET users only. This was good for the BITNET users, but it created a lot of demand among non-BITNET users.

The only `ftpmail` server we will describe here is the one written by one of the authors of this book (RHIP). This server runs on only one host at the time of this writing, but the response time is quite acceptable for the most part, and we invite you, to make whatever use of this server will most please you. The server sends out (as of early 1994) more than one gigabyte of traffic per day; this traffic comprises files that have been retrieved from Anonymous FTP servers, converted from binary to ASCII (actually `uuencode` or `btoa`, if that matters), split into 60 kilobyte chunks, and mailed to users who do not have direct Internet connections.

Following convention, the way to learn about `ftpmail` is to ask it for help, which you can do by sending it a mail message that contains only the line

```
help
```

Subject headers are ignored by `ftpmail`, other than to be included in all of its responses to your request; you can therefore use the subject header as an identifying tag if you ever submit more than one `ftpmail` request at one time. `ftpmail`'s addresses is <ftpmail@pa.dec.com> (or `uunet!decwrl!ftpmail`), which means that the way to get ftpmail to send you its help file is

```
% echo help | Mail -s 'ignore this subject' ftpmail@pa.dec.com
```

As our requisite motivational example, here is the mail message that tells `ftpmail` that you want the latest King James Version of Sendmail:

```
To: ftpmail@pa.dec.com
Subject: kjs

connect gatekeeper.dec.com
binary
uuencode
chdir pub/misc/vixie
get kjs.tar.Z
quit
```

K.6. Reading List

Here is a list of books that most Postmasters will find relevant and that some will even enjoy reading (we did and still do).

Computer Science Research Group, *UNIX System Manager's Manual (SMM)*, 4.4BSD (The USENIX Association and O'Reilly and Associates, Inc, 1994.) Contains two papers written by Eric Allman, "Sendmail Installation and Operation Guide" and "Sendmail — An Internetwork Router."

Carl-Mitchell, Smoot and Quarterman, John S., *Practical Internetworking with TCP/IP and UNIX* (Addison Wesley, 1993.) Covers the general topic of Internet/UNIX system administration and includes a very good chapter on Sendmail as well as background information on rdist, NIS, and quite a few other topics of general interest to Postmasters.

Estrada, Susan, *Connecting to the Internet* (O'Reilly & Associates, 1993.) If you aren't connected to the Internet and would like to be, this book will tell you what you need to know.

Frey, Donnalyn, and Adams, Rick, *A Directory of Electronic Mail Addressing and Networks* (O'Reilly and Associates, 1989.) Is a reference worth having on your bookshelf along side *The Matrix*.

Garfinkel, Simson, and Spafford, Gene, *Practical UNIX Security* (O'Reilly & Associates, 1991.) Is an excellent tour of the various well-worn security holes in UNIX.

Leffler, S. J., McKusick, M. K., Karels, M. J., and Quarterman, J. S., *The Design and Implementation of the 4.3BSD UNIX Operating System* (Addison Wesley, 1989.) While concentrating largely on the kernel, also explains by implication much of the context and culture within which Sendmail exists. It is still timely.

Padlipski, M. A., *The Elements of Networking Style* (Prentice Hall, 1985.) Is required reading. 'nuff said.

Quarterman, John S., *The Matrix* (Digital Press, 1990.) Is the seminal book describing the Internet and many of its gatewayed neighbors. It does so without all the turgid gloss that has come with the recent wave of publicity about this so-called "Information Superhighway" that the politicos would like us to believe they've just invented. It too is still timely.

Rose, Marshall T., *The Internet Message: Closing the Book With Electronic Mail* (Prentice Hall, 1993.) Discusses e-mail mostly from a UA perspective, explains why the OSI model of e-mail is broken, and discusses MIME, PEM, and other extensions to e-mail.

Index